# Reclaiming the Lost Century of Growth

This book, along with any associated content or subsequent updates, can be accessed at https://hdl.handle.net/10986/43280.

Scan to see all titles in this series.

WORLD BANK LATIN AMERICAN AND CARIBBEAN STUDIES

# Reclaiming the Lost Century of Growth

## Building Learning Economies in Latin America and the Caribbean

**William F. Maloney, Xavier Cirera, and Maria Marta Ferreyra**

1 2 3 4 28 27 26 25



ISBN (paper): 978-1-4648-2205-6
ISBN (electronic): 978-1-4648-2244-5
DOI: 10.1596/978-1-4648-2205-6

*Cover image:* Ramon Oviedo (Dominican Republic, 1927–2015), "Untitled," circa 1982. Oil on canvas, 80″ × 130″. © Organization of American States, Art Museum of the Americas Collection. Gift of the Dominican Republic. Photography: Rafa Cruz. Used with permission. Further permission required for reuse. *Cover design:* Bill Pragluski, Critical Stages, LLC.

**Library of Congress Control Number: 2025940216**

# Contents

## Boxes



## Figures

## Map



## Tables

# Foreword

Longstanding problems and new challenges often combine to require urgent solutions. Economic growth rates today in Latin America and the Caribbean (LAC) are low and have been so for too long. This translates into a lower quality of life for its people and limited prospects for its children. At the same time, the region faces the challenges of adapting to changes in the global trade order, seizing the opportunities of new technologies, and leveraging its vast resources for smart energy strategies.

This volume argues that a central reason for the region's tepid economic performance is its inability to "learn how to learn" about and how to exploit the new technologies that drive productivity and seed new areas of comparative advantage. For much of the past two centuries, LAC has been relatively slow at adopting technologies ranging from steamships to computers. This remains the case today, as seen in long adoption lags and incomplete use of even the technologies that have been adopted. Commitments today to finding the frontier technologies of tomorrow are also lagging. Investment in research and development in the region is currently only 0.62 percent of gross domestic product, four times less than the global average. The slow and partial adoption of new technologies explains 83 percent of the divergence in productivity gains between countries in LAC and advanced economies such as Japan, Spain, or Sweden.

But history is not destiny, as late-arriving countries as diverse as Finland, the Republic of Korea, Norway, and Spain suggest. It is what is done today that matters for a better tomorrow. The process of becoming so-called "learning economies" took centuries in the advanced economies. But among the "Asian Tigers," for example, it took just a few decades. There is nothing stopping countries in LAC from changing their approach today to adopting new technologies to achieve higher economic growth tomorrow.

This volume outlines some broad policy guidelines to change the approach. If adopted, they could over several decades transform economic prospects in the region as the payoffs from reform are potentially huge. As a necessary complement to developing market-friendly policies, these guidelines can help countries recognize emerging technological opportunities, develop strategies to exploit them, and then execute them effectively. This process requires learning on the part of the private sector, but also on the part of the government. States need to create an environment to make it easier to adopt new technologies and then encourage learning by firms and potential entrepreneurs.

Learning how to adopt new technologies is critical for the success of economies. Building the capacity to identify, adapt, and implement new technologies is also a critical complement to any successful industrial policy. This is becoming even more true as the accelerating adoption of artificial intelligence transforms how companies operate and how people work. Making changes to how one embraces new technologies can make a huge difference to the lives of citizens today and for their children tomorrow. There is no time to waste.

*Carlos Felipe Jaramillo*
Regional Vice President
Latin America and the Caribbean
World Bank

# Acknowledgments

This report was written by William F. Maloney, Xavier Cirera, and Maria Marta Ferreyra and is a product of the Office of the Chief Economist for Latin America and the Caribbean of the World Bank. We would like to thank Tugba Gurcanlar (World Bank) for contributions in the early part of the project, inputs to chapter 4, and for organizing the field visit to Argentina; to Marcio Cruz (International Finance Corporation), Yuheng Ding (World Bank), and Antonio Martins-Neto (World Bank) for contributions to chapter 2; and to Jose Andree Camarena, Puja Guha, Delfina Muller, and Gabriel Suarez Obando, who provided excellent research assistance.

This volume has benefited from conversations or collaboration with numerous academics and experts over many years: Ufuk Akcigit (University of Chicago), Andres Alvez (Fundação Getulio Vargas), Esteban Anzoise (National Technological University-Mendoza), Patricio Aroca (University Adolfo Ibáñez), Jorge Audy (PUC-Rio Grande do Sul), Edward Beatty (University of Notre Dame), Florencia Barletta (National University of General Sarmiento), José Miguel Benavente (CORFO Chile), Eduardo Bitran (University Adolfo Ibáñez), Georges Blanc (HEC Paris), Nick Bloom (Stanford University), Diego Comin (Dartmouth College), Chiara Criscuolo (IFC/OECD), Augusto de la Torre (Columbia University), Marcela Eslava (University of the Andes), Gustavo Ferro (University of CEMA), Clemente Forero (University of the Andes), Cristobal Garcia (Massachusetts Institute of Technology), Michela Giorcelli (University of California, Los Angeles), Hernando Jose Gomez (former Colombian Minister of Economic Planning and President of the Colombian Council of Competitiveness), Edwin Goñi (Inter-American

Development Bank), Juan Carlos Hallak (University of Buenos Aires), Marcelo Knobel (State University of Campinas), Pravin Krishna (Johns Hopkins University), Yevgeny Kuznetsov (Migration Policy Institute), Santiago Levy (Brookings Institution), Marco Llinas (Economic Commission for Latin America and the Caribbean), Patricio Meller (University of Chile), Juan Carlos Navarro (Inter-American Development Bank), Mariano Pereira (National University of General Sarmiento), Liz Reisberg (Reisberg and Associates), Juan D. Rogers (Georgia Institute of Technology), Jamil Salmi (Center for International Higher Education), Daniel Samoilovich (Columbus Association), Paula Toro (National Planning Department, Colombia; Consejala Manizales, Caldas, Colombia), Felipe Valencia Caicedo (Brown University), John Van Reenen (Massachusetts Institute of Technology), Nick Vornotas (George Washington University), and Gavin Wright (Stanford University).

We also thank our colleagues at the World Bank and International Finance Corporation who have collaborated or discussed these issues with us: Andreas Blom, Oscar Calvo, Paulo Correa, Michael Crawford, Marcio Cruz, Katia Herrera Sosa, Leonardo Iacovone, Somik Lall, Daniel Lederman, Kyungmin Lee, Martha Martinez Licetti, Jose Ernesto Lopez Cordoba, Denis Medvedev, Marcela Melendez, Suhas Parandekar, Heinz Rudolf, Jesica Torres Coronado, and Andres Zambrano.

We thank the following participants in seminars where early versions or sections of this volume were presented: Princeton University; Harvard Kennedy School of Government; the University of Notre Dame; the Escuela de Administración, Finanzas e Instituto Tecnológico in Medellín, Colombia; Escuela Politécnica Nacional in Quito, Ecuador; University of the Andes in Bogotá, Colombia; North American Chapter of the Econometric Society; Center for Monetary and Financial Studies; and Universidad Católica de Chile.

We are grateful to the Ministry of Economics and Finance of Uruguay and Uruguay's Innovation Hub for co-organizing the "Rethinking Innovation in Latin America and the Caribbean" conference held in 2024 in Montevideo, where the volume was soft-launched. Earlier versions or parts were also presented at the OECD/Ministry of Foreign Affairs of Brazil Fourth Ministerial Summit on Productivity (2022); the 2024 Business Association of Latin America "Innovation for Business Ecosystems" conference at the Fundacion Getulio Vargas in São Paulo, Brazil; the 2024 Latin American Network of Innovation Agencies (RELAI) in Santiago, Chile; the 2024

Economic Commission for Latin America and the Caribbean "Connecting the Productivity Challenge with Productive Development Policies in Latin America and the Caribbean" conference; the 2023 Latin American and Caribbean Economic Association conference in Bogotá, Colombia; the 2023 Columbus Association conference in PUC-Rio Grande do Sul; the 2024 Centro Interuniversitario de Desarrollo annual meeting in Santo Domingo, Dominican Republic; the 2024 Pan American Association of Educational Credit Institutions (APICE) in Barranquilla, Colombia; and the 2024 conference on higher education Cooperative University of Colombia in Medellín. We are grateful to the attendees for their reactions and comments.

The work has also benefited from interactions with policy makers and experts from several countries and regions who are working to improve their innovation ecosystems, including CORFO in Chile; the National Planning Department (DNP) and the Administrative Department of Science, Technology, and Innovation (Colciencias) in Colombia; the Ministry of Development, Industry, Trade, and Services (MDIC), the Agency for Industrial Development (ABDI), Support Service for Micro and Small Enterprises (SEBRAE), and the Agency for Research and Industrial Innovation (EMBRAPII) in Brazil; Manizales Más in Caldas, Colombia; Cristobal Garcia and firms and officials in the technology sector in Guadalajara, Mexico; the Ministry of Science, Technology, and Innovation in Argentina (MINCYT); the Peruvian National Council for Science, Technology, and Innovation (CONCYTEC); and the Colombian International Experts Mission on Innovation.

Finally, we would like to thank Jacqueline Larrabure Rivero for excellent project support, Nancy Morrison for editing the report, and Cindy Fisher, Patricia Katayama, and Mark McClure for providing production and acquisitions support.

# About the Authors

**Xavier Cirera** is a senior economist in the Markets, Competition and Technology Global Unit at the World Bank. He has more than 20 years' experience working in different microeconomic areas of development, including innovation and technology policies, productivity, firm-level dynamics, and trade policy. Prior to joining the World Bank, he was a research fellow at the Institute of Development Studies at the University of Sussex. His most recent research focuses on the measurement of firm-level technology adoption; the determinants and impacts of innovation; and the relationship between misallocation, productivity, and firm growth. His most recent policy work centers around the evaluation of innovation and entrepreneurship policies, leading the development of the public Expenditure Reviews in Science, Technology, and Innovation implemented in Brazil, Chile, Colombia, and Ukraine. He is a coauthor of *The Innovation Paradox: Developing-Country Capabilities and the Unrealized Promise of Technological Catch-Up*, *A Practitioner's Guide to Innovation Policy Instruments*, *The Innovation Imperative for Developing East Asia*, and *Bridging the Technological Divide: Firm Technology Adoption in Developing Countries*. He holds a PhD in economics from the University of Sussex.

**Maria Marta Ferreyra** is a senior economist in the Global Engagement and Knowledge unit of the Education Global Practice at the World Bank. Previously, she was a senior economist in the Office of the Chief Economist for Latin America and the Caribbean. Prior to joining the World Bank, she served as a faculty member at the Tepper School of Business at Carnegie Mellon University. Her research specializes in the economics of education.

She is the lead author of *At a Crossroads: Higher Education in Latin America and the Caribbean* and *The Fast Track to New Skills: Short-Cycle Higher Education Programs in Latin America and the Caribbean,* and the co-lead author of *Raising the Bar for Productive Cities in Latin America and the Caribbean.* She has conducted research on school choice, accountability, and finance in primary and secondary education in the United States; childcare markets in the United States; and higher education in Latin America and the Caribbean. She is currently the team lead on a global report on higher education and innovation and supporting higher education operational teams in Latin America and the Caribbean, Eastern Europe and Central Asia, and South Asia. Her research has been published in journals such as *American Economic Journal: Economic Policy, American Economic Review, Journal of Political Economy,* and *Journal of Public Economics.* She holds a PhD in economics from the University of Wisconsin-Madison.

**William F. Maloney** is chief economist for the Latin America and the Caribbean Region of the World Bank. He was previously chief economist for the Equitable Growth, Finance, and Institutions Vice Presidency; chief economist for trade and competitiveness; and lead economist in the Development Economics Research Group. Before joining the World Bank, he was a professor at the University of Illinois Urbana-Champaign. He has published in academic journals, including *American Economic Review: Insights, The Economic Journal, Journal of the European Economic Association, The Review of Economics and Statistics,* and *The Review of Economic Studies,* as well as on issues related to international trade and finance, developing country labor markets, and innovation and growth, and has contributed to several flagship publications of the Latin American division of the Bank. Most recently, he coauthored *The Innovation Paradox: Developing-Country Capabilities and the Unrealized Potential of Technological Catch-Up; Harvesting Prosperity: Technology and Productivity Growth in Agriculture;* and *Place, Productivity, and Prosperity: Spatially Targeted Policies for Regional Development,* as part of the World Bank Productivity Project series, which he directs. He holds a PhD in economics from the University of California, Berkeley.

# Abbreviations

| | |
|---|---|
| AI | artificial intelligence |
| ANID | Agencia Nacional de Investigación y Desarrollo (Chile) |
| CAPES | Coordenação de Aperfeiçoamento de Pessoal de Nível Superior (Brazil) |
| CDIO | conceive, design, implement, and operate |
| CNPq | Conselho Nacional de Desenvolvimento Científico e Tecnológico (Brazil) |
| CONAHCYT | Consejo Nacional de Humanidades, Ciencia y Tecnología (Mexico) |
| CONICET | Consejo Nacional de Investigaciones Científicas y Técnicas (Argentina) |
| CORFO | Corporación de Fomento de la Producción (Chile) |
| CRM | customer relationship management |
| DARPA | Defense Advanced Research Projects Agency (US) |
| ERP | enterprise resource planning |
| ESO | entrepreneurship support organization |
| EU | European Union |
| FAPESP | Fundação de Amparo à Pesquisa do Estado de São Paulo (Brazil) |
| FAT | Firm-level Adoption of Technology survey |

| | |
|---|---|
| FDI | foreign direct investment |
| FINEP | Financiadora de Estudos e Projetos (Brazil) |
| GBF | general business function |
| GDP | gross domestic product |
| HR | human resources |
| ICT | information and communication technology |
| ILO | International Labour Organization |
| IP | intellectual property |
| ISO | International Organization for Standardization |
| IT | information technology |
| LAC | Latin America and the Caribbean |
| MINCIENCIAS | Ministerio de Ciencia, Tecnología e Innovación (Colombia) |
| MIT | Massachusetts Institute of Technology |
| MSI | Millenium Science Initiative |
| NIH | National Institutes of Health (US) |
| NIS | National Innovation System |
| NSF | National Science Foundation |
| OECD | Organisation for Economic Co-operation and Development |
| PEVC | private equity and venture capital |
| PISA | Program of International Student Assessment |
| PNTP | Programa Nacional de Transformación Productiva (Argentina) |
| PPP | purchasing power parity |
| PRI | public research institute |
| R&D | research and development |
| RAIS | Relaçao Anual de Informaçoes Sociais |
| S&T | science and technology |
| SME | small and medium enterprise |
| STEM | science, technology, engineering, and mathematics |

| | |
|---|---|
| TFP | total factor productivity |
| TTO | Technology Transfer Office |
| UC | University of California |
| VC | venture capital |

# Introduction
## Building Learning Economies in Latin America and the Caribbean

*"Knowledge is a free good. The biggest cost in its transmission is not in the production or distribution of knowledge, but in its assimilation. . . ."*

—Kenneth Arrow[1]

## Background

The growth strategy of the Latin America and the Caribbean (LAC) region has come under scrutiny. While there is a growing body of evidence that market-oriented approaches yield better development outcomes than the alternatives (see, for example, Irwin 2020), the indisputable fact is that growth in the region, even in the best-performing countries, remains too low to generate fulfilling jobs and social progress. Before the COVID-19 pandemic, from 2010 to 2018, gross domestic product grew on average 2.2 percent; forecasts today are scarcely better, hovering at about 2.5 percent. Estimates in the *World Development Report 2024* on the middle-income trap (World Bank 2024) suggest that without additional productivity growth, it would take a country like Brazil 30 years to become a high-income country. Further, the region's economy has tended to remain underdiversified and dependent on a small number of commodities. This underperformance has understandably led to a questioning of mainstream economic growth recipes of the last 30 years and given new life to industrial policies.

However, this disappointing growth performance is not a recent problem, nor are its causes new, nor is it particular to one economic model, nor will it be cured by a return to the mechanistic industrial policies of the past. LAC has underperformed across most sectors in the last century and has steadily diverged from advanced economies that were at a similar level of income in 1900. With the exception of episodic booms driven by commodity prices, the history is one of missed opportunities for productivity growth and diversification that extends to recent decades. In the language of the *World Development Report 2024* (World Bank 2024), LAC has experienced a prolonged income trap, although one that has affected the region's relatively wealthy countries and relatively poor countries alike, and over a very long period.

This volume argues that the cause lies in a fundamental disconnect. Countries in the region have faltered in the process of becoming "learning economies": in learning how to learn to identify and exploit technological opportunities.[2] This process took centuries in the advanced countries and miraculously mere decades in the Asian Tigers. Development is fundamentally an experimental process of learning about new technologies or ideas that can lead to more profitable firms or to new firms and areas of comparative advantage. It is not enough for information to flow more freely, as Nobel Prize winner Kenneth Arrow notes. Rather, countries need to learn how to assimilate these technologies—to be able to arbitrage across the expanding technology gap between advanced and follower countries and exploit the new opportunities for growth. This arbitrage process implies placing a series of informed bets, with attendant risk, that require a set of *capabilities*—in the form of basic, technical, managerial, and entrepreneurial human capital—working in an *enabling environment* that includes factor and product markets that function well, along with supporting nonmarket, knowledge-related institutions such as universities and public research entities. Together, these determine a country's capacity for technological absorption: to understand new technologies, evaluate their profitability relative to existing alternatives, finance and implement them over a long gestation period, and manage risk and the potential for failure.

Crucially, these capabilities and supporting institutions need to evolve in order to comprehend and manage the greater complexities that arise as the global leaders in technology advance to new levels—that is, the technological frontier shifts out (Nelson 2005). In LAC, they did not evolve, and the region's lost century of growth arguably arose because it faced the Second Industrial Revolution unarmed: it was unable to "learn how to learn" about the new advances arriving in the Second Industrial Revolution.

Despite notable progress, the region continues to lag. Other fast-growing countries that were at the same level as or behind LAC countries, ranging from Australia, Finland, Norway, and Sweden to the Asian Miracles of Japan, Republic of Korea, and Taiwan, China, sometimes producing the same goods as LAC, mastered frontier technologies and leveraged them to form new businesses and sectors in a race to be full partners at the global frontier. LAC's inability to follow suit resulted in a lack of competitiveness that led not only to low growth but also to an acute sense of dependency and demands for protection that morphed into distortive industrial policies that compounded the shortfalls in capabilities, rather than remedying them.

## LAC Exemplifies the Innovation Paradox

This diagnosis has far-reaching implications. First, it is integral to resolving the conundrum laid out in the *Innovation Paradox: Developing-Country Capabilities and the Unrealized Promise of Technological Catch-up* (Cirera and Maloney 2017). Returns to innovation—adoption of new technologies, processes, and products, as well as invention—can be quite high; they exceed 55 percent in the United States (Bloom, Schankerman, and Van Reenen 2013; Jones and Summers 2020; Lucking, Bloom, and Van Reenen 2019), and appear to increase with distance to the technological frontier, reaching 77 percent in the United Kingdom and 88 percent in Italy (Griffith, Redding, and Van Reenen 2004). Yet LAC, as a region and individual country, invests far less than the advanced economies in innovation of all types. One explanation for this lack of investment is the absence of complementary factors, ranging from credit to skilled labor, risk finance, and other elements of the enabling environment, and distortions more generally, that lower the actual expected return to innovation of all types. Indeed, returns begin to fall, even turning negative at very low income levels, where the most basic elements of the enabling environment and human capital are lacking (Goñi and Maloney 2017). Hence, the concern about establishing healthy market-friendly conditions for the enabling environment remains essential to the growth agenda.

However, much of the low uptake is also due to deficiencies in the capabilities of both the individuals populating this environment and supporting institutions to identify, adopt, and use frontier knowledge and take advantage of new and existing products, processes, and technologies. This volume uses the term "capabilities" to capture the central ingredient for growth and developing learning societies. Capabilities refer to the ability of firms and entrepreneurs to improve firms' outcomes given a set of inputs. These capabilities have been associated with management and organizational capacity as dynamic capabilities (Teece, Pisano, and Shuen 1997). More recently, Verhoogen (2023) has offered a more succinct and formal treatment for the ability of a firm in its overall production technique, which includes the ability to produce at higher quality (Hallak and Sivadasan 2013; Sutton 2007), as well as its organizational capital, including intangible assets, such as management practices or human capital. While the literature uses a variety of different terms—including technological or organizational capabilities, among others—these are all speaking to a broad class of these capabilities (Cirera, Lopez-Bassols, and Maloney 2016). Nurturing and accumulating them, as well as supporting institutions, are the key ingredients for learning societies, and the focus of this volume.

## Growth Policy in the 21st Century Requires Being Prepared to Be Partners at the Technological Frontier

What does this imply for a 21st-century growth strategy—one that also generates maximum development benefits from the energy transition,[3] as well as engendering the nimbleness needed to face a rapidly changing global trade context? Such a strategy will require a set of reforms particularly related to developing this learning capacity and actively seeking insertion in the global knowledge economy. However possible it might have been 100 years ago for countries to erect protectionist barriers, pursue learning by doing, and effectively reinvent frontier technologies, it is far more difficult today.

An example is provided by the current race to master advanced chip manufacturing. The cooperation of the sector leaders in Taiwan, China, with producers in the United States in transferring advanced technologies to US producers makes that project far more feasible than that of mainland China, which cannot count on that transfer (Goldberg et al. 2024). In the natural resources sectors, the analogous example is Norway's collaboration with Esso to transfer oil exploration technology to exploit oil in the North Sea, and then with Mobil to gain field development expertise,[4] a bargain of access to resources for transfer of know-how and of building learning capacity in those sectors. More generally, necessary technologies are easily licensable—but surveys discussed in this volume suggest LAC takes less advantage of such licenses and partnerships than other regions.

Learning to use frontier knowledge and then leveraging that knowledge—whether building efficient suppliers or engendering spin-offs from multinationals to fostering domestic champions in new sectors—requires the participation of both the source and the receiving country. Much knowledge is free and underutilized, as Arrow notes, but in important cases, the possessors of those technologies need to see the value to themselves of their diffusion. Both China with its massive market and Norway with its prized petroleum reserves could strike bargains to transfer capabilities and knowledge over time that only a few countries in LAC will be able to replicate. However, on the demand side, countries need to have as a priority learning from foreign direct investment and other sources of technology and developing the technological and entrepreneurial capabilities to do so.

## Industrial Policy Must Be National Learning Policy

Yet there is a growing trend in LAC and elsewhere in the opposite direction—back toward interventionist industrial policies, relying on trade barriers and subsidies to engineer structural change (figure I.1). The focus on national learning directly challenges this view. If these interventionist policies are not led by other policies redressing deeper shortfalls in the region's capabilities, LAC will again effect only surface-level structural change—applying the veneer of modernity without engaging in the deep changes needed to achieve the actual modernization that will lead to rapid and sustained productivity growth. These shortcomings are highlighted by recent mission-oriented strategies patterned after the massive undertaking by the United States in the 1960s to put a man on the moon—the so-called Moon Shot (Mazzucato 2021). Given the dubious economic value of the lunar landing, it can be argued that the mission's primary goal was precisely demonstrating to the world that the United States possessed these entrepreneurial and technical capabilities, without which any mission in any field will fail. More profoundly, part of the experimental nature of development is precisely in discovering new areas of comparative advantage. The greater the capabilities of the private sector to undertake the risky process of experimentation, albeit subsidized, the less the dependence on the capacities of the public sector to choose. Developing these capabilities needs to be Latin America's mission.

This may be especially the case in the emerging trade in services that is likely to be more important going forward than manufacturing. In this sector, the link between value added and the capabilities of the workforce is direct (Baldwin and Forslid 2023; Nayyar, Hallward-Driemeier, and Davies 2021). Ninety percent of Chinese patents, for example, are joint with Taiwanese or US companies, suggesting that they should be seen more as "exports" of high-end engineering services (Branstetter, Li, and Veloso 2015). India similarly is upgrading from call centers to expanding its technical service exports with major US firms relocating operations there.[5] With the spread of simultaneous translation driven by artificial intelligence, the barriers to being the provider of services across the spectrum will fall, leaving the capabilities of local workers, service firms, and their supporting institutions as the determinant of where LAC inserts itself in the services value chain.

**FIGURE I.1 Industrial Policies and Import Barriers Are Back in Latin America**

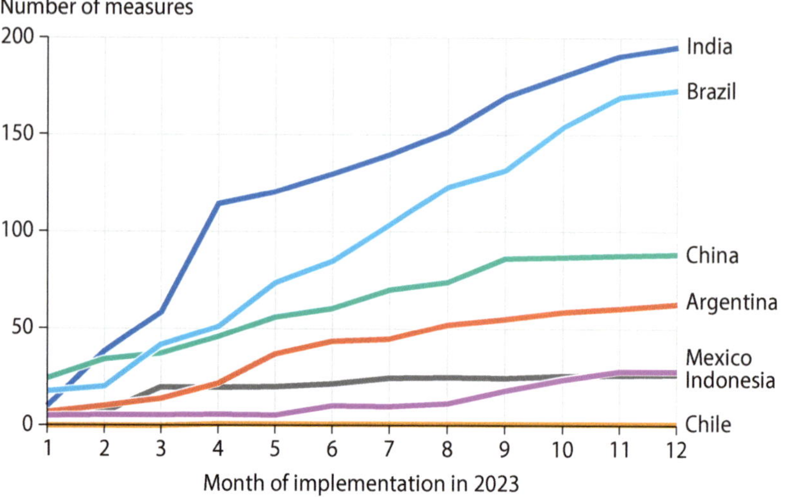


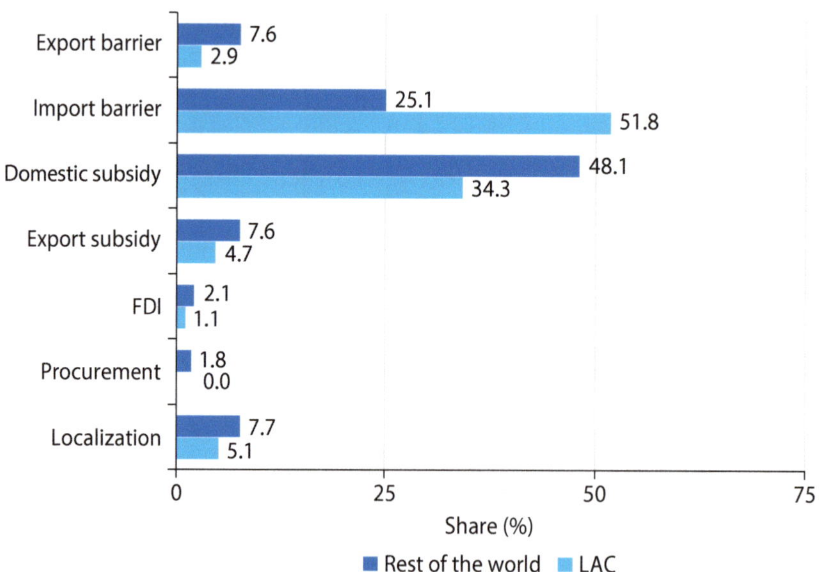


*Source:* Original figure for this volume using data from the New Industrial Policy Database described in Evenett et al. 2024.

*Note:* The figure shows the number of industrial policy measures implemented or announced by month in 2023. FDI = foreign direct investment; LAC = Latin America and the Caribbean.

## Plan of the Volume

Chapter 1, "LAC's Lost Century: A Failure of National Learning," presents a view of Latin America and the Caribbean's development that stresses the inability of the region to learn about the new technologies of the Second Industrial Revolution and apply them—which, in turn, prevented convergence in incomes with successful economies. In the late 1800s and early 1900s, the region had several high-performing countries but then experienced retrocession in industries in which it had long dominated, due to an inability to employ the emerging technologies, and was unable to enter the new industries of the day. As an illustration, the chapter explores differences in how, in this pivotal moment, LAC defined the next century compared to Japan. While Japan invested heavily in capabilities and institutions across the spectrum to become equal partners with foreigners at the technological frontier, LAC ceded to them its most profitable industries.

Chapter 2, "Firms and the Diffusion and Productive Use of Knowledge," explores the extent to which knowledge and technologies are being adopted in LAC today. Using data from the recently fielded World Bank Firm-level Adoption of Technology survey, it measures the diffusion gap and decomposes it into three components: access to new technology; adoption of these technologies; and then effective use. The chapter shows that while some digital technologies are diffusing faster to the region, there are significant gaps in adoption of key technologies, and more importantly significant gaps in their use that could translate into unrealized productivity gains. The chapter then reviews the key barriers to identify, adopt, and use such technologies, emphasizing existing constraints in capabilities, manifested in skills, managerial quality, and organizational capital. Then the chapter documents the ways in which the region's current level of technical education, entrepreneurial skills, and supporting institutions continue to lag. Hence, in addition to the need to continue to improve the business environment, the chapter identifies areas of learning capacity in which progress needs to be made.

Chapter 3, "The Role of Universities and Research Institutes in Learning Economies," focuses on the educational and research institutes in the National Innovation Systems of LAC countries that serve to generate human capital and research, diffuse, and adapt technologies to the local context; and serve as seed beds for new industries. There needs to be a clear and codified understanding that part of the mission of universities, and the unique mission of research institutes, is the resolution of the market failures surrounding knowledge and of supporting the private sector in its development—their "third mission" after teaching and research. This, in turn, requires the need for incentives to ensure the quality of underlying research and its relevance to the private sector, and the cultivation of linkages that guarantee a two-way flow of knowledge. In LAC, academic and research institutes fall short both in quality and in the development of their third mission, leading to unsatisfactory outcomes and weak linkages between their research effort and private sector needs and applications. LAC's failures are not due to not having implemented policies to promote education, research, and knowledge exchange; rather, they are due to having implemented them poorly—without a strategic vision, clear priorities, at sufficient scale, and consistency over time and across space.

Chapter 4, "New Firms, New Sectors: Creating Experimental Economies and High-Quality Entrepreneurship," explores why, despite the vast potential for arbitraging the technological gap, there are relatively few high-quality entrepreneurs doing so in LAC. The chapter offers a simple framework for thinking about what the entrepreneurial ecosystem requires to foster experimentation—learning about possible new firms or industries. This approach implies focusing both on the operating environment—barriers to investment, absence of start-up financing and risk diffusion mechanisms, the presence of less risky alternatives—as well as those related to the characteristics and skills of entrepreneurs, ranging from attitudes to basic technical and administrative skills, to the harder-to-develop skills of distinguishing good new projects and managing the risk and financing. It stresses how the rise of the Latin American unicorns (firms with revenues exceeding US$1 billion) reflect the emergence of high-quality entrepreneurs, but also the importance of international experience in their formation, and global sources of venture capital, which are hard to replicate locally.

Chapter 5, "Policy Guidelines for Creating Learning Economies," concludes with policy proposals.

## Notes

1. Quoted in Stiglitz and Greenwald (2015, 507).
2. For discussions of learning economies or societies, refer to Lundvall and Johnson (1994) and Stiglitz and Greenwald (2015).
3. Refer to *From Resource-Rich to Resource-Smart: LAC's Opportunities in the Energy Transition* (Beylis and Lozano, forthcoming).
4. Refer to https://equinor.industriminne.no/en/partnerships-for-the-future1/ and https://equinor.industriminne.no/en/statfjord-awarded/. Also refer to Ville and Wicken (2013).
5. https://www.nytimes.com/2025/03/26/business/india-jobs-global-capability-center.html?smid=nytcore-ios-share&referringSource=articleShare&sgrp=c&pvid=1F44F94C-13DF-46A7-AF45-304504B7B07A.

## References

Baldwin, R., and R. Forslid. 2023. "Globotics and Development: When Manufacturing Is Jobless and Services Are Tradeable." *World Trade Review* 22 (3–4): 302–11.

Beylis, G., and N. Lozano. Forthcoming. *From Resource-Rich to Resource-Smart: LAC's Opportunities in the Energy Transition.* Washington, DC: World Bank.

Bloom, N., M. Schankerman, and J. Van Reenen. 2013. "Identifying Technology Spillovers and Product Market Rivalry." *Econometrica* 81 (4): 1347–93.

Branstetter, L., G. Li, and F. Veloso. 2015. "The Rise of International Co-Invention." In *The Changing Frontier: Rethinking Science and Innovation Policy*, edited by A. B. Jaffe and B. F. Jones, 135–68. Cambridge, MA: National Bureau of Economic Research.

Cirera, X., V. Lopez-Bassols, and W. F. Maloney. 2016. *Firm Capabilities for Innovation. A Conceptual Framework*. Washington, DC: World Bank. Unpublished.

Cirera, X., and W. F. Maloney. 2017. *The Innovation Paradox: Developing-Country Capabilities and the Unrealized Promise of Technological Catch-Up.* Washington, DC: World Bank.

Evenett, S., A. Jakubik, F. Martín, and M. Ruta. 2024. "The Return of Industrial Policy in Data." *World Economy* 47 (7): 2762–88.

Goldberg, P. K., R. Juhász, N. J. Lane, G. L. Forte, and J. Thurk. 2024. "Industrial Policy in the Global Semiconductor Sector." NBER Working Paper 32651, National Bureau of Economic Research, Cambridge, MA.

Goñi, E., and W. F. Maloney. 2017. "Why Don't Poor Countries Do R&D? Varying Rates of Factor Returns across the Development Process." *European Economic Review* 94: 126–47.

Griffith, R., S. Redding, and J. V. Reenen. 2004. "Mapping the Two Faces of R&D: Productivity Growth in a Panel of OECD Industries." *Review of Economics and Statistics* 86 (4): 883–95.

Hallak, J. C., and J. Sivadasan. 2013. "Product and Process Productivity: Implications for Quality Choice and Conditional Exporter Premia." *Journal of International Economics* 91 (1): 53–67.

Irwin, D. 2020. "The Washington Consensus Stands Test of Time Better than Populist Policies." Realtime Economics (blog), December 4, 2020, Peterson Institute for International Economics, Washington, DC.

Jones, B. F., and L. H. Summers. 2020. "A Calculation of the Social Returns to Innovation." NBER Working Paper 27863, National Bureau of Economic Research, Cambridge, MA.

Lucking, B., N. Bloom, and J. Van Reenen. 2019. "Have R&D Spillovers Declined in the 21st Century?" *Fiscal Studies* 40 (4): 561–90.

Lundvall, B.-A., and B. Johnson. 1994. "The Learning Economy." *Journal of Industry Studies* 1 (2): 23–42.

Mazzucato, M. 2021. *Mission Economy: A Moonshot Guide to Changing Capitalism.* Penguin UK.

Nayyar, G., M. Hallward-Driemeier, and E. Davies. 2021. *At Your Service? The Promise of Services-Led Development*. Washington, DC: World Bank.

Nelson, R. R. 2005. *Technology, Institutions, and Economic Growth.* Cambridge, MA: Harvard University Press.

Stiglitz, J. E., and B. C. Greenwald. 2015. *Creating a Learning Society: A New Approach to Growth, Development, and Social Progress.* New York: Columbia University Press.

Sutton, John. 2007. “Quality, Trade and the Moving Window: The Globalization Process.” *Economic Journal* 117 (524): F469–98.

Teece, D. J., G. Pisano, and A. Shuen. 1997. “Dynamic Capabilities and Strategic Management.” *Strategic Management Journal* 18 (7): 509–33.

Verhoogen, E. 2023. “Firm-Level Upgrading in Developing Countries.” *Journal of Economic Literature* 61 (4): 1410–64.

Ville, S., and O. Wicken. 2013. “The Dynamics of Resource-Based Economic Development: Evidence from Australia and Norway.” *Industrial and Corporate Change* 22 (5): 1341–71.

World Bank. 2024. *World Development Report 2024: The Middle-Income Trap.* Washington, DC: World Bank.

# 1 LAC's Lost Century
## A Failure of National Learning

*"Subdesenvolvimento não se improvisa, é obra de séculos."*

*["Underdevelopment is not improvised; it is the work of centuries."]*

—Nelson Rodrigues[1]

## Introduction

In 1850, the average income in the Latin America and the Caribbean (LAC) region was on a par with that of Japan, Spain, and Sweden at about 40 percent of the United States's income, and substantially above that of Korea (figure 1.1, panel a). Viewing the subsequent evolution, the central growth question centers not so much on the lost decade of the 1990s, when the region slipped from 30 percent to 20 percent of US income, but rather why, beginning at the turn of the 20th century, the Asian and Nordic comparators, as well as the colonial mother countries of Portugal and Spain, were able to catch up to about 60 percent of US levels. At the same time, LAC's relative position remained unchanged.

Disaggregating further deepens the mystery by revealing a group of Latin American superstars (Argentina, Uruguay, and to a lesser extent Chile) that reached about 60 percent of US income levels, and were tied with France and Germany at the end of the 19th century (1890), while a second group of relatively poor countries (including Brazil, Colombia, Mexico, and Peru) remained at 25 percent (figure 1.1, panel b). The early world-class performance of the superstars and the fact that Portugal and Spain behaved like "median" LAC countries until 1950 militates somewhat against a

**FIGURE 1.1 LAC Has Underperformed for More than a Century**

a. LAC region's income versus European and Asian comparators
relative to the United States, 1850–2020


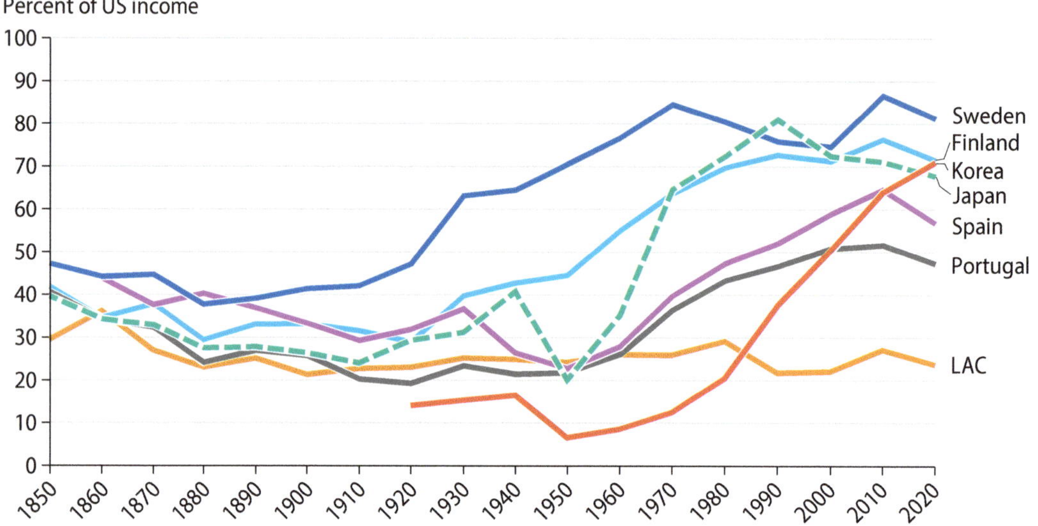


**b. Individual LAC countries' income versus Germany and France comparators relative to the United States, 1850–2020**

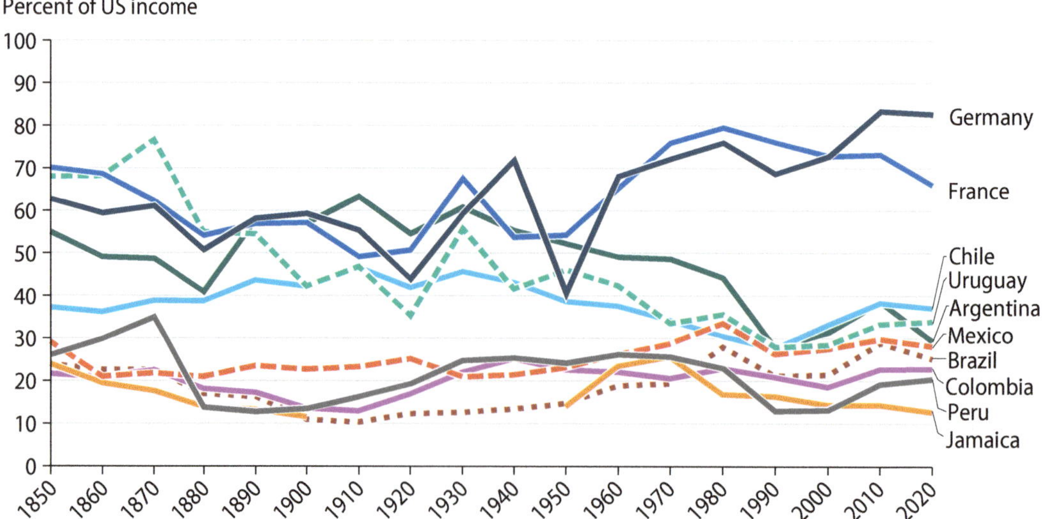


*Source:* Original figure for this volume based on 2023 Maddison Project Database (https://www.rug.nl/ggdc/historicaldevelopment/maddison/releases/).

*Note:* In both panels, income refers to gross domestic product per capita. In panel a, Korea refers to the historical Korea until 1948, and the Republic of Korea after that. LAC = Latin America and the Caribbean.

view that there are idiosyncratic factors particular to the region that would obviously condemn it to underperformance.

However, with the advent of the Second Industrial Revolution around 1880, the LAC superstars began to lose ground relative to the United States. Further, while some of the laggards grew very well (Brazil tied Portugal, Spain, and Sweden at increasing income 11 times across the 20th century), most grew less than the frontier countries (France, Germany, and the United States) and far below the century's catch-up miracles like Finland, Japan, and later the Republic of Korea—and hence did not converge. Viewed through this lens, LAC did not lose two decades in the 1980s and 1990s; it lost the 20th century. In the language of the *World Development Report 2024* (World Bank 2024), the LAC superstars hit a middle-income trap around 1900, while the poorer group grew well, but just not better than the frontier countries in other regions.

## The Mechanics of Lost Growth: LAC's Inability to Adopt the Technologies of the Second Industrial Revolution

Economic convergence is driven by firms and farms adopting frontier technologies, enabling growth rates faster than those of the countries that are inventing these technologies. Small differences in rates of adoption can result in large divergence (Parente and Prescott 1994, 2002). A large share of productivity growth in the Organisation for Economic Co-operation and Development (OECD) is attributed to technology diffusion (Eaton and Kortum 1999). Historically, adoption of new technologies is not only risky but requires a trial-and-error process in the organization of production that, in turn, leads to heterogeneity across firms facing the same technological opportunities and slow convergence in productivity gains across time (Juhász, Squicciarini, and Voigtländer 2024). Figure 1.2 suggests that for much of the past two centuries, LAC has been relatively slow at adopting technologies ranging from steamships to computers. Simulations suggest these lags can explain 83 percent of this lack of convergence or divergence (Comin and Mestieri 2018).

Historical case studies of particular industries offer insight into how this process unfolded on the ground. A particularly striking example is the evolution of the emblematic mining sector, in which Latin America excelled for centuries before losing with catastrophic economic and, in some cases, political consequences. Chile's copper industry dominated world markets in the mid-19th century, but lost global market share (figure 1.3, dotted line),

**FIGURE 1.2 Latin America Has Lagged in Adopting New Technologies**

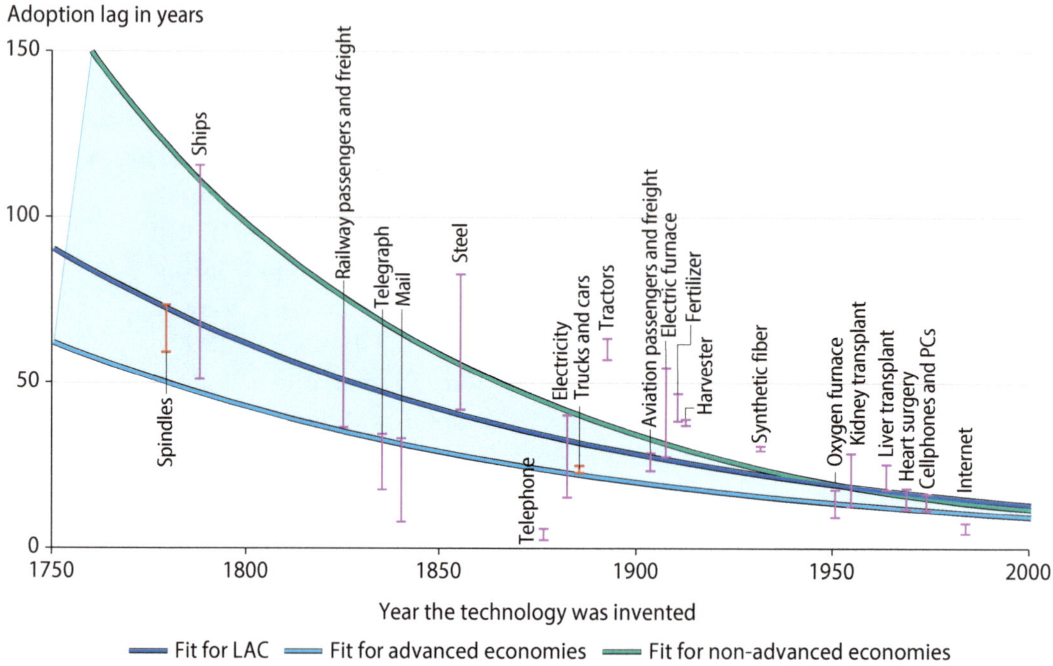

Adoption lag in years
150
100
50
0
1750
1800
1850
1900
1950
2000
Year the technology was invented
Spindles
Ships
Railway passengers and freight
Telegraph
Mail
Steel
Telephone
Electricity
Trucks and cars
Tractors
Aviation passengers and freight
Electric furnace
Fertilizer
Harvester
Synthetic fiber
Oxygen furnace
Kidney transplant
Liver transplant
Heart surgery
Cellphones and PCs
Internet
Fit for LAC
Fit for advanced economies
Fit for non-advanced economies


*Source:* Original figure for this volume based on Comin and Mestieri 2018.
*Note:* The figure shows the evolution over time of adoption lags, the difference in the years in the adoption between advanced economies and LAC for specific technologies. LAC = Latin America and the Caribbean; PCs = personal computers.

**FIGURE 1.3 Chile Ceded Its Domestic Dominance in Copper Production to Foreign Technology and Know-How Over the Course of a Century**

Percent of world production
Copper production (metric tons)
70
60
50
40
30
20
10
0
7,000
6,000
5,000
4,000
3,000
2,000
1,000
0
Introduction of new technologies
1870
1880
1890
1900
1910
1920
1930
1940
1950
1950
1970
Percent of world production (left scale)
Copper production (right scale)


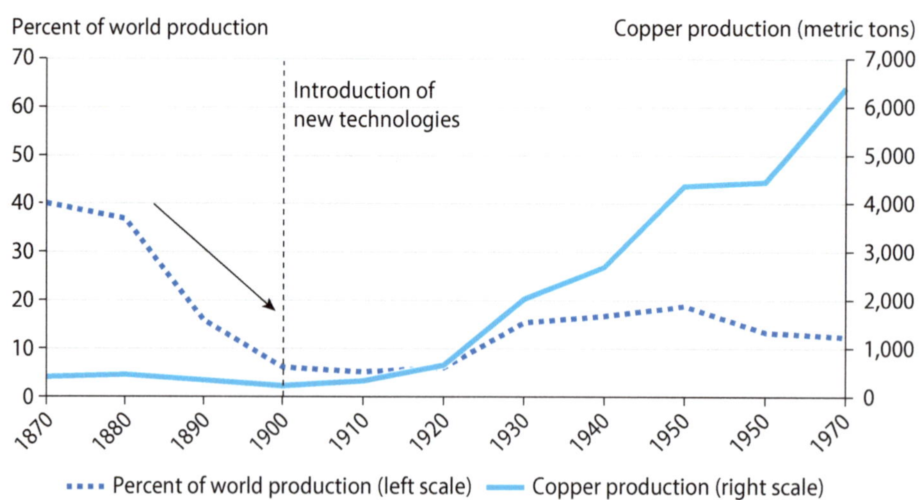

*Source:* Maloney and Valencia Caicedo 2022.

and production stagnated so much (solid line) that the industry was declared bankrupt by 1900 by the leading industrial association SOFOFA. It was revived only by the infusion of foreign technology and know-how by US firms, which would grow to completely dominate the sector (Maloney and Valencia Caicedo 2022).

This dynamic was replicated throughout the region and can be seen with more granularity in the gold and silver industry in Mexico (figure 1.4). In the 19th century, local and foreign patenting were of similar orders of magnitude, suggesting similar levels of innovation. However, the introduction of the MacArthur-Forrest cyanide separation process in 1903 led to an explosion of patents for new techniques related to the refining of gold and silver ores, which was entirely due to foreigners. As Beatty (2015a) notes, the fact that Mexican technicians, miners, and mining engineers played no part is striking given the long history of Mexican mining expertise: Mexico produced the dominant refining technology three centuries earlier. In the late 18th century, it was home to the first technical school in the Americas—Royal Mining College. As late as the 1870s and 1880s, as in Chile, local miners and engineers

**FIGURE 1.4 Domestic Innovation Stalled in Mexico with the Advent of New Industrial Processes**

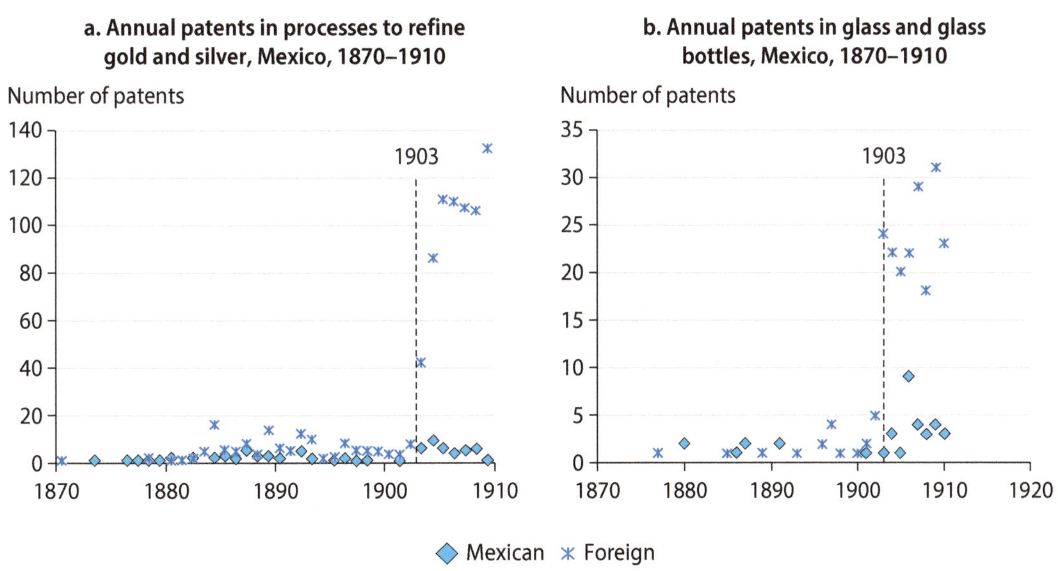


*Source:* Beatty 2015a.
*Note:* The panels show the number of patents filed each year by locals and foreigners after the introduction of new technologies. The year 1903 (vertical dotted line) marked the introduction of radical new technology.

directed most of the nation's mining and refining activity. However, the introduction of the cyanide process was part of the shifting technological frontier during the Second Industrial Revolution and was dependent on the newly emergent fields of industrial chemistry, electricity, and machine building. The epicenter of expertise shifted to mining colleges in Britain, Germany, and the United States. Mining had radically changed from a speculative short-term activity to an industrial science, and in fact, one of the most technically advanced sectors of the time (Beatty 2015a, 60; Tortella Casares 2000).

Clearly, neither case of national retrogression in mining offers any support to the idea of a resource curse—a low growth trajectory intrinsic to these products (for a review, refer to Lederman and Maloney 2007); identical products yielded very different outcomes in local versus foreign hands. Further, mining had very different development impacts in other countries. Stanford University economic historian Gavin Wright cites the US experience with copper as an example of "how nations learn." Exploiting copper gave impetus to schools of mining, for instance, at Columbia University and the University of California, Berkeley, which would later morph into major research universities at the frontier of metallurgy and chemistry, which in turn would lay the foundation for diversified industrialization. "The United States did more than passively live off the rents from these resources, but this unique resource base served as the foundation for an advanced national technology and applied science oriented toward this particular bundle of resources" (Wright 1987, 168). Similarly, Japan, perhaps contrary to its image as a manufacturing miracle, leveraged its position as a major copper producer in the same period into broader-based growth: high-tech conglomerates Fujitsu, Hitachi, and Sumitomo all began as copper mining companies (Maloney and Zambrano 2022).

Latin America lacks any comparable legacies. In fact, by 1900, mining across the continent had passed almost entirely into foreign hands, leaving the host nations with an acute feeling of dependency and a limited indigenous technical base upon which to diversify their economies. As late as 1952, Chileans had no capacity to monitor, let alone run, the giant foreign mines in the Norte Grande, and would not until 1965.[2] By 1945, 96 percent of investment in the Mexican mining industry would be in foreign hands (Maloney and Zambrano 2022). Similarly, Colombians clearly saw a lack of technical expertise as a barrier to taking back control of their petroleum industry (Murray 1997).

### What Matters Is Not What a Country Produces, but How

The preceding discussion reveals with blinding clarity how industrial policy discussions focusing primarily on an artificially induced structural change—defined as changing country baskets of production or exports—are fatally incomplete and misleading. Producing a homogenous product like copper or silver that has not changed substantially since the Big Bang spewed these minerals across the universe can yield very different development paths; success depends on the ability of firms and nations to identify and apply the right technologies to their production. It is not what a country produces, but how (Lederman and Maloney 2012).

This applies to manufacturing, as well. One frequently studied example is how the 19th-century synthetic dye industry in the United Kingdom fell behind the surging competition from Germany (Murmann 2003). Similarly, Southern US industrial sectors lagged the North, most emblematically in the failing Birmingham Steel company in Alabama. As steel mogul Andrew Carnegie mocked, "You have all the ingredients, but you cannot make steel." (Wright 1986, 171). Latin America's limited manufacturing sectors at the turn of the 20th century experienced retrogression similar to that in mining and would struggle to introduce new industries. Mexico again offers a granular example with clear parallels to the current nearshoring movement. The appearance in 1903 of the Owens automated glass blowing machine revolutionized the bottling industry in Mexico, but as figure 1.4, panel b shows, 87 percent of patents in Mexico would be filed by foreigners, concentrated in mechanical improvements, while the few patents filed by Mexicans were in decoration (Beatty 2015a). Similarly, no improvements occurred in productivity or technology adaptation in Mexico's textile industry in the 19th century (Gómez-Galvarriato 2007). In Minas Gerais, Brazil, nascent textile and steel industries fell behind global competitors from 1830 to 1880, experiencing a "retrogression of technique" (Rogers 1962, 183). Again, this is not a problem of the production basket—Japan during this period became a textile powerhouse, while Denmark grew rapidly by innovating in "low-tech" industries related to food, textiles, and furniture (Lundvall 2013).

In each of the preceding cases, distinct experiences with very similar products suggest tremendous missed opportunities for more dynamic and diversified development, and a short-circuiting of an organic process of structural change. Indeed, historian Guido Di Tella (1985, 51) explains the relative decline of Argentina relative to other resource-rich countries fundamentally as a function of its inability to transition from relying on the continued expansion of the frontier to a growth model driven more by technology and innovation. "To the extent that development was based on innovation, [the United States and Canada] were switching to an alternative and unlimited source of growth. To the extent that [Argentina's development] was based on collusion, it opened up a limited, alternative path."

## Facing the Second Industrial Revolution Unarmed: LAC Lags in Technical and Entrepreneurial Capabilities

Moving to a growth model based on learning and innovation begins by recognizing that technology transfer, and even more so invention, is not a disembodied flow of ideas; it is affected by individuals—entrepreneurs, scientists, and skilled workers working within supporting entrepreneurial and innovation systems—placing risky bets that experimenting with new ideas will pay off. This phenomenon has sometimes been called "absorptive capacity." The possession of these capabilities and institutions was essential to benefiting from and competing in the Second Industrial Revolution, but LAC effectively faced this revolution unarmed.

### Weak Technical Capabilities and Institutions

This is illustrated well by one proxy for technological capabilities, the density of domestically trained engineers, which captures both the presence of technical capabilities as well as the institutions that would train them, undertake research, and interact with the global scientific community.[3] Despite Argentina and Chile having similar income levels as Denmark and Sweden around 1900, consistent with figure 1.5, panel a, those Nordic countries have levels near that of the United States—and five times the engineering density as the average Latin American country. This gap immediately makes technical capabilities a prime suspect for driving the divergence in technology adoption seen in figure 1.5, panel b. The fact that the US South is closer to Latin America than the US North helps explain the frequent similarities of experience. As Wright notes, "the distinctive resources base of the South required adaptations in technology, but the South lacked a strong indigenous community of engineers and mechanics devoted to these tasks" (Wright 1986, 167).

**FIGURE 1.5 LAC Had Low Technical Capacity and Technology Adoption Compared to Other Countries at Its Income Level around 1900**

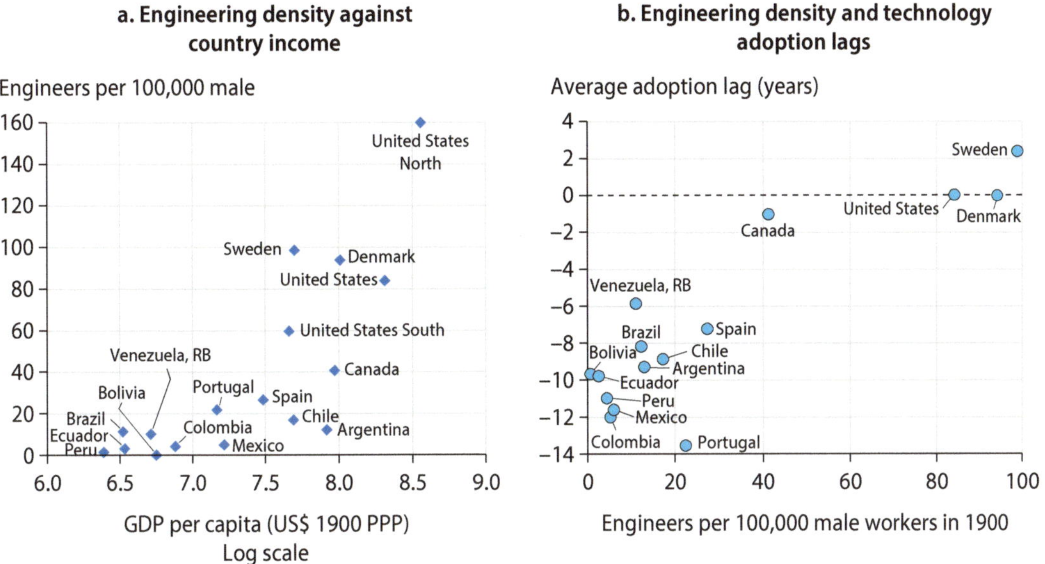


*Sources:* Original figure for this volume based on Maloney and Valencia Caicedo (2022) (panel a); and Alfaro and Comin (forthcoming), based on Comin and Mestieri (2018) and Maloney and Valencia Caicedo (2022) (panel b).
*Note:* Panel b plots the average adoption lag in the United States minus the lag in each country for technologies invented after 1900 against the number of engineers per 100,000 male works in each country in 1900. GDP = gross domestic product; LAC = Latin America and the Caribbean.

Figure 1.5, panel b, shows that Comin and Mestieri's (2018) estimates of slow LAC average adoption lags in 1900 are correlated with lower engineering density (Maloney and Valencia Caicedo 2022). At a more granular subnational level, the 50 states of the United States offer evidence of the importance of such skills. Across the US states, the adoption of new corn varieties, tractors (mechanized farming), and personal computers, as well as the number of inventors even today is highly correlated with engineering density in 1900 (figure 1.6). At the firm level, evidence from global gold mining firms in 1900 shows that engineering presence on the management teams was the most important determinant of the rate of adoption of new technologies (Solares and Beatty 2024). Spain's shift toward an outward orientation, openness to foreign direct investment (FDI), and local procurement set-asides led to growth precisely because Spanish engineering firms were able to assimilate imported knowledge and new capabilities and converge to the frontier (Álvaro-Moya 2014; Calvo-Gonzalez 2021). This "upper tail" human capital is as or more important than basic literacy

**FIGURE 1.6 Higher Technical Capabilities Lead to Faster Adoption**

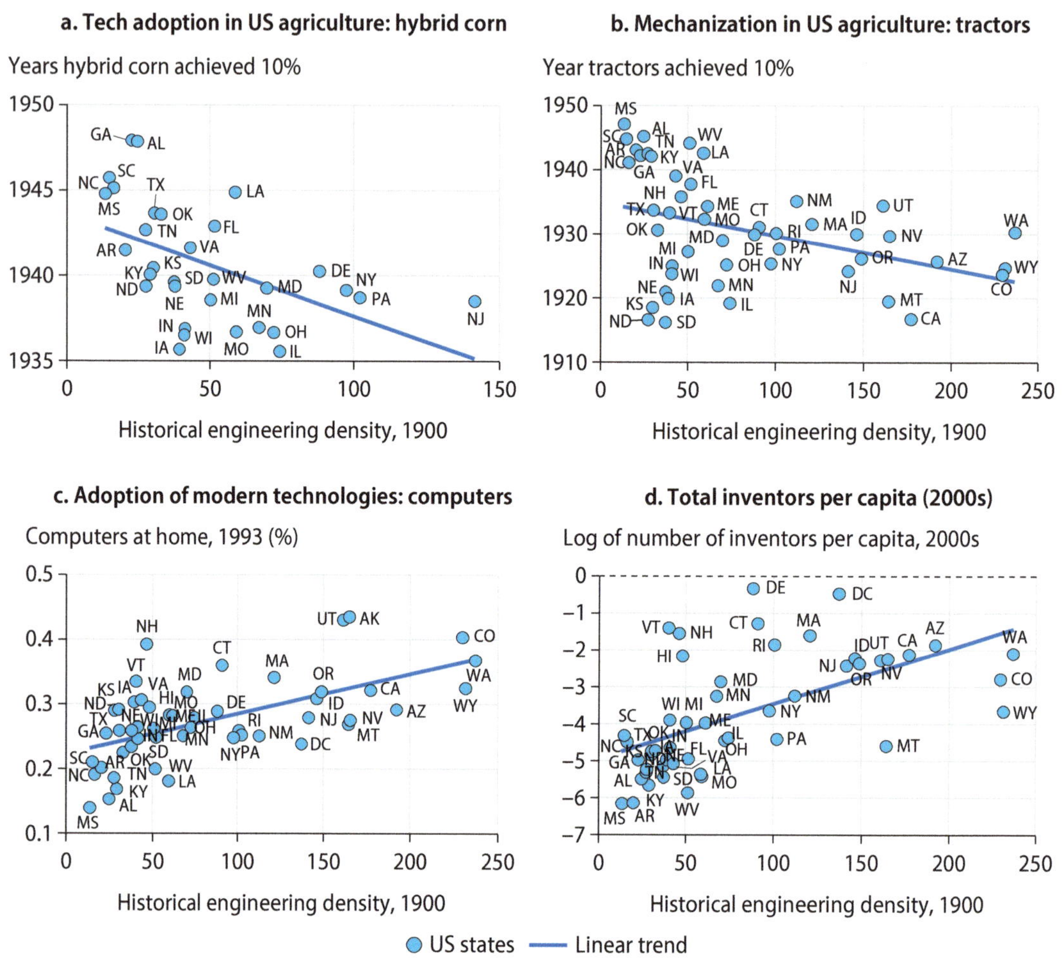


*Sources:* Maloney and Valencia Caicedo 2022. Adoption data are from Skinner and Staiger 2007.

*Note:* US state-level engineering density in 1900 versus year in which 10 percent of cropland was planted with hybrid corn (panel a); year in which tractor use achieved 10 percent of farms (panel b); percentage of population living in homes with a personal computer in 1993 (panel c); total inventors per capita in the 2000s (panel d). US = United States.

or basic education. In 1900, the United States had a well-articulated engineering community, while about 10 percent of the population over the age of 25 had received at least a lower secondary education.

Ideally, such engineering statistics would be adjusted for quality of scientific human capital.[4] One ingredient highlighted to explain the emerging dominance of the German scientific establishment in the late-19th century was its excellent primary and secondary school system, which served as a talent feeder to higher education institutions (Murmann 2003). If, as table 1.1 suggests, only one-third of LAC's population was

**TABLE 1.1 Literacy Rates in about 1850 and the Early 1900s**

*Percent of the population that is literate*

| Country | Year | Literacy rates circa 1850 | Year | Literacy rates circa the early 1900s |
|---|---|---|---|---|
| **European, North American, and Asian comparators** | | | | |
| Sweden | 1850 | 90 | 1900 | 99 |
| Germany | 1850 | 85 | 1900 | 90+ |
| Denmark | 1850 | 70 | 1900 | 90+ |
| France | 1850 | 61 | 1901 | 83.5 |
| United Kingdom | 1850 | 52 | 1900 | 97 |
| Japan | 1868 | 25–40 | 1912 | 70+ |
| Spain | 1860 | 27 | 1900 | 41.3 |
| Portugal | 1850 | 15 | 1900 | 26.6 |
| Korea[a] | n.a. | n.a | 1930 | 22 |
| United States[b] | 1870 | 80 | 1900 | 89.3 |
| **LAC countries** | | | | |
| Uruguay | n.a | n.a | 1900 | 54 |
| Argentina | 1869 | 24 | 1900 | 52 |
| Costa Rica | 1892 | 24 | 1900 | 33 |
| Paraguay | 1886 | 19 | 1900 | 30 |
| Chile | 1865 | 18 | 1900 | 43 |
| Jamaica | 1871 | 16 | 1911 | 47.2 |
| Brazil | 1872 | 16 | 1900 | 25 |
| Mexico | n.a | n.a | 1900 | 22 |
| Honduras | 1887 | 15 | 1925 | 29 |
| Guatemala | 1893 | 11 | 1925 | 15 |

*Source:* Original table for this volume. Refer to annex 1A.
*Note:* LAC = Latin America and the Caribbean.
a. Korea refers to the historical Korea.
b. Data for the United States for 1900 refer to the native white population with native parentage.

functionally literate in 1900 while virtually the entire population was in Germany and Scandinavia, the pool from which the latter countries could draw top scientific talent to its universities was three times larger. While some countries in Latin America made great progress in education in the latter half of the 19th century, the extraordinarily high levels of literacy in Denmark and Sweden even in 1850 suggests that lying behind the similarities in 1900 gross domestic product (GDP) per capita with Argentina, Chile, and Uruguay in figure 1.1 lay vast differences in human capital across the spectrum. LAC's low literacy rates may be the proximate result of deeper exclusionary forces in the sense of Acemoglu, Johnson, and Robinson (2005), although, again, Portugal and Spain show very similar levels of literacy in 1850 and 1900, suggesting a high inherited component of growth impeding attitudes and institutions.

More direct evidence suggests the low performance of universities and other institutions in LAC in their role as conduits and facilitators of technology transfer to the private sector and as participants in the global networks of knowledge generators. In Mexico, the disconnect between scientific institutes and centers and the productive sector was a partial motivation for the Banco de México, in collaboration with the Illinois-based Armour Research Foundation (now IIT), to form the Mexican Institute of Technological Investigations (Instituto Mexicano de Investigaciones Tecnológicas) in 1944 in a project to remedy the "profound lack of knowledge of the potential for industrial development through the application of better technologies" (Gómez-Galvarriato Freer 2020, 1252).[5] Meller (2001, 44) argues that "in the 1950s one could have learned more about Chilean copper in foreign libraries and universities than in Chilean ones."[6] By contrast, in Japan, the massive effort in translation of technical literature in the mid-Meiji period suggests a much stronger national effort to link domestic agents with global technologies. The stock of technical literature translated into Japanese was similar to what existed in English globally by 1870 and appears to be more highly correlated with the country's industrial take-off than any other reform of the period (Juhász, Sakabe, and Weinstein 2024).

Again, historical case studies provide evidence that this lack of technical capability curtailed the evolution of the regional economies. Progress in Brazilian agriculture was slowed by the virtual absence of journals that were ubiquitous even in the lagging US South—few Brazilians could read them (Graham 1981). Explaining the industrial retrogression in Minas Gerais, Brazil, Birchal (1999, 183) concludes: "Mineiro firms relied strongly on foreign technologies and skilled personnel. … The existing informal and spontaneous technological innovation system was not developed enough to take the process of technological assimilation farther in the direction of a profound modification of existing foreign technologies or to create a more complex indigenous technological alternative." The most successful Mineiro foundries in the first three-quarters of the 20th century were set up by foreigners with extensive knowledge of metallurgy. In Mexico's first wave of industrialization, from 1890 to 1930, its almost total dependence on foreign technology and firms, Haber (1995) argues, led to an inability to export, a need for protection, oligopolistic structures, and eventually but inexorably led directly to the stagnation of the 1970s. Arguably, a lack of technological capabilities at the dawn of the Industrial Revolution led to pressures for protection, high levels of concentration, and the low growth rates seen today.

## Lack of Experimenting Entrepreneurs

Why these disparities in technical capabilities existed at the turn of the last century is an open question. On the one hand, the similarly low engineering and literacy levels in Portugal and Spain suggests that the mother countries had little tradition to hand down to their colonial outposts, leaving them far from the technical frontier. But the question also remains as to why there was no demand by local entrepreneurs—for instance, in the established mining sector—for such skills, despite the obvious money to be made by adapting emerging technologies and industries to the local context. Again, the innovation paradox arises. Why didn't LAC entrepreneurs follow the US elites when they were exploiting copper, and invest massively in technical universities like the Colorado School of Mines, Columbia, or the University of California, Berkeley? Or invest in the technologies that would take Hitachi from making motors for the local mine of the same name to a major high-tech conglomerate?

Adopting or inventing new technologies is fundamentally a process of placing risky bets that an investment of long duration and great uncertainty will pay off (refer to box 1.1). A substantial literature, for instance, points to risk and uncertainty more generally as a major barrier to adoption of technologies that impede catch-up across all sectors (see, for example, Foster and Rosenzweig 2010; Gorodnichenko and Schnitzer 2013; Greenwood and Jovanovic 1990; Krishna et al. 2023).

### BOX 1.1 Culture or Learning Development Trap? The Role of Entrepreneurial Capital

Latin America's loss of key industries and slow take-up of the industrialization project may be the result of an inability to use arriving information to evaluate the risk or return profiles of possible new investments in risky innovation projects or sectors—what Maloney and Zambrano (2022) term "entrepreneurial capital." This can be modeled as strong prior beliefs about likely profitability that do not alter much with the arrival of new information, and an openness to new ideas versus being resistant to them. This may not only deter entry into new activities or application of new

(Continued on next page)

**BOX 1.1 Culture or Learning Development Trap? The Role of Entrepreneurial Capital *(continued)***

technologies but may also discourage investing in the ability to weigh and respond to future information—that is, in *learning how to learn* about more profitable but potentially more complex opportunities that might arise.

This potentially leads to a development trap: entrepreneurs cannot see the potential in an industrialization project and hence do not invest in the ability to interpret the associated new "signals" surrounding its benefits—and hence stay with safe traditional activities. Without such investment, as modernization proceeds and new projects become more complex, locals' skills in interpreting these signals will deteriorate relative to the frontier, potentially leading entrepreneurs and countries to abandon established industries as they become more sophisticated, as was the case in Brazil, Chile, and Mexico.

Modeling the investment process suggests several factors driving decisions. First is the cost of accumulating the ability to use new information. In the absence of local business skills or a community of frontier businesses, catching up may have been very costly. Certainly, the prohibition on local elites engaging in trade during the colonial period would have made impossible the learning that the North American colonies had from transacting with advanced economies.

The second factor is how far local managers were from the "entrepreneurial frontier." Even if the investment costs were at US levels, when confronted with the new technologies of the Second Industrial Revolution, it is possible that Latin Americans saw themselves as too far from the frontier to catch up and hence deferred to foreigners with the experience—thereby foreclosing participation in more complex projects in the future.

Finally, in a variant on the resource curse related to learning, the obvious profitability of mineral exports may have made it seem unnecessary to invest in entrepreneurial capital to weigh mining against alternative investment options.

Chile's history suggests that retrocession in mining and other industries was importantly due not to cultural aversions but to an erosion of entrepreneurial capital as the frontier shifted out. In Chile, as soon as Spanish restrictions on trade were

*(Continued on next page)*

**BOX 1.1 Culture or Learning Development Trap? The Role of Entrepreneurial Capital *(continued)***

lifted after independence, exports from Chile—and Latin America more generally—boomed. Chilean entrepreneurs were the second largest presence in Peruvian nitrate fields, ahead of the British, and pioneered copper mining in their home country. They aggressively responded in mining and agricultural to global price movements. As many as 50,000 Chileans sailed to San Francisco to search for gold and brought mining technologies to their Anglo counterparts.

However, locals observed a decline in entrepreneurship at the end of the 19th century. Writing in 1900, Mac-Iver (1900, 10–11) noted that "Chilenos didn't lack either an entrepreneurial spirit, nor the energy to work, characteristics which are incarnate in the first railroads and telegraphs, in ports and piers, the irrigation canals in the central valley. But these qualities have been lost." Writing a few years later, in 1911, Encina concurred, adding that the Chileans lacked the technical and managerial skills to enter modern sectors (Encina 1911, 195). Decades later, Silva Vargas (1977, 50) noted the lack of "the basic theoretical knowledge of credit, simple and compound interest, amortization, capitalization, banks, etc. . . ." This missing entrepreneurial and technological capital would have been essential to moving from the customary high-return, short-horizon mining investments to the evaluation and planning of more complex projects with longer gestations emerging from the Second Industrial Revolution.

By contrast, the foreign entrepreneurs arriving in Valparaiso after independence had precisely this entrepreneurial capital. Villalobos and Beltrán (1990, 99) note that "the empresarial spirit united with the motivation to apply new techniques was almost always the result of initiatives on the part of foreigners who came to Chile and *saw* opportunities [italics added] to develop or solutions to problems based on practical experience. They brought a greater tradition of information, spirit of action, attention to detail, and urgency to capitalize on the results or resources generated; these were not common traits of the average inhabitant of the country."

Cultural inheritance, of course, can be a cost of accumulating entrepreneurial capital. But the observed loss of entrepreneurial spirit over a matter of decades, to be partly regained again a few decades later, seems more consistent with falling behind, and then catching up, in entrepreneurial skills.

*Source:* Maloney and Zambrano 2022.

Here the ability of the enabling environment to minimize and help manage and diffuse risk is critical, as Mokyr (2004, 27) noted for the Industrial Revolution. "British institutions did what institutions are supposed to do: they reduced uncertainty ... [Britain] provided a healthy environment for would-be entrepreneurs who were willing to take risks and work hard." By contrast, traditional agricultural interests resisted reforms to the mining code in Chile that would facilitate consolidation of mining claims and the establishment of limited liability corporations that would reduce risk to an individual entrepreneur. In the bigger picture, the US government's efforts to cultivate the sector as a source of growth rather than purely tax revenue allowed US mining to progressively dominate technologically beginning in the 1860s while Chile retrogressed (Culver and Reinhart 1989).

While such sector-specific institutional factors—limiting the diffusion of risk and amassing the financing needed for modern mining—are clearly important impediments to technological adoption, the issue of retrogression and missed opportunities is so widespread across sectors and across the region as to prompt the search for other factors as well.

One possibility is that the low average level of education prevailing in the region meant that the density of high-quality entrepreneurs was below the mass necessary for such investments. But another possibility is that those who had driven development up to that point lacked the higher-order entrepreneurial capital to take the next step: to recognize the new possibilities presented by the Second Industrial Revolution, evaluate and manage the risk around them, and then implement a plan of long gestation (Maloney and Zambrano 2022). The ability to recognize opportunities is partly a function of technical abilities. In Germany, for instance, schools, polytechnics, and universities were established in order to "train scientists capable of conducting industry-related research *[and] industrial managers capable of appreciating their discoveries*" (Trebilcock 1981, 62, cited in Juhász and Steinwender 2023; italics added).

However, recognizing opportunities is also a function of managerial practices per se. This includes basic management skills (Bloom and Van Reenen 2007)—what the management literature calls "ordinary capabilities," or the ability to produce things efficiently and maintain quality control. Beyond this are what some have called "dynamic capabilities," which entails the ability on the part of entrepreneurs and firms to manage new product (and process) development, unique managerial orchestration processes, a change-oriented organizational culture, and a prescient assessment of the business environment and technological opportunities (Teece, Pisano, and Shuen 1997). A substantial literature, discussed in chapter 2, shows that such capabilities have driven faster growth and higher productivity, more and higher quality exports to more sophisticated markets, and more innovation in China, Colombia, India, Italy, and Portugal, among others.

That local entrepreneurial capabilities, however adequate in the 19th century, were no longer so in the twentieth is suggested both by the episodes of retrogression in LAC discussed earlier as well as by the fact that industrialization and the wholesale adoption of the new technologies of the Second Industrial Revolution were largely driven by foreigners and immigrants, far out of proportion to their share of the population and without obvious favorable financial or other conditions (figure 1.7). A vast literature indicts cultural characteristics of the Creole landowning elites and the inheritance of a Roman and then Spanish distaste for applied activities (refer to Cusolito and Maloney 2018; Maloney and Zambrano 2022; Safford 1976; Stein and Stein 1970). However, these same elites had been very entrepreneurial in the early 19th century, building vast mining empires and related industries—which would imply that a relatively sudden cultural regression seems unlikely. Nor was a similar disdain for entrepreneurial activity reputedly embodied in Confucianism a barrier to Chinese, Japanese, Korean, and Taiwanese industrialization (Baumol 1990).[7]

**FIGURE 1.7 Immigrants and Foreigners Drove Industrialization in LAC around 1900**

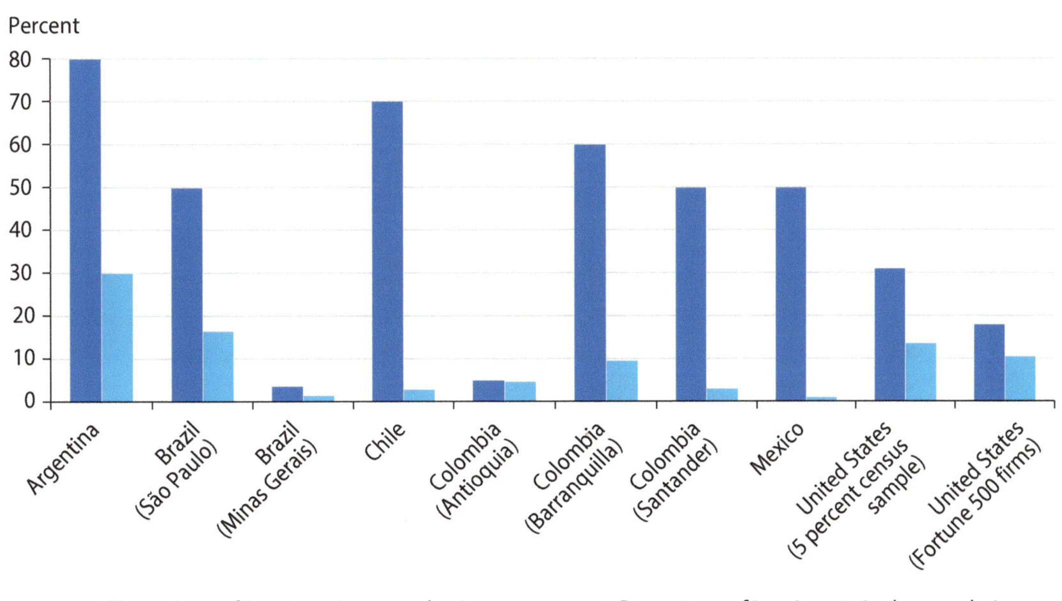


*Source:* Maloney and Zambrano 2022.

One possibility is that LAC fell into an entrepreneurial trap, brought on by the obvious profitability of mineral sectors that discouraged investment in the kind of "entrepreneurial capital" in learning how to learn that would allow the evaluation of the increasingly complex new industrialization opportunities arriving (box 1.1). A related explanation might be traced to barriers to interaction with the principal poles of the Industrial Revolution, both as explicit prohibitions by colonial Portugal and Spain on local elites to engage in direct international trade—even to the relative backwater of Cadiz, Spain, in the case of Spanish colonies in LAC, and even to domestic industrial production, in the case of Brazil—compounded by the fact that Portugal and Spain were far from significant players in this revolution in the first place. These historical legacies left locals in the region unprepared to rapidly accumulate the entrepreneurial capital needed as the managerial frontier shifted out in the Second Industrial Revolution.[8] That is, the forces at work were less an adverse attitude toward applied activities by locals than the possession by immigrants of some skills or a worldview that permitted them to see opportunities to adopt technologies and industries at the dawn of the Second Industrial Revolution that locals no longer had.

Some of what immigrants brought was actual market knowledge. The textile industries in Argentina and Mexico were energized by Syrian Jewish immigrants who emigrated from the declining textile centers of Aleppo and Damascus via the Arab Republic of Egypt and then Manchester, Great Britain, and eventually moved on to Latin America before the first world war. However, many migrants entered sectors in which they had no prior experience, suggesting the importance of entrepreneurial skills per se. Andrew Carnegie's background was in textile weaving and accounting before he became a steel magnate. George Edwards, founder of the Edwards dynasty in Chile, was trained as a doctor but became involved in sectors ranging from mining to newspapers. Elon Musk began in electronic payments before moving to space travel. This suggests that a broader ability to recognize new opportunities and to evaluate and manage risk may be more important than specific sectoral expertise.

The bottom line then and now is that increasing the density of entrepreneurs with these abilities and their supporting institutions is necessary to raise the rate of entry of higher productivity firms and drive the creative destruction that drives growth.

### The Role of Workers in the Learning Process

The collective learning process happens at the worker level, as well. In the US South, deficient worker skills also impeded the management of new technologies in the 19th century (Wright 1986). Measured by literacy levels, this is likely to have been the case in LAC as well, which lagged far behind Europe and the United States and catch-up countries like Denmark, Japan, and Sweden.[9] In addition, advanced and convergent countries have had extensive vocational training programs. Germany provided vocational education at all levels from primary to higher education; educational spending between 1872 and 1914 almost reached the level of military spending (Trebilcock 1981, 63). In a similar vein, Japan also provided vocational training in industrial skills, initially in schools attached to government industrial establishments (Crawcour 1997, cited in Juhász and Steinwender 2023).

### Importing Modernity versus Modernization

This focus on technical and entrepreneurial capabilities, and the academic and financial institutions that support them, highlights the shortcomings of just focusing on technology transfer itself. It is not the arrival of imported machinery per se, but rather the cultivation of a societal ability to demand it, modify it to local conditions, and improve upon it, that leads to a deeper process of modernization. Merely importing foreign technology amounts to applying the veneer of modernity rather than actually modernizing firms, along with the larger economy and society.

As an example, under threat of Western domination, often symbolized by the arrival of Admiral Perry's Black Ships in the 1850s, Japan took on the mission to reach the West's technological and entrepreneurial frontiers and built a strong industrial economy in a single generation. The country advanced from building manufacturing and financial industries on top of its mining industry, to building a world-beating textile industry, to defeating a western Navy by 1905, and then flying the most advanced fighter plane in the world at the beginning of World War II. The trappings of modernity were undergirded by a deep modernization of norms, education, and innovation institutions that facilitated uptake of technology, and then building upon it. As journalist George Rittner noted admiringly in 1904, "In less than 20 years, Japan has acquired the knowledge it has taken us centuries to learn" (Rittner 1904, 142). A similar compressed process of learning is clear in Korea (box 1.2) which, in 1950, had both literacy and income levels below those of Latin America, yet in three decades caught up with the global frontier.

## BOX 1.2 Korea Followed Japan's Capability Accumulation Strategy

Recent literature has sought to rigorously document the positive effects of Korean industrial policy, and particularly the heavy and chemical industry drive from 1973 to 1979 (Choi and Shim 2024a; Lane 2022). Developing the capability to adopt and use technologies was a critical ingredient.

Korea's development strategy was patterned on the Meiji restoration (Studwell 2013), drew on industry experience from Japanese colonization, and was similarly motivated by a concern with national defense (Lane 2022). Central to the industrial policy supporting heavy manufacturing was reaching the technological frontier, captured by its slogan "nation building through science and technology, and technological self-reliance" (Choi and Shim 2024a). Like Japan, Korea did not base its development strategy on foreign direct investment, but instead actively invested in national learning capabilities and licensing agreements. Government subsidies to adoption, in particularly access to scarce foreign exchange, had the effect of not only increasing adoption but in turn increasing adoption rates in subsequent periods, while also inducing other companies to adopt, raising the overall rate of productivity growth in what has been termed a technological "big push" (Choi and Shim 2024a). Over time, subsidies were shifted from adoption to invention (Choi and Shim 2024b), much as has been discussed in the *World Development Report 2024* on the middle-income trap (World Bank 2024).

Critical to this was the accumulation across the entire spectrum of human capital (Soh, Koh, and Aridi 2023). Literacy was only 22 percent in 1930 but at present is at 98 percent, while the managerial and technical capital supported a rise in research and development, progressively driven more by the private sector, to the second highest levels in the world, at more than 4.5 percent of gross domestic product. Thirty percent of its college graduates major in science, technology, engineering, and mathematics fields, while the Brain Korea 21 program aims to develop world-class research-oriented universities and educate high-caliber research workers (master's and doctoral students and post-doc researchers) (Soh, Koh, and Aridi 2023).

In the early phases, Korea actively used targeted and interventionist industrial policies to support specific firms but combined these with discipline through tightly monitored export targets (Soh, Koh Aridi 2023; Studwell 2013). As capabilities to compete has grown, protection has been gradually phased out. Tariffs fell from a

*(Continued on next page)*

**BOX 1.2 Korea Followed Japan's Capability Accumulation Strategy *(continued)***

simple average rate of 23.7 percent in 1983 to 8 percent in 1994, and then to 5 percent for consumption and 3 percent for other goods by 2019 (Soh, Koh, and Aridi 2023).

To ensure continuity in technology policy over time, beginning in 2003, every 5 years, the government has published a Science and Technology Master Plan, the nation's most important action plan on development of its science, technology, and innovation system.

It has been argued that these types of measures have enabled the Republic of Korea to "leapfrog" to the technology frontier (Lee 2013, 2021; Lee and Lim 2001) and thus avoid succumbing to the middle-income trap. Notable examples of leapfrogging include steel (POSCO outperforming Nippon) and mobile telephony (Samsung overtaking Nokia) (Lee 2021).

*Source:* Original analysis for this volume and Soh, Koh, and Aridi 2023.

By contrast, when the same Admiral Perry invaded Tabasco as part of the effort that took half of Mexico's territory, the response of President Porfirio Diaz was radically different: Mexico engaged in massive importation of foreign technologies by foreigners but neglected both indigenous capabilities and the machine tool and capital goods industries. As Beatty (2015b) describes in his *Technology and the Search for Progress in Modern Mexico*, Mexico chose a path to modernity without societal modernization. Both new and old industries became dominated by foreign capital and expertise, while Mexican capabilities developed during its long history either atrophied or were displaced. Government policies that promoted local learning and the development of local technology were few and largely ineffective. As with the US South (Wright 1986), Mexico developed limited machine tool and capital goods industries. As Beatty (2015b, 205) explained, "Mexico's technology policy consisted of little more than consistent and concerted efforts to promote technology imports. Weak state capacity—both fiscal and administrative—were partly to blame. More importantly, a short time horizon and the imperative of intermediate growth in the international context of late development governed all key political decisions. In the short term, policy makers' primary objective was to ease access to the importation of new machines, tools, processes, and knowledge. Although Mexican officials and commenters voiced concern about falling 'tributary' to more powerful economies—and especially to their northern neighbor—they expressed less concern about dependence on foreign expertise." Parkes (1969, 309) concludes that Diaz, "in his eagerness for industrial development, had failed to protect Mexican interests and to safeguard Mexican sovereignty. He had not insisted that Mexicans learn the new techniques; foreigners monopolized every responsible position."

It is not clear why, faced with similar challenges to national sovereignty, Japan and Mexico would choose such disparate paths, one learning to learn and joining the advanced world in a generation, the other predictably leading to a troubled industrialization. However, returning to the discussion in box 1.1, Diaz may have felt the country was just too far from the frontier to advance in a reasonable period of time. In 1900, Japan had literacy rates twice those of Mexico and could count on a well-educated and disciplined class of former samurais who comprised perhaps half the emerging entrepreneurial class. Further, Japan established high-level universities and sought tight links with centers of learning in, particularly, the United Kingdom. But passing up the challenge of learning to learn to manage new technologies, much as Chile did with nitrates and copper, left Mexico dependent and without the managerial and technical capabilities to develop extensive indigenous industries.

An alternative path emerges from Antioquia, Colombia, one of the three industrial growth poles in LAC identified by Hirschman (1968) and one of two in figure 1.7, where local entrepreneurs drove the industrialization process with foreigners as only supporting actors. Hypotheses abound as to why, but two factors may be key. First, Antioquians managed the entire chain of gold mining from excavation to market after independence and hence learned frontier business skills. Second, two prominent citizens, Pedro Nel and Tulio Ospina, attended the fledgling University of California, Berkeley College of Mining, returned, and established the Antioquia School of Mines, which trained generations of engineers and managers.

## Developing National Learning Does Not Happen Naturally

These examples underscore the deliberate nature of "national learning": it does not happen naturally; it is chosen. This conscious path provides the second necessary caveat to arguments that producing "rich country" or high-tech or high value-added goods is central to the development strategy. Having a good produced on national territory, be it copper or electronics assembly, does not automatically generate the capabilities to either defend against future technology shocks or to diversify into new sectors. This is especially relevant to the current efforts in the region to leverage nearshoring or the new demand for green transition minerals or new sectors like green hydrogen to generate more value added.[10] Either countries must invent the related technologies to create forward and backward linkages, or they must convince foreign companies to transfer the necessary technologies—a prospect that is made more likely with the technical capability of the local entrepreneurs.

Hence the misguidedness of regional governments seeking to diminish foreign dominance and diversify their economies by erecting massive protective barriers. Import substitution industrialization strategies gave local entrepreneurs breathing room, but rather than encouraging the accumulation of capabilities necessary to eventually rejoin the global economy and promote productivity growth, this approach shielded inefficient industries from competition, making it unnecessary to accumulate them. In fact, the process may have been self-reinforcing. The movement toward protectionism happened early in the 20th century, before the Great Depression (refer to Coatsworth and Williamson 2004; Gómez-Galvarriato 2007; Lederman 2005), around the time that many industries were losing competitiveness and retrogressing.

Similarly, attempting to achieve technological independence before dominating existing technologies will likely lead to uncompetitiveness. While, as box 1.2 shows, Korea sought technological "independence," it first subsidized the rapid adoption of foreign technologies. By contrast, as the *World Development Report 2024* (World Bank 2024) notes, Brazil after the 1970s placed a 10 percent tax on licensing foreign technologies and subsidized indigenous innovation, which led to an expansion of low-quality patenting but neither technological mastery nor independence.

## Where Is LAC Today? Still Trapped in the Innovation Paradox

This history speaks directly to the region today, where Latin industries perform less dynamically relative to international comparators. Colombia's flagship textile industry emerging from the Antioquian miracle described earlier would serve the US market, producing uniforms for the US Army during World War II, but would eventually be displaced by Asian competitors paying similar wages, partly due to weak managerial practices (Morawetz 1980). Korea and Mexico would both start assembling electronics in the early 1980s. But Korea would leverage electronic assembly into major industries while, despite the presence of Hewlett-Packard and IBM for 50 years in Guadalajara, there is yet no Mexican analogue to the Samsung Galaxy. More generally, in the same way that the early-20th-century cycle of FDI or nearshoring of the Diaz era was not sufficient to prime the pump of indigenous management of new technologies today, countries tend to view FDI more as a source of jobs or tax revenue than as a vector of national learning the way, for instance, China has.

Both Norway and Brazil have sought to leverage their oil and gas reserves to more diversified industries. Norway developed its own school of oil exploration, including related electronic industries, and now specializes in rough water platforms. Brazil's attempt to enter ship and platform building foundered due importantly to deficient engineering and design capabilities (Alves, Vonortas, and Zawislak 2021).

The challenge of assimilating and managing technologies to infuse dynamism in local industries is not restricted to LAC. In *The Rise of Ersatz Capitalism in South East Asia,* Yoshihara Kunio (1988) argues that Indonesia, Malaysia, the Philippines, and Thailand were "technology-less" developers that could not follow the Asian Miracles of Japan, Korea, and Taiwan, China (cited in Studwell 2013). Again, they are all exporting advanced manufactures, but they have not developed the kind of innovative dynamism that allowed the Asian Miracles to catch up.

The bottom line is that the low rates of productivity growth in the region suggest that LAC continues to struggle with adopting technologies across the board. It remains trapped in the innovation paradox of not investing in technological capabilities despite theoretically high returns.

The fact that the region is still not placing the necessary technological bets can be viewed through the lens of product quality which, like efficiency, is a component of overall productivity (total factor productivity, TFP) and is frequently measured as the price a good commands in the market (Krishna et al. 2023). Similar to efficiency, the quality of the basket of a country's exports increases with economic development (figure 1.8), and its growth is similarly driven by the same bets on new products, processes, and technologies. What is clear is that the rate of growth of quality rises

**FIGURE 1.8 The Quality of a Country's Exports Increases with Economic Development and Risk**

**a. Quality increases with growth**

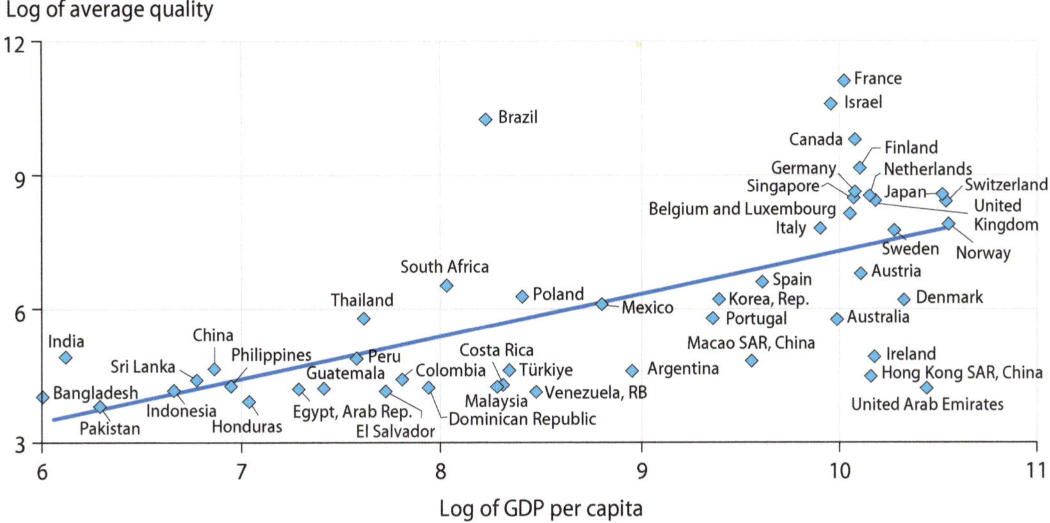


**b. Quality growth increases with risk**

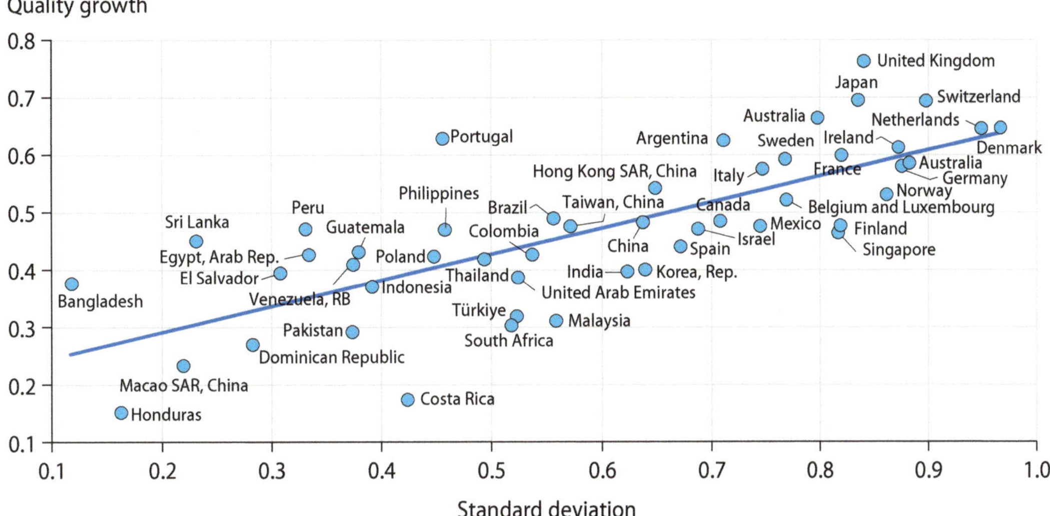


*Source:* Krishna et al. 2023.

*Note:* For panel a, the figure plots average cross-good unit values standardized by the 90th value of HS-10 against log GDP per capita for countries with more than 50 products, log of average quality versus log of gross domestic product per capita. Slope = 0.956 (*t*-statistic = 5.73). HS-10 = 10-digit level of disaggregation in the Harmonized System of industrial classification. GDP = gross domestic product.

sharply with the variance of that growth, a measure of risk suggesting the customary risk-return trade-off. It is also clear that richer countries, at the high end, show higher growth rates in quality, signifying that they are taking on more risk, and that Latin America, by contrast, is a middling risk taker. Though some goods do show greater potential for upside risk, and hence, in principle, are more desirable sectors, most variance is driven by within-sector differences in risk-taking.[11]

Updating a standard measure of investment in technological capacity and absorptive capacity, research and development (specifically, research and development [R&D] expenditures as a share of GDP) in LAC remains average for countries of its level of income, with the exceptions of Chile and Colombia on the higher side and Barbados, Trinidad and Tobago, and Uruguay on the lower side (figure 1.9). The countries far above the average for their level of income are in Asia and Europe. The exception is Brazil, but even here, it has been argued that these resources are often channeled to less productive uses and/or universities with limited linkages to the productive sector (de Souza 2023).

**FIGURE 1.9 LAC Does Not Invest Enough in Expertise for Technological Catch-Up**

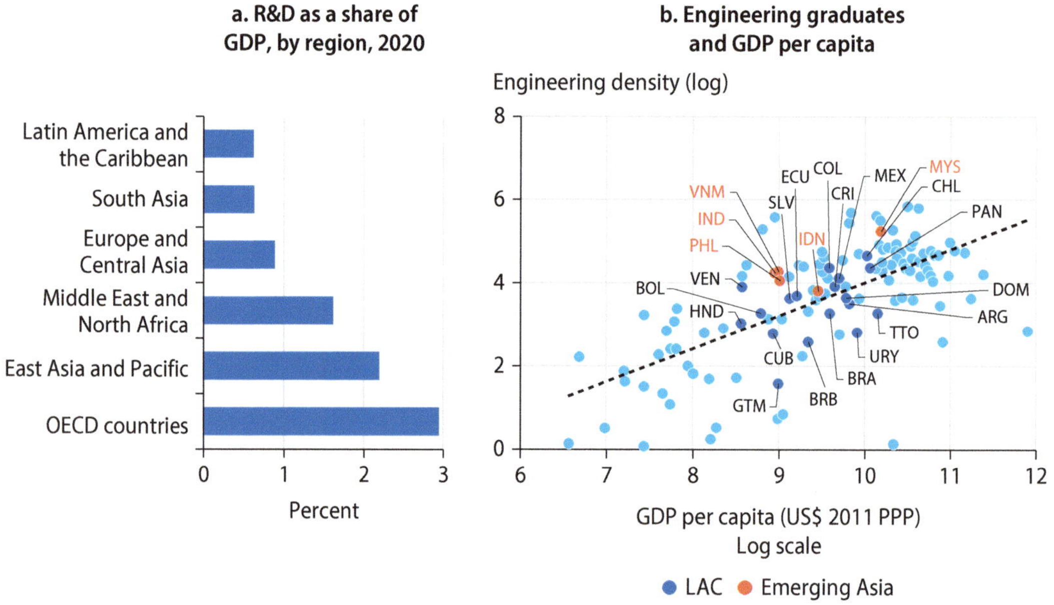

a. R&D as a share of GDP, by region, 2020

Latin America and the Caribbean
South Asia
Europe and Central Asia
Middle East and North Africa
East Asia and Pacific
OECD countries
0
1
2
3
Percent

b. Engineering graduates and GDP per capita

Engineering density (log)
8
6
4
2
0
6
7
8
9
10
11
12
GDP per capita (US$ 2011 PPP)
Log scale
VNM
IND
PHL
VEN
BOL
HND
ECU
SLV
COL
CRI
IDN
MEX
MYS
CHL
PAN
DOM
ARG
TTO
URY
BRA
BRB
CUB
GTM
LAC
Emerging Asia

*Source:* Original figure for this volume based on World Bank World Development Indicators data (https://databank.worldbank.org/source/world-development-indicators) (panel a); and UNESCO data (https://databrowser.uis.unesco.org/) (panel b).
*Note:* The comparators in emerging Asia have income levels similar to those of LAC countries. For country abbreviations in panel b, refer to International Organization for Standardization (ISO), https://www.iso.org/obp/ui/#search. GDP = gross domestic product; LAC = Latin America and the Caribbean; OECD = Organisation for Economic Co-operation and Development; PPP = purchasing power parity.

Mexico remains an exemplary case of the paradox (figure 1.10). Even adjusting for differences in economic structure from the average member country of the OECD, Mexico's R&D intensity is the lowest, at about 70 percent of the level of Greece, Portugal, or Spain and 10 percent of the level of the highest countries (Austria, Finland, France, Sweden).[12] Further, the share of R&D financed by the government ranges from 60 percent in Brazil to almost 80 percent in Mexico compared to 20 percent in China, Korea, and the United States, suggesting that LAC industries are investing proportionately far less. Mexico may represent the most extreme case of the innovation paradox. Geographically it sits immediately below the largest generator of new technology progress in the history of humankind yet somehow invests very little in the human capital or R&D needed to access it.

In fact, there appears to be a clear disconnect between investments in absorptive capacity and technology adoption (figure 1.11). China's imports

**FIGURE 1.10 The R&D Intensity of LAC Countries over the Development Process Is Very Low**

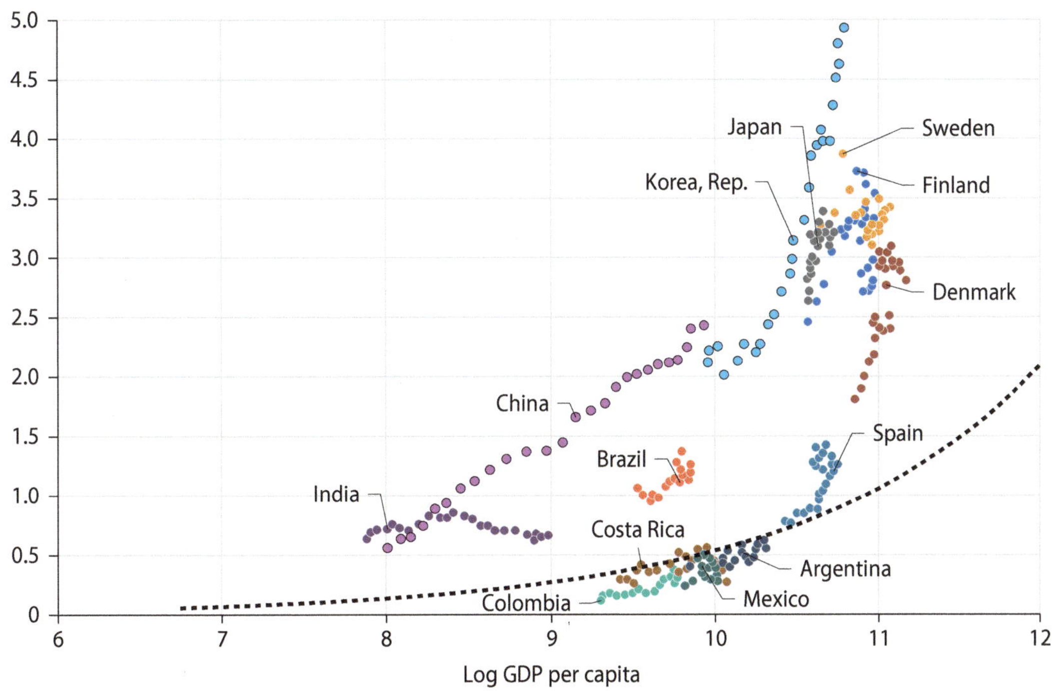


*Source:* Original figure for this volume based on World Bank World Development Indicators data (https://databank.worldbank.org/source/world-development-indicators).

*Note:* The dotted line plots the fitted line of R&D expenditure (as a percentage of GDP) for 146 countries during the period 1996–2022. GDP = gross domestic product; LAC = Latin America and the Caribbean; R&D = research and development.

**FIGURE 1.11 Even as LAC Countries Increase Their Licensing of Foreign Technology, Their Expenditure on R&D Remains Low**

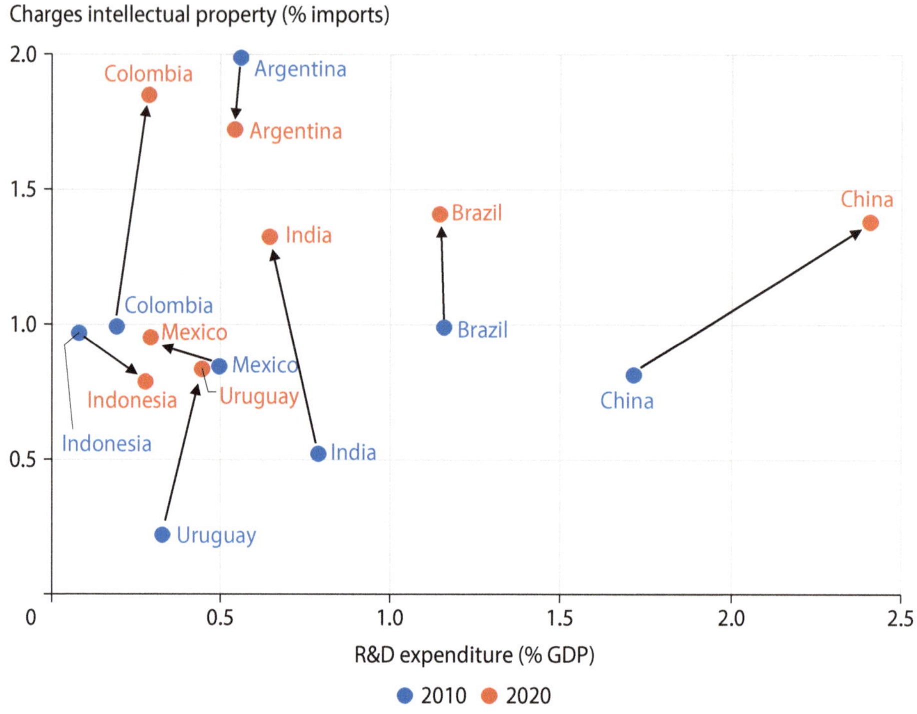

*Source:* Original figure for this volume based on World Bank World Development Indicators data (https://databank.worldbank.org/source/world-development-indicators).

*Note:* The figure shows charges for intellectual property (licensing fees) as a percentage of imports versus expenditure on research and development (R&D) as a percentage of GDP. For Indonesia, R&D expenditure as a percentage of GDP refers to the values from 2009 rather than 2010. GDP = gross domestic product; LAC = Latin America and the Caribbean.

of foreign technologies have been accompanied by a strong investment in R&D that enables the "learning" from FDI and licenses. In LAC, while in the last decade there has been an important increase in licensing, R&D spending has been low and, in some cases, falling, raising the fear that the region is repeating the 19th-century pattern epitomized by President Porfirio Diaz.

## Agriculture: Success Stories from which to Learn

One area where some parts of LAC has shown success as a learning economy has been in agriculture, although with great variation across the region. From 1960 to 2022, TFP in agriculture tripled in Brazil and quadrupled in Chile. This achievement was partly attributable, in Brazil, to EMBRAPA, the Brazilian Agricultural Research Corporation, which for a time was the model research or extension institution, and in Chile to close international collaboration with external research centers, particularly in California. Progress was lower in parts of the region, with TFP in the Caribbean growing 3 percent across the same period. At 1.2 percent of agricultural GDP, LAC's investment in R&D is twice the average of the global south and half that of the global north, despite estimated returns of 30–40 percent (Fuglie et al. 2019; Fuglie, Morgan, and Jelliffe 2024).

## Mapping the Expanded National Innovation System: Capabilities and the Enabling Environment Required for National Learning

Focusing on these capabilities does not negate the long-standing emphasis on removing distortions and remedying market failures in the enabling environment or business climate. In fact, if we consider innovation—including both technological adoption and invention—as the accumulation of knowledge, analogous to accumulation of any other factor of production and subject to all of the customary barriers, then the complementarity between capabilities and the emphasis on market-friendly reforms to remove such barriers are clear.

Figure 1.12, based on *The Innovation Paradox* (Cirera and Maloney 2017), provides a map of these interactions and broadly of the themes and interconnections in this volume. It tracks the demand and supply for knowledge capital (innovation, broadly construed), which together underlie a nation's ability to learn. On the right are firms, incumbents or start-ups, and their demand for factors of production (capital, human capital, and knowledge capital). On the left, broadly speaking, are the supply factors. The center panel makes the point that innovation policy must deal with barriers to all types of accumulation, both because physical capital is a complement and because the accumulation of knowledge capital is subject to all the same accumulation barriers as physical capital—shallow capital markets and the inability to diffuse risk, barriers to entry and exit, an unfriendly business and regulatory climate, and so on. Hence low investment in managerial capabilities or technology may be due to a variety of general accumulation investment barriers that are commonly discussed and thoroughly examined in the World Bank Business Ready analyses (B-READY),[13] rather than to market or systemic failures related to innovation per se.

**FIGURE 1.12 The Expanded National Innovation System**

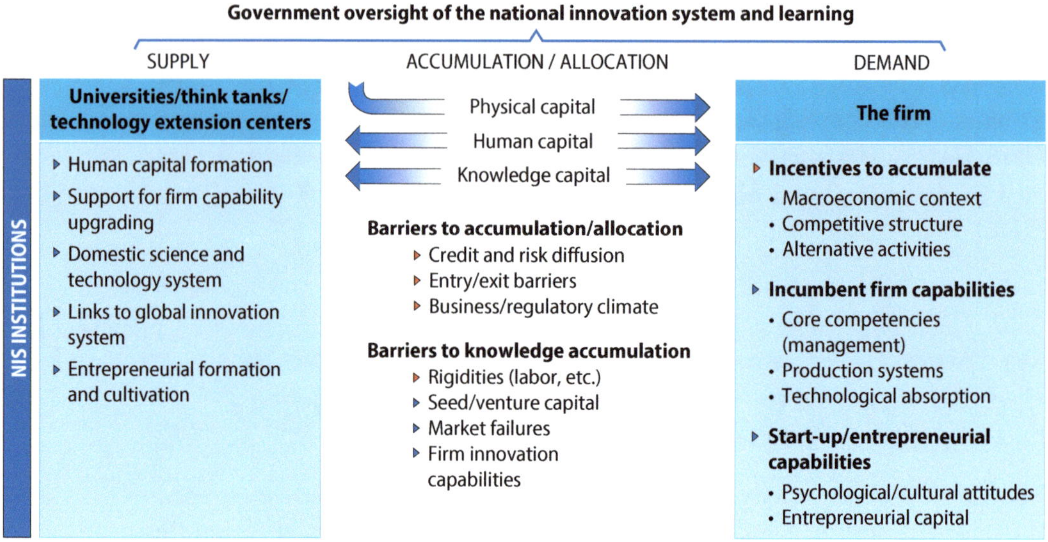

*Source:* Original figure for this volume based on Cirera and Maloney 2017.
*Note:* NIS = National Innovation System.

Clearly, innovation-specific barriers to accumulation are still important, and they are captured in the next group down in the figure. For instance, there may be specific restrictions on the workforce restructuring required for firms to adopt new technologies. In addition, there may be an absence of seed or venture capital that would enable new innovative start-ups to emerge and existing firms to place new innovative bets. Finally, there are all the standard information-related market failures discussed earlier: those related to the appropriation of knowledge, which have prompted an array of R&D subsidies and tax incentives, and to intellectual property rights systems.

The first group of variables on the demand side comprises the overall set of incentives for firms and farms to invest and accumulate. This includes the macro context, competitive structure, trade regime, and international networks that determine whether firms seek to innovate. The second set of variables captures firm capabilities. In incumbent firms, firm capabilities include the core managerial competencies, production systems, and higher-end capabilities for technological absorption and innovation that enable a firm to recognize an opportunity and mobilize itself to take advantage of it. Of particular salience is the ability to quantify and manage the risk intrinsic to any project. These capabilities can be seen as increasingly demanding in sophistication as "innovation" moves from simple improvements to actual long-term R&D. For entering firms, both psychological or cultural factors, and specific early-stage entrepreneurial skills are critical.

Critical on the supply side are all the sources of knowledge that support firm demand. This begins with the basic supply of human capital, from the worker level to the entrepreneur to engineers and scientists. The second set are institutions that support firms, including the kinds of productivity and quality extension services found around the world, services to disseminate new technologies or best practices, and higher-end consulting services in specialized topics. The science and technology (S&T) system, including universities and publicly supported research institutes, adapts existing knowledge or generates new knowledge for the use of firms, and as discussed, shares the risk.

Finally, the international innovation system generates most new knowledge; therefore, being firmly plugged in along manifold dimensions in international markets is key. Because many of these institutions are nonmarket (government research institutes, universities, and so on), the question about what mechanisms and incentives link them to one another is prominent in the National Innovation System (NIS) literature.

Overall, the concept of the NIS provides a framework to understand the environment within which firm innovation takes place. It also highlights how demand for innovation—specifically, the ability of the firm to recognize, articulate, and execute an innovation-related project—is at the center of the discussion. This view requires a deeper examination of firm capabilities and a recognition that innovation occurs along a continuum of sophistication ranging from basic business practices to more advanced production systems (such as just-in-time methods) to technical literacy to manage formal R&D. Evolving into more R&D–intensive products also requires a greater set of skills and contracting institutions for managing technological complexity (Krishna and Levchenko 2013); financial literacy and deeper capital markets for managing riskier products (Acemoglu and Zilibotti 1997; Krishna et al. 2023); greater technological literacy; and high-quality S&T institutions. Overseeing this evolution and the overall functioning of the NIS is the government, which is also tasked with the resolution of market and systemic failures and coordination among various actors and is the steward of raising overall national learning capabilities.

The chapters that follow utilize the structure depicted in figure 1.12. The next chapter focuses on the role of firms in the production and diffusion of knowledge and discusses some of the barriers listed in the center of the figure.

## ANNEX 1A Sources for Data on Literacy Rates

### Sources circa 1850

For Denmark: Ford, Ranestad, and Sharp (2022).

For England, France, and Germany: Gawthrop (1987).

For Japan: Taira (1971).

For Latin America and the Caribbean and the United States: Beltrán Tapia et al. (2021); Mariscal and Sokoloff (2000).

For Portugal: Goulart and Bedi (2017).

For Spain: Beltrán Tapia et al. (2021).

For Sweden: Henrekson and Wennström (2022).

### Sources circa 1900

For historical estimates specific to LAC countries, the data set uses Mariscal and Sokoloff (2000).

For France, Portugal, and Spain: UNESCO (1953).

For Jamaica, Korea, and Sweden: Harvard Business School (No date).

For Japan: Taira (1971).

For the United Kingdom: Lloyd (2007).

For the United States (aggregated): National Center for Education Statistics, National Assessment of Adult Literacy.

For the United States (disaggregated): IPUMS USA, Population, U.S. Census, 1910: Volume 1, Chapter 13, page 1195.

## Notes

1. Refer to https://www.goodreads.com/author/quotes/52349.Nelson_Rodrigues.
2. "The fact that in 1952 the Controller General admitted that he had no idea of what went on in the companies suggests that part of the feeling of vulnerability and dependency must be attributed to the lack of advanced science capacity to monitor and confidently critique the actions of the Gran Mineria. It was not until 1955 that the Copper Department was created to oversee US firms' copper operations, and a bureaucracy established of Chilean professionals, engineers, and economists with the local Chilean expertise. 'In short', Meller argues, 'it took about 40 years, from 1925 to 1965, to develop a domestic capacity to analyze the role of copper and

to educate Chilean professionals and technicians in the management of the [large copper firms]'" (de Ferranti et al. 2002, 61, citing Meller 2001).

3. As an historical example of another measure, the presence of individuals in France in the mid-1700s with subscriptions to the famous Encyclopédie that sought diffusion of the scientific learning of the Enlightenment on a grand and international scale is closely correlated with the growth of cities in France over time (Squicciarini and Voigtländer 2015). General literacy was correlated with level of income, but not with growth.
4. On the role of knowledge networks for growth, refer to Rosenberger, Hanlon, and Hallmann (2024).
5. In Spanish, "profundo desconocimiento de sus potencialidades de desarrollo industrial mediante la aplicación de mejores tecnologías."
6. By comparison, the stock of technical literature translated into Portuguese and Spanish is far below the stock in English globally.
7. In China, enterprise was not only frowned upon, ranking very low in the Confucian social order, but was also subjected to impediments deliberately imposed by officials, at least after the 14th century AD, Baumol (1990) notes. The road to riches ran through the Mandarin bureaucracy that, he argues, allowed for confiscation of rents of others' ingenuity. Yet the dismissive view of enterprise ran throughout many countries and areas influenced by Confucianism, including Japan, the Korean peninsula, the island of Taiwan, and what is now Viet Nam—areas that today are or are rapidly becoming entrepreneurial.
8. In fact, there is evidence of substantial latent entrepreneurial energy in the region, but also of high costs of investment in entrepreneurial capital posed by the business and institutional climate of the colonial period. Aspiring Creole merchants were severely constrained by both the legal requirement to trade primarily with Spain, a country that came exceptionally late to the Industrial Revolution, and even this trade was prohibited except through peninsular intermediaries. Hence, local entrepreneurs would never even see the relatively backward port of Cadiz, let alone Manchester. However, the demand for greater commercial interaction was keen. In the 1720s and 1730s, the merchant classes of Mexico City and Peru, among the most developed in the region, sought direct trade with Spain but were rebuked, and a vigorous contraband trade prevailed throughout the Caribbean (McFarlane 2002). In Brazil, until the end of the 18th century, even the establishment of domestic industries was prohibited by the Portuguese colonial government, but industries were latent, as in much of the region, emerging upon independence (Birchal 1999). By contrast, the northern US colonies were tightly integrated into England's industrialization process, sharing extensive trade and travel, engaging in industrial espionage, and accumulating knowledge and entrepreneurial capital (Maloney and Zambrano 2022).
9. Recent literature points to the accumulation of human capital as driving 50 percent of structural change (Porzio, Rossi, and Santangelo 2022).
10. Refer to Beylis and Lozano, forthcoming.
11. Supporting the view that "what you export matters," there are some goods that offer combinations of higher risk and return, and Latin America is average in this dimension as commodities, for instance, have modest upside risk. But well over half of the overall pattern is due to the fact that developing countries engage less in high-risk, high-return projects within finely disaggregated sectors. Again, what matters is not what is produced, but how.

12. https://www.oecd-ilibrary.org/docserver/9789264268821-en.pdf?expires=1729966203&id=id&accname=guest&checksum=96015F692E7440D6850ECC2735D451D9.
13. Refer to the B-READY website: https://www.worldbank.org/en/businessready.

## References

Acemoglu, D., S. Johnson, and J. A. Robinson. 2005. "Institutions as a Fundamental Cause of Long-Run Growth." In *Handbook of Economic Growth*, vol. 1A, edited by P. Aghion and S. N. Durlauf, 385–472. Amsterdam: Elsevier.

Acemoglu, D., and F. Zilibotti. 1997. "Was Prometheus Unbound by Chance? Risk, Diversification, and Growth." *Journal of Political Economy* 105 (4): 709–51.

Alfaro, L., and D. Comin. Forthcoming. *Macroeconomics*. Oxford, UK: Oxford University Press.

Álvaro-Moya, A. 2014. "The Globalization of Knowledge-Based Services: Engineering Consulting in Spain, 1953–1975." *Business History Review* 88 (4): 681–707.

Alves, A. C., N. S. Vonortas, and P. A. Zawislak. 2021. "Mission-Oriented Policy for Innovation and the Fuzzy Boundary of Market Creation: The Brazilian Shipbuilding Case." *Science and Public Policy* 48 (1): 80–92.

Baumol, W. J. 1990. "Entrepreneurship: Productive, Unproductive, and Destructive." *Journal of Political Economy* 98 (5): 893–921.

Beatty, E. 2015a. "Globalization and Technological Capabilities: Evidence from Mexico's Patent Records ca. 1870–1911." *Estudios de Economía* 42 (2): 45–65.

Beatty, E. 2015b. *Technology and the Search for Progress in Modern Mexico*. Oakland, CA: University of California Press.

Beltrán Tapia, F. J., A. Diez-Minguela, J. Martinez-Galarraga, and D. A. Tirado-Fabregat. 2021. "The Uneven Transition towards Universal Literacy in Spain, 1860–1930." *History of Education* 50 (5): 605–27.

Beylis, G., and N. Lozano. Forthcoming. *From Resource-Rich to Resource-Smart: LAC's Opportunities in the Energy Transition*. Washington, DC: World Bank.

Birchal, S. 1999. *Entrepreneurship in Nineteenth-Century Brazil: The Formation of a Business Environment*. New York: Springer.

Bloom, N., and J. Van Reenen. 2007. "Measuring and Explaining Management Practices across Firms and Countries." *Quarterly Journal of Economics* 122 (4): 1351–408.

Calvo-Gonzalez, O. 2021. *Unexpected Prosperity: How Spain Escaped the Middle-Income Trap*. Oxford, UK: Oxford University Press.

Choi, J., and Y. Shim. 2024a. "Industrialization and the Big Push: Theory and Evidence from South Korea." IMF Working Paper 2024/259, International Monetary Fund, Washington, DC.

Choi, J., and Y. Shim. 2024b. "From Adoption to Innovation: State-Dependent Technology Policy in Developing Countries." IMF Working Paper 2024/154, International Monetary Fund, Washington, DC.

Cirera, X., and W. F. Maloney. 2017. *The Innovation Paradox: Developing-Country Capabilities and the Unrealized Promise of Technological Catch-up*. Washington, DC: World Bank.

Coatsworth, J. H., and J. G. Williamson. 2004. "Always Protectionist? Latin American Tariffs from Independence to Great Depression." *Journal of Latin American Studies* 36 (2): 205–32.

Comin, D., and M. Mestieri. 2018. "If Technology Has Arrived Everywhere, Why Has Income Diverged?" *American Economic Journal: Macroeconomics* 10 (3): 137–78.

Crawcour, E. S. 1997. "Industrialization and Technological Change, 1885–1920." In *The Cambridge History of Japan, Part III–Economic Development*, edited by P. Duus, 50–115. Cambridge, UK: Cambridge University Press.

Culver, W. W., and C. J. Reinhart. 1989. "Capitalist Dreams: Chile's Response to Nineteenth-Century World Copper Competition." *Comparative Studies in Society and History* 31 (4): 722–44.

Cusolito, A. P., and W. F. Maloney. 2018. *Productivity Revisited: Shifting Paradigms in Analysis and Policy.* Washington, DC: World Bank.

de Ferranti, D., G. E. Perry, D. Lederman, and W. F. Maloney. 2002. *From Natural Resources to the Knowledge Economy: Trade and Job Quality.* World Bank Latin American and Caribbean Studies. Washington, DC: World Bank Group.

de Souza, G. 2023. "R&D Subsidy and Import Substitution: Growing in the Shadow of Protection." *SSRN Electronic Journal* 4587133. doi:10.2139/ssrn.4587133.

Di Tella, G. 1985. "Rents, Quasi-Rents, Normal Profits and Growth: Argentina and the Areas of Recent Settlement." In *Argentina, Australia and Canada: Studies in Comparative Development 1870–1965*, edited by D. C. M. Platt and G. Tella, 37–52. London: Palgrave Macmillan UK.

Eaton, J., and S. Kortum. 1999. "International Technology Diffusion: Theory and Measurement." *International Economic Review* 40 (3): 537–70.

Encina, F. A. 1911. *Nuestra Inferioridad Economica, sus Causas, sus Consequencias.* Santiago, Chile: Coleccion Imagen de Chile.

Ford, N., K. Ranestad, and P. Sharp. 2022. "Leaving Their Mark: Using Danish Student Grade Lists to Construct a More Detailed Measure of Historical Human Capital." *Rivista di storia economica* 38 (1): 29–56.

Foster, A. D., and M. R. Rosenzweig. 2010. "Microeconomics of Technology Adoption." *Annual Review of Economics* 2 (1): 395–424.

Fuglie, K., M. Gautam, A. Goyal, and W. F. Maloney. 2019. *Harvesting Prosperity: Technology and Productivity Growth in Agriculture.* Washington, DC: World Bank.

Fuglie, K., S. Morgan, and J. Jelliffe. 2024. *World Agricultural Production, Resource Use, and Productivity, 1961–2020.* Economic Information Bulletin No. 268. Washington, DC: USDA (United States Department of Agriculture) Economic Research Service.

Gawthrop, R. L. 1987. "Literacy Drives in Preindustrial Germany." In *National Literacy Campaigns*, edited by R. F. Arnove and H. J. Graff, 29–48. Boston, MA: Springer.

Gómez-Galvarriato, A. 2007. "The Political Economy of Protectionism: The Mexican Textile Industry, 1900–1950." In *The Decline of Latin American Economies: Growth, Institutions, and Crises*, edited by S. Edwards, G. Esquivel, and G. Márquez, 363–406. Chicago: University of Chicago Press.

Gómez-Galvarriato Freer, A. 2020. "La construcción del milagro mexicano: el Instituto Mexicano de Investigaciones Tecnológicas, el Banco de México, y la Armour Research Foundation." *Historia Mexicana* 69 (3): 1247–309.

Gorodnichenko, Y., and M. Schnitzer. 2013. "Financial Constraints and Innovation: Why Poor Countries Don't Catch Up." *Journal of the European Economic Association* 11 (5): 1115–52.

Goulart, P., and A. S. Bedi. 2017. "The Evolution of Child Labor in Portugal, 1850–2001." *Social Science History* 41 (2): 227–54.

Graham, R. 1981. "Slavery and Economic Development: Brazil and the United States South in the Nineteenth Century." *Comparative Studies in Society and History* 23 (4): 620–55.

Greenwood, J., and B. Jovanovic. 1990. "Financial Development, Growth, and the Distribution of Income." *Journal of Political Economy* 98 (5, Part 1): 1076–107.

Haber, S. 1995. *Industry and Underdevelopment: The Industrialization of Mexico, 1890–1940.* Redwood, CA: Stanford University Press.

Harvard Business School. No date. "Adult Literacy Rates: Adult Total, 1870–2010." Historical Data Visualization. https://www.hbs.edu/businesshistory/courses/teaching-resources/historical-data-visualization/details?data_id=31.

Henrekson, M., and J. Wennström. 2022. *Dumbing Down: The Crisis of Quality and Equity in a Once-Great School System—And How to Reverse the Trend*, 1–9. Cham, Switzerland: Springer International.

Hirschman, A. O. 1968. "The Political Economy of Import-Substituting Industrialization in Latin America." *Quarterly Journal of Economics* 82 (1): 1–32.

IPUMS USA. No date. *Population, U.S. Census, 1910: Volume 1.* https://usa.ipums.org/usa/resources/voliii/pubdocs/1910/Vol1/36894832v1ch14.pdf.

Juhász, R., S. Sakabe, and D. Weinstein. 2024. "Codification, Technology Absorption, and the Globalization of the Industrial Revolution." NBER Working Paper 32667, National Bureau of Economic Research, Cambridge, MA.

Juhász, R., M. P. Squicciarini, and N. Voigtländer. 2024. "Technology Adoption and Productivity Growth: Evidence from Industrialization in France." *Journal of Political Economy* 132 (10): 3215–59.

Juhász, R., and C. Steinwender. 2023. "Industrial Policy and the Great Divergence." *Annual Review of Economics* 16: 24–57.

Krishna, P., and A. A. Levchenko. 2013. "Comparative Advantage, Complexity, and Volatility." *Journal of Economic Behavior & Organization* 94 (C): 314–29.

Krishna, P., A. A. Levchenko, L. Ma, and W. F. Maloney. 2023. "Growth and Risk: A View from International Trade." *Journal of International Economics* 142: 103755.

Kunio, Yoshihara. 1988. *The Rise of Ersatz Capitalism in South East Asia.* Oxford, UK: Oxford University Press.

Lane, N. 2022. "Manufacturing Revolutions: Industrial Policy and Industrialization in South Korea." *SSRN Electronic Journal* 3890311. https://dx.doi.org/10.2139/ssrn.3890311.

Lederman, D. 2005. *The Political Economy of Protection: Theory and the Chilean Experience.* Stanford, CA: Stanford University Press.

Lederman, D., and W. F. Maloney. 2007. "Neither Curse nor Destiny: Introduction to Natural Resources and Development." In *Natural* Resources: *Neither Curse nor Destiny*, edited by D. Lederman and W. F. Maloney, 1–14. Washington, DC: World Bank and Stanford, CA: Stanford University Press.

Lederman, D., and W. F. Maloney. 2012. *Does What You Export Matter? In Search of Empirical Guidance for Industrial Policies.* Washington, DC: World Bank.

Lee, K. 2013. *Schumpeterian Analysis of Economic Catch-Up: Knowledge, Path-Creation, and the Middle-Income Trap.* Cambridge, UK: Cambridge University Press.

Lee, K. 2021. "Economics of Technological Leapfrogging." In *The Challenges of Technology and Economic Catch-Up in Emerging Economies*, edited by J. D. Lee, K. Lee, D. Meissner, S. Radosevic, and N. Vonortas, 123–59. Oxford, UK: Oxford University Press.

Lee, K., and C. Lim. 2001. "Technological Regimes, Catching-Up and Leapfrogging: Findings from the Korean Industries." *Research Policy* 30 (3): 459–83.

Lloyd, A. J. 2007. *Education, Literacy and the Reading Public. British Library Newspapers*, 2. Detroit: Gale.

Lundvall, B.-A. 2013. "The Danish Model and the Globalizing Learning Economy." In *Development Success: Historical Accounts from More Advanced Countries*, edited by A. K. Fosu, 115–39. Oxford, UK: Oxford University Press.

Mac-Iver, E. 1900. *Discurso sobre la crisis moral de la república (1900).* Santiago, Chile: Biblioteca La Revista de Chile, Imprenta Moderna.

Maloney, W. F., and F. Valencia Caicedo. 2022. "Engineering Growth." *Journal of the European Economic Association* 20 (4): 1554–94.

Maloney, W. F., and A. Zambrano. 2022. "Learning to Learn: Experimentation, Entrepreneurial Capital, and Development." Documentos CEDE 19940, Universidad de los Andes, Facultad de Economía, CEDE.

Mariscal, E., and K. L. Sokoloff. 2000. "Schooling, Suffrage, and the Persistence of Inequality in the Americas, 1800–1945." In *Political Institutions and Economic Growth in Latin America: Essays in Policy, History, and Political Economy*, edited by S. Haber, 159–217. Stanford, CA: Hoover Institution Press.

McFarlane, A. 2002. *Colombia before Independence: Economy, Society, and Politics under Bourbon Rule.* Cambridge Latin American Studies, 17. Cambridge, UK: Cambridge University Press.

Meller, P. 2001. "Chilean Copper: Facts, Role and Issues." Universidad de Chile Facultade de Ciencias Fisicas y Matematicas, Departmento de Ingenieria Industrial/ World Bank, Washington, DC.

Mokyr, J. 2004. "Accounting for the Industrial Revolution." In *The Cambridge Economic History of Modern Britain, Vol. 1: Industrialisation, 1700–1860*, edited by R. Floud and P. Johnson, 1–27. Cambridge, UK: Cambridge University Press.

Morawetz, D. 1980. *Why the Emperor's New Clothes Are Not Made in Colombia: A Case Study in Latin America and East Asia Manufactured Exports.* New York: Oxford University Press for the World Bank.

Murmann, J. P. 2003. *Knowledge and Competitive Advantage: The Coevolution of Firms, Technology, and National Institutions.* Cambridge, UK: Cambridge University Press.

Murray, P. S. 1997. *Dreams of Development: Colombia's National School of Mines and Its Engineers, 1887–1970.* Tuscaloosa, AL: University of Alabama Press.

National Center for Education Statistics. No date. "A First Look at the Literacy of America's Adults in the 21st Century." https://nces.ed.gov/naal/lit_history.asp#illiteracy.

Parente, S. L., and E. C. Prescott. 1994. "Barriers to Technology Adoption and Development." *Journal of Political Economy* 102 (2): 298–321.

Parente, S. L., and E. C. Prescott. 2002. *Barriers to Riches.* Cambridge, MA: MIT Press.

Parkes, H. B. 1969. *A History of Mexico.* Boston, MA: Houghton Mifflin.

Porzio, T., F. Rossi, and G. Santangelo. 2022. "The Human Side of Structural Transformation." *American Economic Review* 112 (8): 2774–814.

Rittner, G. H. 1904. *Impressions of Japan.* London: J. Murray.

Rogers, E. 1962. "The Iron and Steel Industry in Colonial and Imperial Brazil." *The Americas* 1 (2): 172–84.

Rosenberger, L., W. W. Hanlon, and C. Hallmann. 2024. "Innovation Networks in the Industrial Revolution." NBER Working Paper 32875, National Bureau of Economic Research, Cambridge, MA.

Safford, F. 1976. *The Ideal of the Practical: Colombia's Struggle to Form a Technical Elite.* Austin, TX: University of Texas Press.

Silva Vargas, F. 1977. *Comerciantes, habilitadores y mineros: una al estudio de la mentalidad empresarial en los primeros años de chile republicano (1817–1840).* Santiago, Chile: Empresa Privada.

Skinner, J., and D. Staiger. 2007. "Technology Adoption from Hybrid Corn to Beta-Blockers." In *Hard-to-Measure Goods and Services: Essays in Honor of Zvi Griliches*, edited by E. R. Berndt and C. R. Hulten, 545–70. Chicago: University of Chicago Press.

Soh, H. S., Y. Koh, and A. Aridi. 2023. *Innovative Korea: Leveraging Innovation and Technology for Development.* Washington, DC: World Bank.

Solares, I. G., and E. Beatty. 2024. "Engineers & Corporate Management, ca 1870–1930: The Invisible Hand Redux." *Enterprise & Society* 25 (2): 486–511.

Squicciarini, M. P., and N. Voigtländer. 2015. "Human Capital and Industrialization: Evidence from the Age of Enlightenment." *Quarterly Journal of Economics* 130 (4): 1825–83.

Stein, S. J., and B. H. Stein. 1970. *The Colonial Heritage of Latin America: Essays on Economic Dependence in Perspective.* New York: Oxford University Press.

Studwell, J. 2013. *How Asia Works: Success and Failure in the World's Most Dynamic Region.* New York: Grove Press.

Taira, K. 1971. "Education and Literacy in Meiji Japan: An Interpretation." *Explorations in Economic History* 8 (4): 371.

Teece, D. J., G. Pisano, and A. Shuen. 1997. "Dynamic Capabilities and Strategic Management." *Strategic Management Journal* 18 (7): 509–33.

Tortella Casares, G. 2000. *The Development of Modern Spain: An Economic History of the Nineteenth and Twentieth Centuries.* Cambridge, MA: Harvard University Press.

Trebilcock, C. 1981. *Industrialisation of the Continental Powers 1780–1914.* Oxfordshire, UK: Routledge.

UNESCO (United Nations Educational, Scientific, and Cultural Organization). 1953. *Progress of Literacy in Various Countries: Preliminary Statistical Study of Available Census Data since 1900.* Paris: UNESCO.

Villalobos, S. R., and L. Beltrán. 1990. *Historia de la Ingeniería en Chile.* Santiago, Chile: Hachette.

World Bank. 2024. *World Development Report 2024: The Middle-Income Trap.* Washington, DC: World Bank.

Wright, G. 1986. *Old South, New South: Revolutions in the Southern Economy since the Civil War.* New York: Basic Books.

Wright, G. 1987. "The Economic Revolution in the American South." *Journal of Economic Perspectives* 1 (1): 161–78.

# Firms and the Diffusion and Productive Use of Knowledge

# 2

*"Ahí mismo, al otro lado del rio, hay toda clase de aparatos mágicos…"*

["There, on the other side of the river, are all manner of magical apparatuses…."]

—José Arcadio Buendia in *Cien Años de Soledad*[1]

## Introduction

As chapter 1 stressed, the production of identical goods, whether copper or electronic devices or soybeans, can have a radically greater development impact if combined with frontier knowledge. Technological adoption also ensures competitiveness and productivity growth in industries and generates the spin-offs and linkages that can ensure more diversified and dynamic economies. But it is not enough to know, as José Acadio Buendia did, that such magical apparatuses exist on the other side of the river. Bringing them across is made possible only by firms that possess the entrepreneurial and technical skills that can identify and exploit opportunities for technological arbitrage, operating in a framework that supports placing informed bets and diversifying risks. Latin America and the Caribbean (LAC) has, historically, not had enough of these firms.

This chapter uses new firm-level data from the World Bank Firm-level Adoption of Technology (FAT) survey, a comprehensive data set that covers the patterns of diffusion and use of technology by firms in their main tasks or business functions (business administration, supply chain management, production planning, sales methods, marketing, and quality control; for a more detailed description of the data, refer to Comin, Cirera, and Cruz 2025). The chapter draws extensively on survey data for Brazil and Chile (annex 2). It first considers the diffusion chain—the process from identification of a technology to its adoption and use—and highlights three types of gaps in that process: (1) the identification of a new idea or opportunity at the national level and the ability to access it (access to frontier technology gap); (2) the diffusion across similar firms and sectors (the adoption gap); and, finally, (3) incomplete utilization within firms (the use gap) (figure 2.1). Looking across several sectors reveals that while some technologies, especially digital ones, are diffusing faster in the region across the first two gaps, especially after the COVID-19 pandemic, for many other technologies, diffusion is far from complete across all three gaps.

In a narrower framing of the innovation paradox, the question becomes what explains this incomplete diffusion when the returns should, in fact, be very high. As discussed in chapter 1, factors in the enabling environment external to the firm—including shallow financial markets, distorted factor and product markets, barriers to external trade and investment, lack of qualified workers, absence of or too much competition—effectively reduce the expected return or make it impossible to invest. But there are also factors related to capabilities within the firm, including the availability of technical, managerial, and organizational capital, the links to universities and other learning centers (chapter 3), and the quality of entrepreneurs (chapter 4) that impede the full diffusion of technologies.

**FIGURE 2.1 Three Gaps Hamper Diffusion of Technology to Existing Firms**

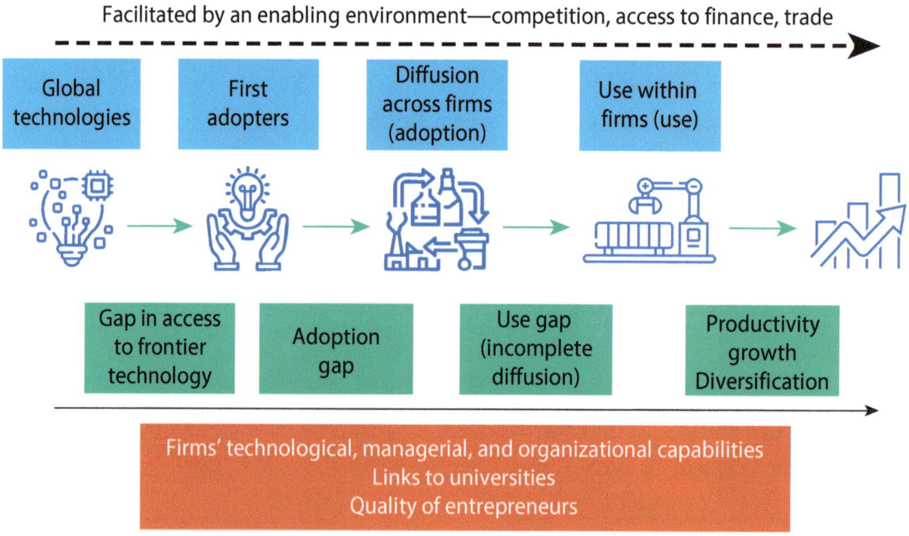

*Source:* Original figure for this volume.

## Gaps in Technology Diffusion in Latin America

The reduction in information and trade costs is increasing the speed at which technologies are recognized and adopted by first movers within countries around the world (figure 1.2 in chapter 1). However, the share of firms that follow and adopt the technology within countries is not growing at the same pace as in high-income countries (figure 2.2). This widening gap in use can, in simulations, explain 75 percent of the divergence between LAC and advanced economies (Comin and Mestieri 2018).

This increasing awareness of new technologies but increasingly incomplete adoption can be seen, for instance, in the purchase of technology licenses that give domestic firms the right to use technologies developed by foreign companies. Although LAC has significantly reduced the length of adoption lags over time, overall spending on foreign technologies is low (figure 2.3). In France and Germany, nearly 10 percent of firms have licenses. This percentage understates technology flows from the frontier because these countries produce a lot, as well. By contrast, in Colombia, less than

**FIGURE 2.2 The Diffusion of Technology Is Accelerating, but the Intensity of Use across Firms Is Diverging**

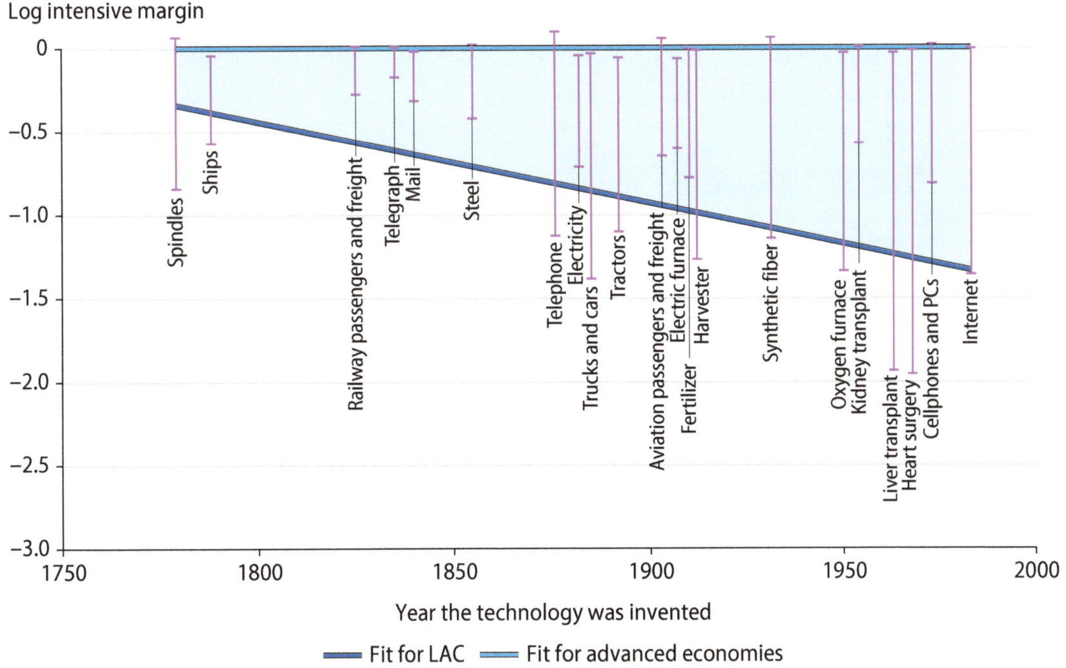


*Source:* Original figure for this volume based on Comin and Mestieri 2018.
*Note:* The y-axis label (log intensive margin) refers to the measure of intensity of use in Comin and Mestieri (2018). LAC = Latin America and the Caribbean; PCs = personal computers.

**FIGURE 2.3 The Share of Firms Using Licenses for Foreign Technology Is Relatively Low in LAC Countries**

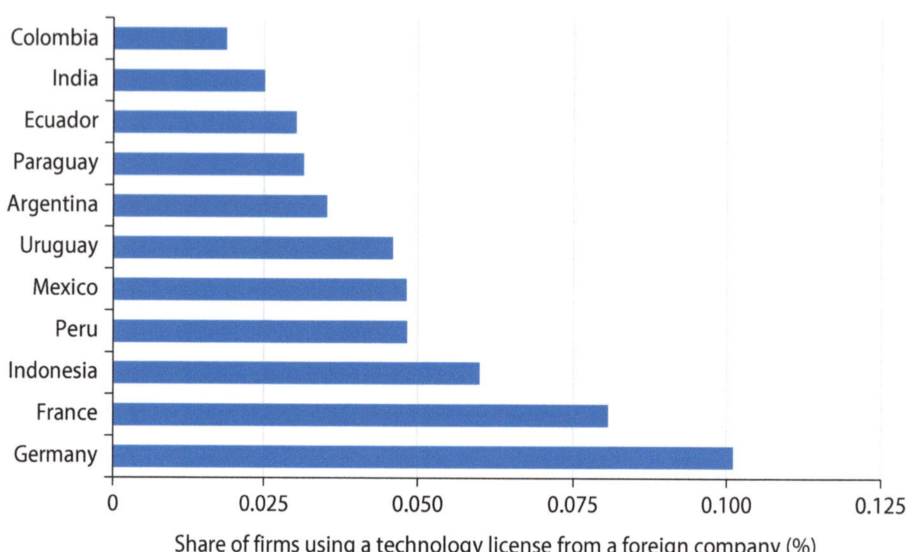


*Source:* Original figure for this volume based on World Bank Enterprise Survey data (https://www.enterprisesurveys.org/en/enterprisesurveys).
*Note:* Estimates for each country are based on Enterprise Survey data for the following years: 2017 (Argentina, Colombia, Ecuador, Paraguay, Peru, Uruguay); 2021 (France, Germany); 2022 (India); 2023 (Indonesia, Mexico). LAC = Latin America and the Caribbean.

2.5 percent of firms have licenses. Even in Mexico, despite a massive influx of foreign direct investment and proximity to the United States, only about 5 percent of firms have licenses.

## Lifting the Hood on Adoption Gaps

The FAT survey allows us to more deeply explore both the degree of adoption by firms (the adoption gap) and then, once adopted, how these technologies are actually used within firms (the use gap). Technology diffusion curves allow us to map the degree of adoption by following the cumulative share of firms adopting a particular technology over time. Figure 2.4, panel a, for example, shows the diffusion curve for the adoption of two digital technologies: enterprise resource planning (ERP)—software designed to integrate business administration and production planning tasks such as production, human resources, or supply chains (such as SAP, Oracle Net, and Microsoft Dynamic 365); and customer relationship management (CRM) software, which helps businesses manage customer interactions and data. Some LAC countries do not lag in adoption. Brazil and Chile do fairly well. For ERP, Brazil overtook Poland in 2006 and the Republic of Korea in 2010 (figure 2.4, panel a). For CRM, both Brazil and Chile overtook Korea in 2015 (figure 2.4, panel b).

**FIGURE 2.4 LAC Countries Do Well in the Diffusion of Relatively Accessible and Inexpensive Technologies**

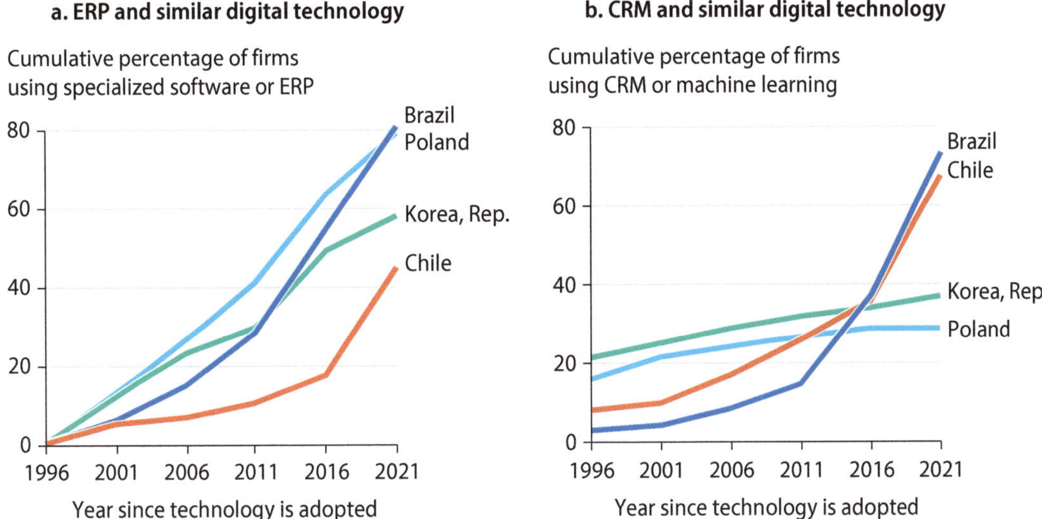


*Source:* Original figure for this volume based on the World Bank Firm-level Adoption of Technology survey.
*Note:* In panel a, the figure plots the share of firms adopting advanced technologies for business administration for each country and year. Advanced technologies include enterprise resource planning (ERP) and similar software. In panel b, the figure plots the share of firms adopting advanced technologies for marketing and product development for each country and year. Advanced technologies include customer relationship management (CRM) software or machine learning.

However, such technologies are mature, easily identifiable, and customizable via software suppliers, and they are relatively inexpensive to purchase and install. Longer delays, both in initial adoption and subsequent diffusion across firms, occur in more sector-specific, complex, and costlier technologies.[2] For example, in the textile-related sectors, by 2021, only 20 percent of Brazilian firms had adopted automated sewing machines, compared to 50 percent in Korea and 70 percent in Poland (figure 2.5, panel a). Similarly, as of 2016, very few firms had adopted quality control techniques in the pharmaceutical sector in Chile. By 2021, they had reached 20 percent of firms, while the share in Korea was 35 percent, and in Poland was 80 percent (figure 2.5, panel b). In each case, both LAC countries are substantially behind other comparable countries.

**FIGURE 2.5 LAC Countries Lag in the Adoption of Advanced Production Technologies**

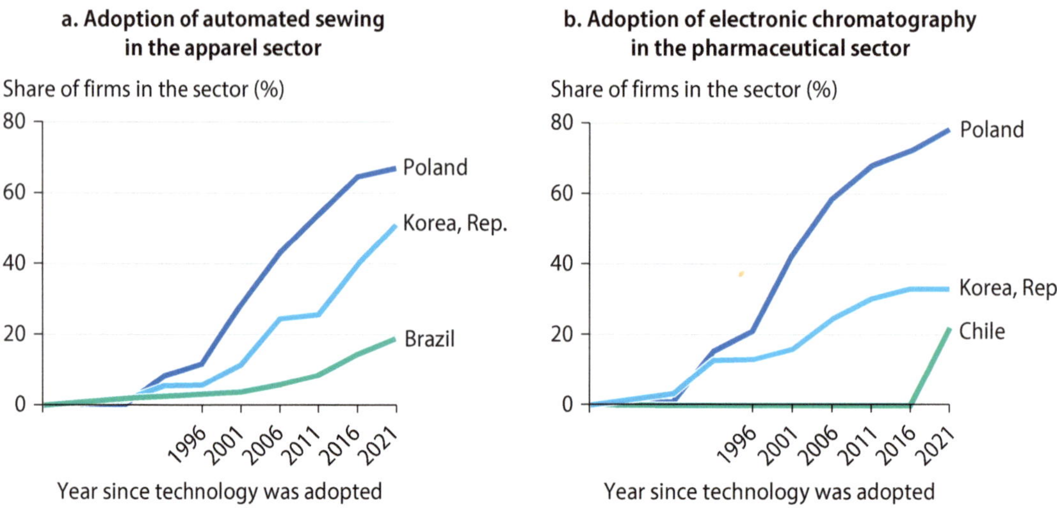


*Source:* Original figure for this volume based on calculations from the World Bank Firm-level Adoption of Technology survey.
*Note:* Panel a: Advanced technology refers to the cumulative percentage of firms using semi-automated, automated, or 3D knitting machines for sewing in the apparel sector. Panel b: Advanced technology refers to the cumulative percentage of firms using electronic chromatography with or without data acquisition for quality control in the pharmaceutical sector.

## Decomposing the Adoption Gap and the Productive Use Gap of Technologies

Having examined the rate of initial uptake and the adoption intensity of digital technologies, the analysis turns to the final component of the diffusion chain—the use gap, or how productively new technologies are used once they are adopted. Figure 2.6 decomposes the three gaps. A firm is considered fully digitalized in production planning, for example, when it intensively uses ERP or advanced digital production planning tools. A first barrier to digitalization is a lack of access to internet connectivity. In the case of Brazil and Chile, the gap in access to internet connectivity is negligible, with less than 1 percent of firms not having access in both countries. Access to internet connectivity is almost universal among formal firms in these countries. However, the gap in adoption of ERP and advanced production planning technologies is 39 percent in Brazil and 49 percent in Chile—nearly half of firms choose not to adopt.

The final use gap is measured by the share of firms that have adopted an advanced digital technology, but are not using it intensively: that is, they use other digital technologies more frequently to perform the same tasks. Despite some early adoption, for 36 percent of firms in Brazil and 28 percent of firms in Chile, some barriers within the firm—lack of training or know-how, or organizational barriers—lead the majority of the firm units to use

**FIGURE 2.6 The Digital Gap in Production Planning among Firms in Brazil and Chile Is Mainly Explained by Lack of Adoption and Productive Use**

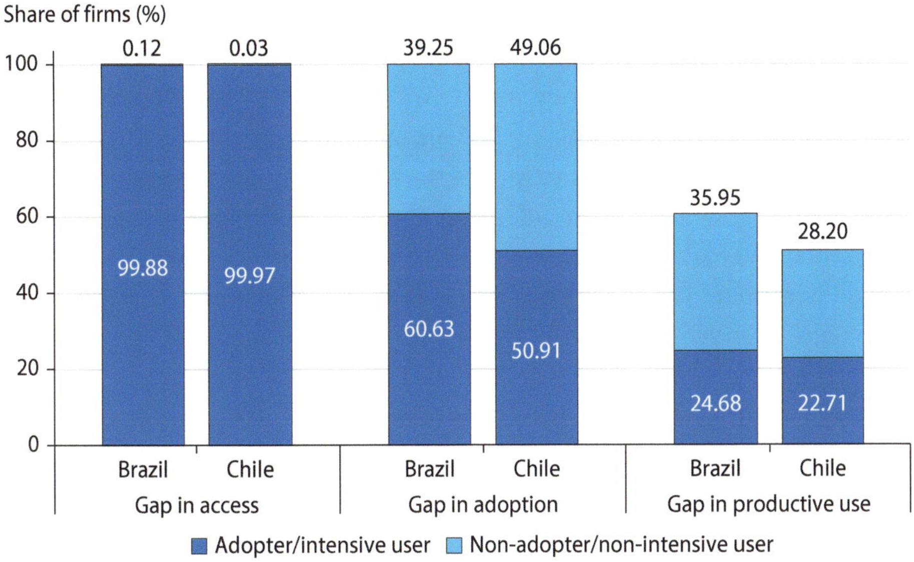

*Source:* Original figure for this volume based on calculations from the World Bank Firm-level Adoption of Technology survey.
*Note:* The figure plots the share of firms that have access to internet connectivity and computers (access); whether they have then adopted advanced digital technologies (adoption); and conditional on having adopted advanced technologies, whether they use them more intensively (productive use).

more familiar manual or basic computer technologies that already exist in the firm (Comin, Cirera, and Cruz 2025).

This pattern of incomplete digitalization also applies to other business functions and tasks and tends to be persistent among some small and medium enterprises (SMEs) (box 2.1). When considering all business functions, the share of firms overall that are "incompletely digitized"—where at least one business function is not using the new technology—is high (88 percent in Brazil and 80 percent in Chile), for a set of relatively cheap, proven, and accessible technologies.[3]

The implications of these gaps for individual firm productivity are significant, providing microevidence for the Comin and Mestieri (2018) simulations discussed in the previous chapter. Controlling for firm characteristics, sector, and size, labor productivity is lowest in those firms that use manual control systems, about average for firms adopting basic and advanced ERP, and highest for firms using advanced ERP intensively throughout the organization (figure 2.7). Hence, incomplete diffusion along each of the gaps is associated with losses in productivity (Comin, Cirera, and Cruz 2025).

### BOX 2.1 Incomplete Digitalization: Slow Diffusion or a Persistent State?

A major reason that firms do not fully utilize digital technologies that they have adopted is because technologies may require a process of integration in the firm, changes in organization, and training of workers. That is, the intensive use of technology does not happen automatically once the technology has been adopted. This can result in time lags between adoption and use. To explore these lags, figure B2.1.1 plots how many years have passed since the year a firm adopted an advanced digital technology, focusing on firms in Brazil that adopt and do not use these technologies intensively.

The plot shows how in most cases, firms adopted advanced digital technology more than 3 years earlier, with 4–5 years elapsing for most firms. In cases where firms need to undertake training and organizational arrangements to complement the adoption of the technology, the firm can be expected to implement the arrangements before it adopts the technology or during an initial period of adoption. However, in most cases, adoption occurred more than 5 years earlier. This suggests that incomplete digitalization is likely to reflect cases where firms are struggling to integrate and productively use such technology, and in some cases may have abandoned the technology. This incomplete diffusion is likely to be persistent for many establishments.

**FIGURE B2.1.1 Incomplete Digitalization in Brazil**

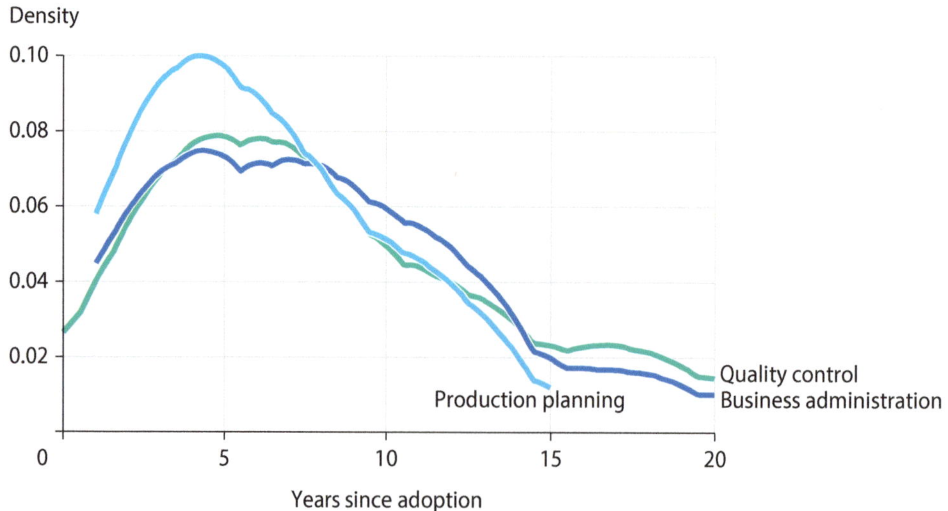


*Source:* Original figure for this volume based on the World Bank Firm-level Adoption of Technology survey.
*Note:* The figure plots the distribution of the number of years of adoption for different business functions for firms with incomplete digitalization.

**FIGURE 2.7 Labor Productivity Lags Further with Each Successive Gap in Technology Adoption**

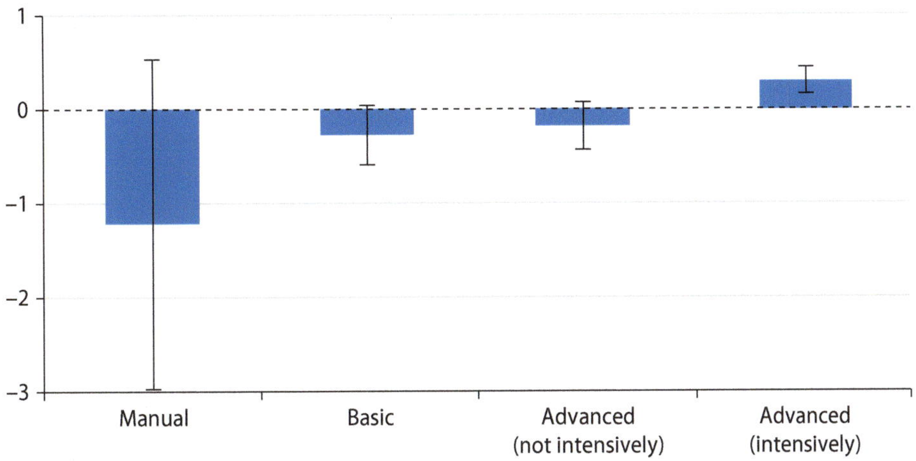


*Source:* Original figure for this volume based on the World Bank Firm-level Adoption of Technology survey.
*Note:* Estimated levels of a linear regression correlating labor productivity (measured as standard deviations from the country mean) with firms' size, sector, location, and the different levels of digitalization in business administration for firms in Brazil and Chile.

What is preventing Latin American firms from fully utilizing existing technologies? Figure 1.12 in chapter 1 highlights two sets of barriers to firms demanding new knowledge and technologies, whether imported or invented.

First are factors internal to the firm: the firm's capabilities to recognize relevant technologies, evaluate the risk-return profiles relative to other options, and adapt them to and implement them in the local context. This requires a variety of educational, technical, managerial, and organizational skills.

Second are factors external to the firm: the traditional incentives to the accumulation of knowledge and capital ranging from macroeconomic stability to trade openness to the overall competitive structure; as well as the barriers to realizing that demand—indeed, to any type of accumulation—such as finance or costs of doing business.[4]

The literature describing and documenting the negative effects of distortionary and unpredictable macroeconomic and business climates on all types of accumulation is substantial and will not be repeated here. However, there are important complementarities between the enabling environment and these capabilities that have been underemphasized in the literature. The discussion that follows reviews both internal and external barriers related to the ability to recognize and use knowledge intensively, as well as barriers related to the incentives to adopt and use knowledge.

## Barriers to Technology Diffusion: Factors Internal to the Firm–The Foundations of Firm Capabilities to Identify, Adopt, and Use Technologies

The ability to identify, adopt, and use technologies depends on three main types of factors: (1) human capital, both that of the manager and the technical skills of workers; (2) the quality of managerial practices and related behavioral biases; and (3) organizational capital. More educated managers are better equipped to identify knowledge and assess risk, employ better workers, and adopt and implement the management practices and organizational structures required to adopt and use complex knowledge. These capabilities reflect different dimensions, including human capital and skills, entrepreneurial ability (discussed in chapter 4), managerial quality, and organizational capital (Verhoogen 2023). LAC lags in these foundations of capabilities. In addition, behavioral biases prevent some entrepreneurs and managers from being able to identify the potential returns to investment. This is most likely to occur when managers overestimate their managerial or technological capabilities. In the case of LAC, this type of overconfidence is quite high and poses a serious constraint to knowledge diffusion.

### Human Capital

#### *Managers' Human Capital*

Managers' human capital is an important factor explaining firms' technology adoption and use. Using data from the FAT survey, figure 2.8 shows that controlling for other factors, firms in LAC that have a main manager who has a university degree adopt and use more sophisticated technologies. Out of an index of sophistication 1 to 5, for firms with a college-educated manager, the index measures are between 0.2 and 0.3 higher for both general and sector-specific business functions. College-educated managers are also associated with higher sophistication in the technologies that firms use intensively, although this correlation is mainly significant for technologies in general business functions. Similar results are found when using a related proxy for human capital: whether the manager has studied abroad. In fact, the correlations are higher, likely because in addition to the improvements in capabilities through an increase in human capital, managers gain information by being more exposed to international technologies and managerial practices.

**FIGURE 2.8 Firms in LAC with College-Educated Managers Who Have Studied Abroad and Have Experience in Large Firms Adopt and Use More Sophisticated Technology**

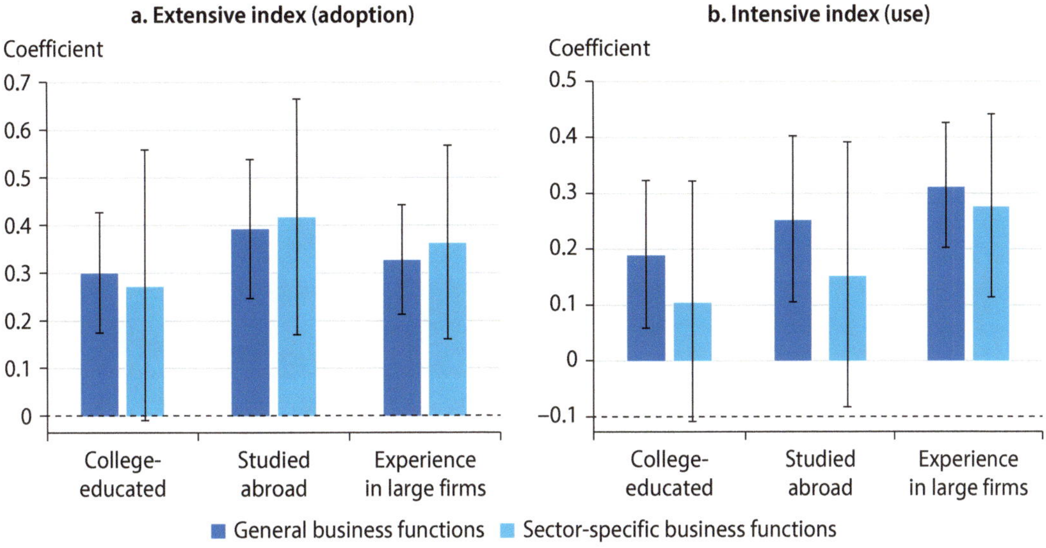

*Source:* Original figure for this volume based on the World Bank Firm-level Adoption of Technology survey.
*Note:* The y-axis gauges the difference on the degree of technology sophistication of the firm of different levels of education, with the estimated standard errors. Panel a is based on technologies adopted (extensive margin), while panel b is based on the most sophisticated technology that is used more intensively (intensive margin). LAC = Latin America and the Caribbean.

Education is not the only way that managers can accumulate capabilities that are relevant for technology use and production. Experience in large companies and access to value chains are also important channels of knowledge diffusion. Giorcelli (2021), for example, documents the role of US firms in the diffusion of management practices in both Europe and Japan after World War II. Figure 2.9 shows that managers who have previous experience working in large companies or as suppliers to global value chains are also more likely to adopt and use more sophisticated technologies. This experience seems to play a role especially when it comes to the use of these more sophisticated technologies, potentially as a result of accumulating tacit knowledge and learning in using these technologies.

The preceding evidence that higher levels of technical and managerial capital are critical for closing the three gaps provides microsupport for a broader literature linking human capital to firm performance. In general, firms with more educated main managers start out larger, grow more over the life cycle, and are more likely to be innovative from the time of entry (see, for example, Queiró 2022). But more importantly, they also grow much larger (figure 2.9, panel a) and become more innovative over the life

**FIGURE 2.9 In Brazil, Highly Educated Managers Run Firms That Grow and Innovate More**

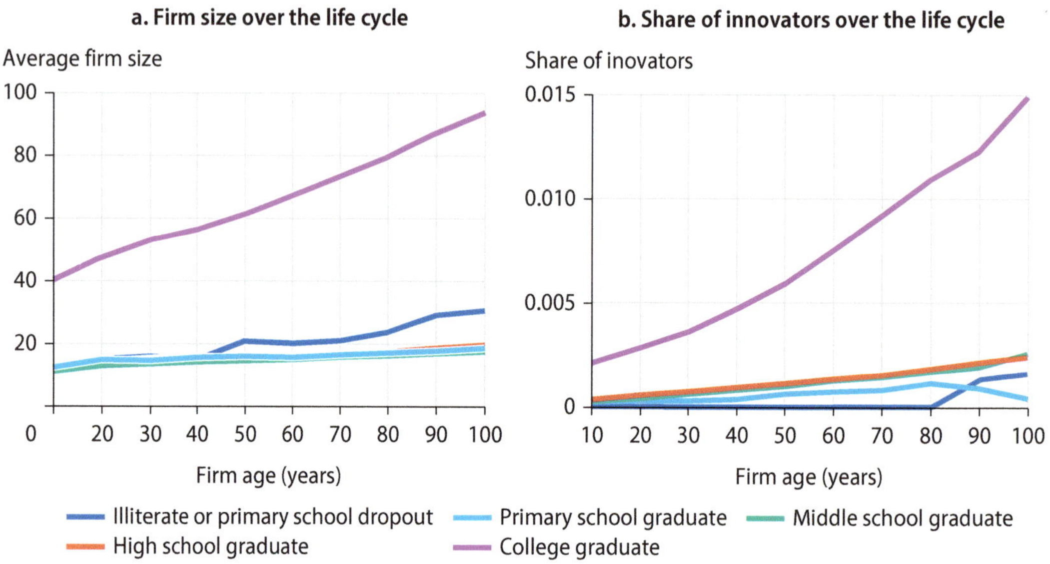

*Source:* Original figure for this volume based on data for Brazil from the Relação Anual de Informações Sociais Annual Social Information Report.

*Note:* Panel a shows firms' average size (in terms of number of workers) by top manager's education for new firms. The sample includes only new establishments with top managers. Panel b shows the share of patenting firms for new firms by top manager's education. The sample includes only new establishments with top managers. The figure covers all firms in Brazil with an identified top manager.

cycle (figure 2.9, panel b). While differences are not large for firms with main managers who have education levels of high school or less, there are large differences in firm performance and innovation at inception and over the life cycle when the main manager has a college degree. Highly educated managers run firms that perform better.

Highly educated managers are also more likely to be able to identify and manage more complex knowledge. Data from Brazil show that controlling for other factors, highly educated managers are more likely to have more complex organizational capital and manage firms that patent and export (figure 2.10). Strong foundational skills of managers are critical.

### *Workers' Human Capital and Technical Skills*

Almost half of LAC companies report difficulty finding capable workers, compared to one-third of firms in member countries of the Organisation for Economic Co-operation and Development. In countries that are most constrained, such as Argentina, this issue affects almost 60 percent of firms, while in Colombia and Peru, it affects approximately half of firms. Garcia Sanchez (2024) suggests that the lack of skills is related to an insufficient

**FIGURE 2.10 In Brazil, Firms with Highly Educated Managers Are More Likely to Patent and Export**

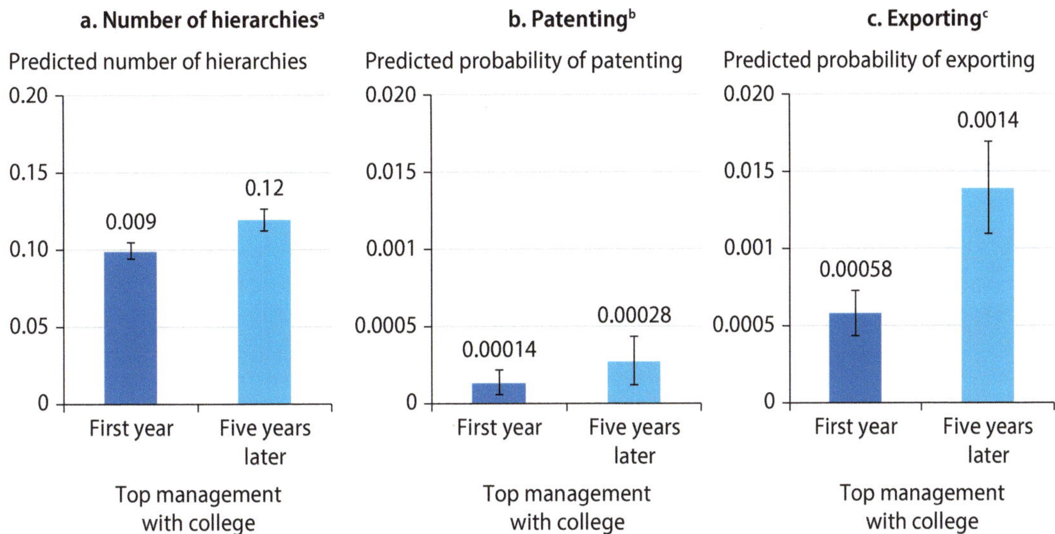


*Source:* Original figure for this volume based on data for Brazil from the Relação Anual de Informações Sociais Annual Social Information Report.

*Note:* The samples in each panel include only new establishments with top managers. The results compare the probability in the first and fifth years since the establishment started operating.

a. Panel a shows the coefficients of the number of hierarchies (organizational levels) in the firm for top managers with a college education. The number of hierarchies aims to capture the vertical depth of the organization. The figure defines firms' "number of hierarchies" based on occupational categories according to the Brazilian Code of Occupations, which is composed of nine different categories according to similar levels of authority, skills, and competencies. Based on this classification, firms have at least one and up to five hierarchies (Cirera, Cruz, and Martins-Neto, forthcoming). Confidence intervals from linear regressions control for sector, size, cohort, region, and average wage.

b. Panel b shows the predicted probability of patenting by top manager education group. Confidence intervals from Probit regressions control for sector, size, cohort, region, and average wage.

c. Panel c shows the predicted probability of exporting by top manager education group. Confidence intervals from Probit regressions control for sector, size, cohort, region, and average wage.

number of graduates in tech-related areas. For example, in Guadalajara, a world-class hub for technology in LAC, Garcia Sanchez (2024) notes that demand for engineers can exceed supply by three times. This shortage is even worse in Central America and the Caribbean (Alfaro de Morán and Amo 2021).

Technical skills are critical for innovation. Using data from the employer-employee database in Brazil (Relação Anual de Informações Sociais [RAIS], Annual Social Information Report),[5] we calculate a measure of the technical skill content of establishments, PoTec, based on the share of workers in the establishment with skills critical to guiding complex innovation projects: specifically, researchers, engineers, research and development (R&D) directors and managers, and scientific professionals.[6] Figure 2.11, panel a shows that the probability of having obtained at least one patent after 1 year

**FIGURE 2.11 Firms with Workers with the Skills to Manage Complex Innovation Projects Innovate Earlier and More Often throughout Their Life Cycle**

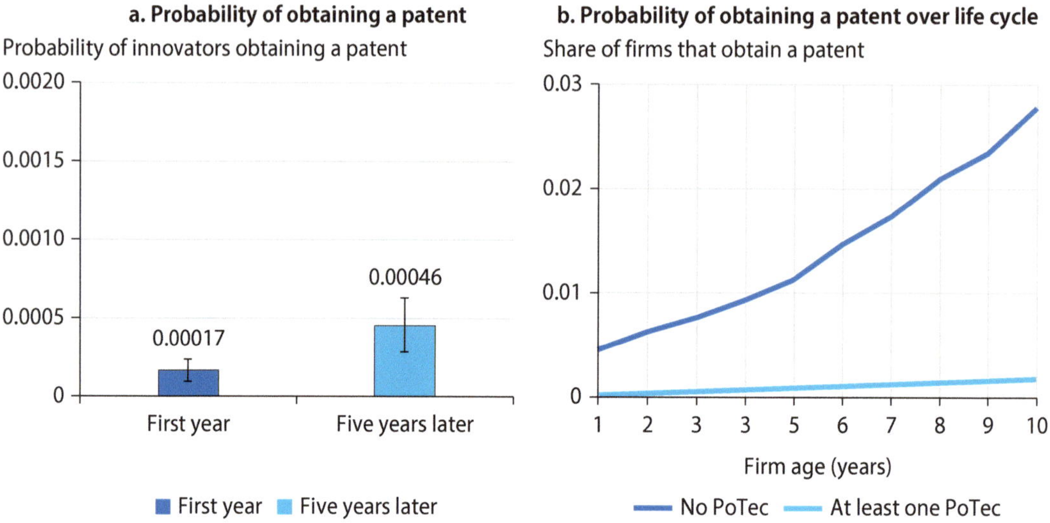

*Source:* Original figure for this volume based on data for Brazil from the Relação Anual de Informações Sociais Annual Social Information Report.

*Note:* In panel a, the probability of obtaining a patent is for firms with at least one technical worker compared to no technical worker after the first and fifth year of operation. In panel b, the probability of obtaining a patent over 10 years is for firms with no or at least one technical worker. PoTec refers to the technical skill content of establishments. PoTec workers are researchers, engineers, research and development directors and managers, and scientific professionals.

is low, but is 0.017 percent larger for establishments that have at least one PoTec worker, and more than doubles after 5 years. Figure 2.11, panel b shows that the firms' patenting probability increases significantly over the life cycle for firms that have at least one technical worker at inception.

## The Quality of Managerial Practices and Related Behavioral Biases

Central to the ability to use knowledge productively is the ability to seek, identify, and use this knowledge in firms. While some of these issues are discussed in chapter 4, especially in relation to entrepreneurial traits, an emerging literature on managerial quality (Bloom et al. 2013; Bloom and Van Reenen 2007; Grover and Karplus 2021; Maloney and Sarrias 2017) stresses the importance of sound business strategies and human resources policies, along with long-term strategic planning and ability to cope with crises. The importance of management quality and its role in the innovation paradox is stressed in Cirera and Maloney (2017) and in explaining high-growth firms in Grover Goswami, Medvedev, and Olafsen (2019). Both studies emphasize the importance of building managerial capabilities as a critical complement to innovation as part of a strategy for generating healthy firm dynamics.

The growing literature of Bloom, Van Reenan, and others suggest that better-quality management translates into higher productivity and growth. At the firm level, Bloom, Sadun, and Van Reenen (2012), Bloom and Van Reenen (2007), Fernandez, Iacovone, and Maloney (forthcoming), Giorcelli (2019), McKenzie (2021), and others show that the introduction of improved management practices increases firm performance. Differences in firm-embedded productivity (management practices, other intangible capital) account for one-third of cross-country variance in output per worker across countries, Alviarez, Cravino, and Ramondo (2023) find. Relaxing barriers on higher managerial quality in multinational corporations in developing countries is estimated to raise developing country gross domestic product (GDP) by 12 percent (Burstein and Monge-Naranjo 2009).

Various studies have found a specific channel through which improved management quality leads to improvements in innovation and productivity. For instance, in Portugal, higher-skilled entrepreneurs head faster-growing and more innovative and productive firms, Queiró (2022) finds. More generally, better-managed firms are more likely to patent and invest in more R&D, controlling for firm characteristics, Cirera, Maloney, and Sarrias (2017) show (figure 2.12).

**FIGURE 2.12 Better-Managed Firms Are More Likely to Patent and Invest in More R&D**

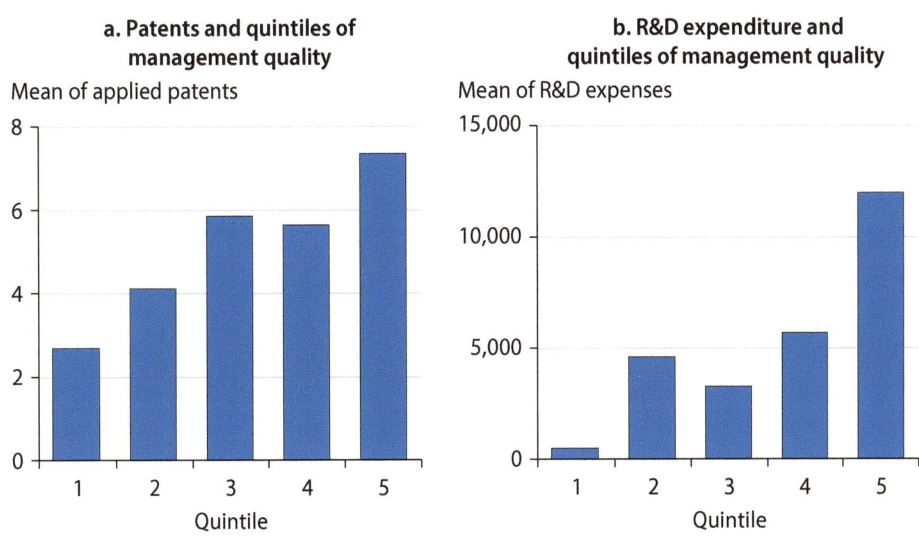


*Source:* Cirera, Maloney, and Sarrias 2017.
*Note:* R&D = research and development.

Export data provide additional confirmation. Better-managed firms in China and the United States export more and to more sophisticated and more diverse markets, Bloom et al. (2021) find. Fernandez, Iacovone, and Maloney (forthcoming) confirm this for Colombia and show that an important channel is through undertaking investment in innovation. Further, referring back to figure 2.10, panel c, firms that export higher-quality goods are also better managed, providing support that it is not only the ability to diversify risk through the financial sector that matters, but also the firm's ability to manage risky innovation projects.

LAC firms continue to lag in both management and organizational quality. Figure 2.13 shows that for the LAC countries with data available in the World Management Survey, only Mexico has management scores that exceed the level its GDP per capita would predict. Argentina, Brazil, and Chile significantly underperform, A Deloitte report on cost management practices in 2020–21 adds granularity, finding in its own survey that "only 17% of companies in Latin America rate their cost management maturity as high—much lower than in the United States (50%) and globally (35%)." Survey respondents report a lack of strategic plans as the top internal challenge (23 percent), followed closely by liquidity and financial position (22 percent), and lack of controls (19 percent) (Deloitte 2020). In general, LAC firms tend to use less of the structured management practices that are important for firm performance and also to successfully manage R&D projects (Bloom and Van Reenen 2007).

More recently, Dahlstrand et al. (2025) find that developing countries also have a scarcity of management "leaders" that the authors associate with higher productivity. This lack of management "leaders" is especially high in Brazil, the only LAC country in their sample. Not only are these types of managers hard to find but they often do not lead the firms that would benefit the most in terms of performance.

An expanding literature has sought to measure how to raise the level of these capabilities (Cirera and Maloney 2017; McKenzie and Woodruff 2015; Verhoogen 2023 for a review). Figure 2.14 plots the probability distribution functions of the management scores of Latin American countries and compares them to the frontier—the United States. Firms at all levels of sophistication are lagging, and in some cases even firms at higher deciles of the distribution have larger management quality gaps with US firms (Maloney and Sarrias 2017). This pattern suggests that simply trimming the left tail—eliminating the laggards—but increasing competition will not be sufficient. Consistent with the findings of Bloom et al. (2012), the share

**FIGURE 2.13 Managerial Skills Are Low in LAC**

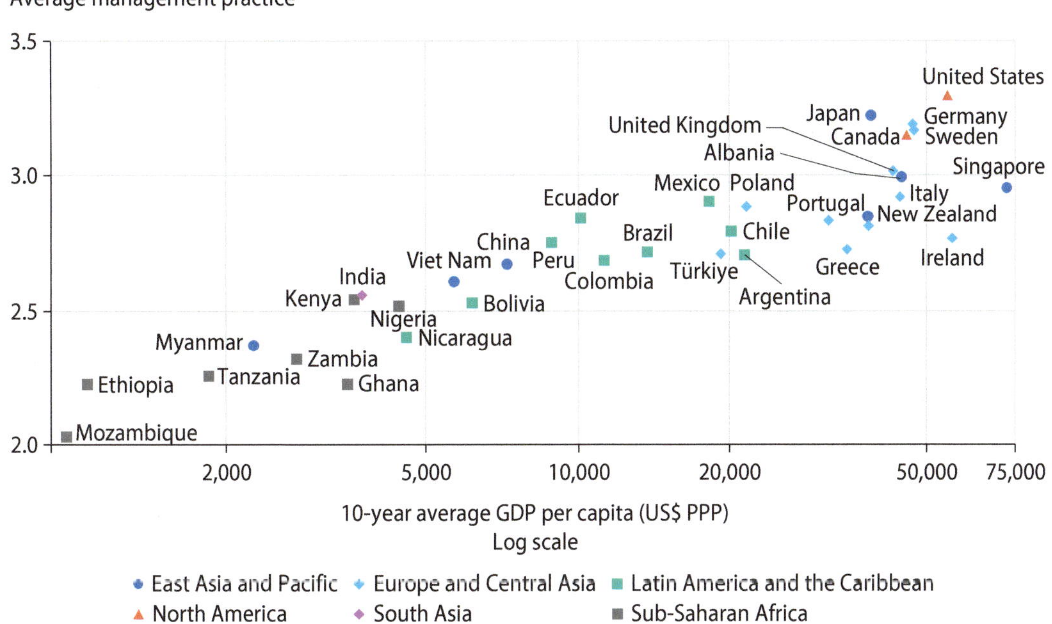


*Sources:* Modified from Bloom et al. 2014b based on World Management Survey data (https://worldmanagementsurvey.org/) and World Bank World Development Indicators (https://databank.worldbank.org/source/world-development-indicators).
*Note:* The y-axis shows country-level average management score over manufacturing firms; for every firm, an average score is computed over multiple management practices. Data years: 2004–22; GDP per capita is the average for 2012–21. GDP = gross domestic product; LAC = Latin America and the Caribbean; PPP = purchasing power parity.

of both employees and managers with a college degree is correlated with better management practices, especially among the best firms. Whether the manager studied abroad has the greatest magnitude among the best firms.

Evidence from around the world suggests that basic management skills can be taught to existing firms, and their positive effects can be long-lasting. Random control trials in India show large and persistent increases in performance measures of improving management quality in apparel firms, including exports (Bloom et al. 2020). A similar experiment in Colombia shows positive results, especially where the consulting was directed to a group of managers and workers (Iacovone, Maloney, and McKenzie 2022). An examination of the long-term effects of the Marshal Plan's Productivity Program (1952–58) finds that firms that received management training under the program in postwar Italy were 29 percent more likely to be exporting 15 years after the program ended and export volumes were 17 percent higher among participating exporters (Giorcelli 2019). Raising quality for exporters works better when the support program combines support

**FIGURE 2.14 Gaps in Management Quality Are Evident in Firms at All Levels of Sophistication in Various LAC Countries**

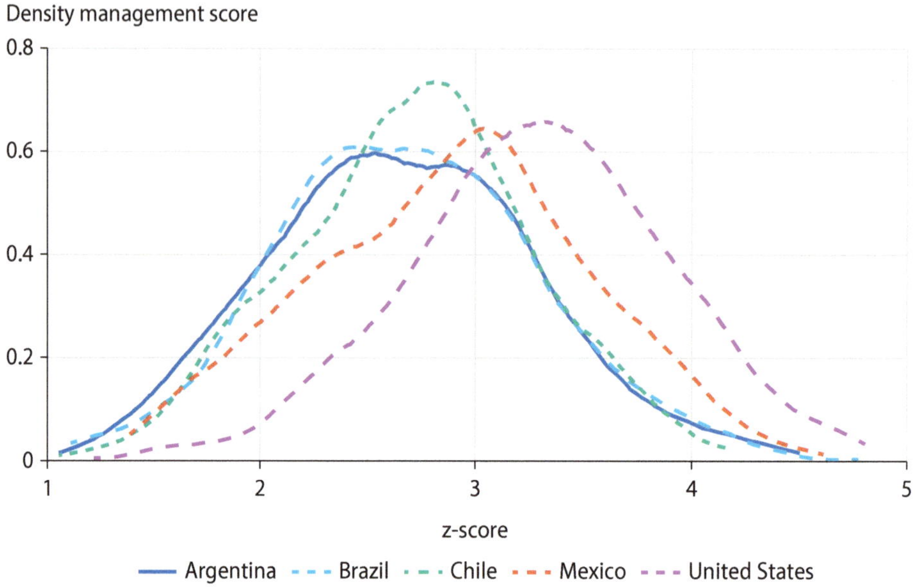

*Source:* Original figure for this volume based on World Management Survey data (https://worldmanagementsurvey.org/).

*Note:* The figure shows the distribution of management quality z-scores—ranging from 1 (worst practice) to 5 (best practice) across 18 key management practices.

to managerial quality to generate more exports. Exporting can generate important knowledge transfer that increases the quality of products, Atkin, Khandelwal, and Osman (2017) find.

The vast majority of advanced and Asian economies have agencies dedicated to providing extension services for firms, often providing public subsidies. The returns can be quite high, especially when extension is implemented by private consultants. Bloom et al. (2020) find that privately supplied management extension to Indian textile firms by Accenture increased production 11 percent in 1 year, paying for the full cost of the program. This raises another aspect of the innovation paradox. Why, if the returns are so high, do firms not invest themselves? This lack is especially puzzling among the "best" firms, which, despite presumably having the resources, often lag their global benchmarks the most.

### *Behavioral Barriers and Overconfidence or Information Asymmetries*

One potential explanation of firms' lack of investment is related to a lack of information as to where the benchmark is. But more profoundly, firms may be hampered by behavioral biases both in their own evaluation of the quality of their managers and in their assessment of their overall proximity to the frontier. One such bias is related to overconfidence in one's ability with respect to other competitors. This tendency is known in the behavioral literature as "reference group neglect" (Camerer and Lovallo 1999). Entrepreneurs may believe themselves to have a particular skill, but may neglect to realize that they are competing with others who also possess that skill. This tendency is related to the Dunning-Kruger effect (Kruger and Dunning 1999), in which people with limited competence in a particular domain overestimate their abilities. For example, if a firm believes that it is already adopting more sophisticated technologies—whether managerial or technological—relative to its competitors, it is unlikely that it will invest to upgrade.

Data from the World Management Survey suggest that contrary to firms having rational views of their managerial capabilities, the worse the objective measure of actual firm performance (horizontal line), the higher the manager's own (subjective) measure of his or her ability (vertical line). This is shown in figure 2.15, with height above the 45-degree line—subjective higher than actual assessment—marking increasing subjective and overconfident assessments. Moreover, countries with the average highest overconfidence are concentrated in Latin America—Argentina, Brazil, Chile, and Mexico. These findings suggest that poor management skills not only lower productivity, but also prevent the firm from having a clear view of how it could improve.

The FAT survey also asks managers to self-assess their technological level relative to peers and finds such overconfidence may be a major barrier to technological adoption (figure 2.16). Again, the self-assessment is weakly correlated—or, in Chile's case, negatively correlated—with the objective measure of the sophistication of the technology that firms use to conduct general business functions. Here, also, excess confidence or reference group neglect is larger for those firms that use less sophisticated technologies. This overconfidence in Latin America ranks among the highest in overoptimism in the FAT data set. The roots of this regional overconfidence are not clear, but they may be related to the dearth of entrepreneurial capital discussed in chapter 1—an inability to use information to alter preconceptions around the benefits in investing in new technologies versus the status quo. A key, therefore, to invest in upgrading capabilities in LAC lies in reducing these subjective biases via benchmarking tools that provide objective information to managers about their actual capabilities.

**FIGURE 2.15 Latin American Firms Are Especially Overconfident of Their Management Ability**

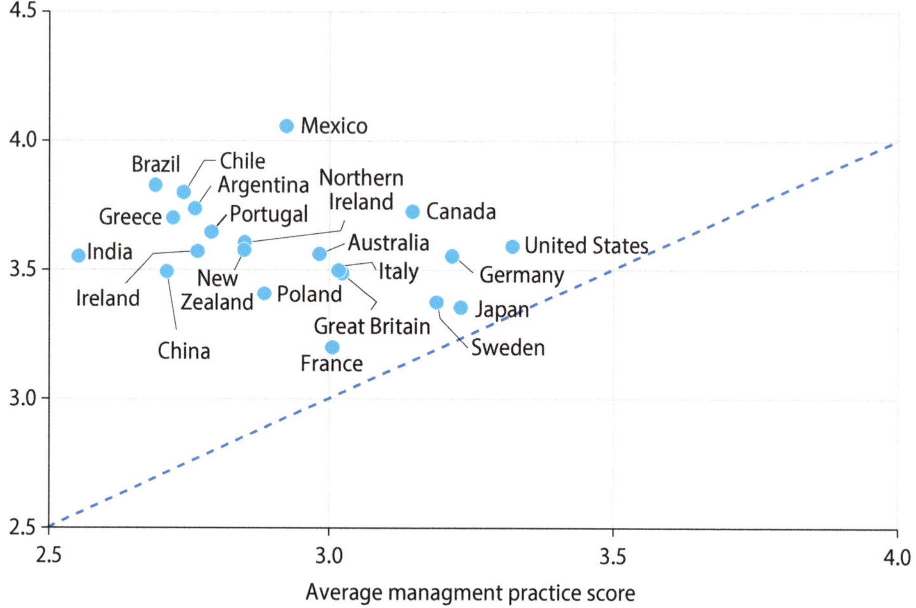


*Source:* Cirera and Maloney 2017, based on Bloom and Van Reenen 2007, using World Management Survey data.

**FIGURE 2.16 Firms in Brazil and Chile Are Overconfident of the Sophistication of Their Technology in Relation to Other Firms in the Country**

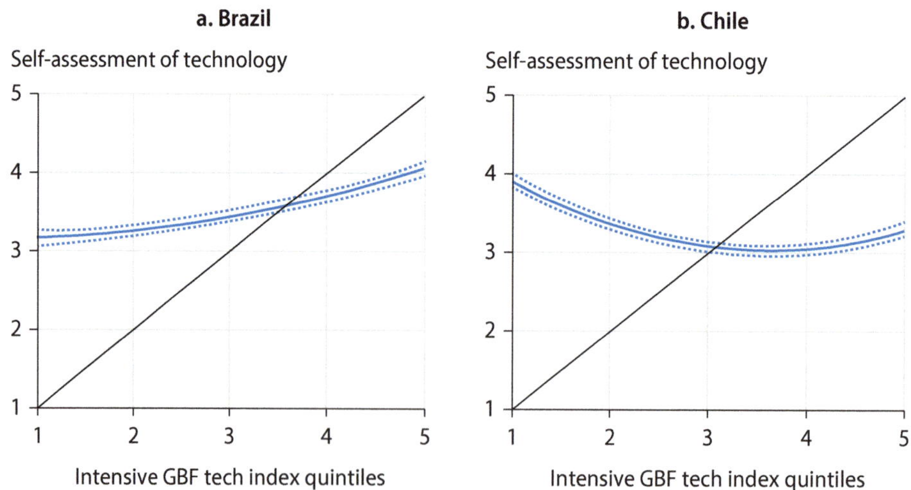


*Source:* Original figure for this volume based on the World Bank Firm-level Adoption of Technology survey data for Brazil and Chile.

*Note:* The figure focuses on the sophistication of technology for general business functions (GBFs). The blue lines show the quadratic fit with 95 percent confidence intervals of the scatterplot of firms' self-assessment versus actual technology sophistication. Above the 45-degree line, self-assessment is higher than the actual sophistication index.

## Organizational Capital and Productive Use of Knowledge

Beyond individual managerial capabilities, a growing literature highlights the role of organizational capital. Acquiring the knowledge needed to use new technologies and innovate is costly, and managers and workers are limited by their time and capabilities to address complex problems. Different organizational structures divide tasks among staff in ways that can relax this individual-level constraint and boost firm-level problem-solving capabilities. For instance, in firms with a pyramid-shaped knowledge-based hierarchy that organizes workers into layers of different sizes, where higher layers are smaller but include more knowledgeable employees, if a problem falls outside staff's ability, they can seek help from specialized workers one or more layers above.[7]

Adding new layers allows workers to specialize in more specific tasks, increases monitoring, and facilitates the efficient use of knowledge by reallocating problems to a few individuals instead of incurring the cost of having to requalify all production workers. These changes have positive implications for firms' performance. Recent evidence shows a positive association between the number of layers and productivity (Caliendo et al. 2020; Garicano and Hubbard 2016); value added (Spanos 2019); and export performance (Caliendo, Monte, and Rossi-Hansberg 2017; Cruz, Bussolo, and Iacovone 2018; Spanos 2016). For instance, firms with a greater number of layers report higher performance levels and engage in exports to a larger number of destinations (Spanos 2016). Similarly, firms that enter export markets tend to be more inclined to introduce additional layers to their organizational structure than non-exporting firms to deal with more complex demands (Caliendo, Monte, and Rossi-Hansberg 2017).[8]

There is an intrinsic complementarity between technology and innovation and firms' organization. On the one hand, the use of information and communication technology (ICT) has significant implications for firms' organizations. Better communication technologies lower the interaction cost between layers such that production workers can more frequently rely on specialized workers to deal with exceptional problems. Similarly, improvements in information technologies allow top-layer workers to leverage more of their available time to solve problems (Mariscal 2018). For instance, information technologies such as ERP allow managers to handle more requests from subordinates (Bloom et al. 2014a). At a lower level in the hierarchy, advanced technologies for fabrication and quality control increase the autonomy of production workers, allowing workers to deal with more complex problems and reducing the need for managers to monitor work activities (Dixon, Hong, and Wu 2021). Across an organization, advanced communication technologies can also increase firms' geographic span of control by reducing internal communication costs, Jiang (2021) and Kang and Suh (2022) find.

On the other hand, the use of more advanced technologies also requires changes in organization. "Firms do not simply plug in computers or telecommunications equipment and achieve service quality or efficiency gains" as Bresnahan, Brynjolfsson, and Hitt (2002) note. Instead, firms go through a number of changes in their organization in order to successfully adopt and integrate new technologies. Recent evidence suggests a link between technology adoption and new work practices (Bartel, Ichniowski, and Shaw 2007) and indicates that the gains from ICT are closely linked to how firms organize themselves (Bloom et al. 2012; Brynjolfsson, Hitt, and Yang 2002). For instance, using data on technology adoption in police departments in the United States, Garicano and Heaton (2010) show the importance of aligning technology adoption with appropriate organizational and management practices. They find that technology's positive impact on performance is contingent upon the presence of specific organizational and management practices that complement its implementation.

These organizational changes are required not only to manage more complex knowledge but also to create the incentives to implement new technologies successfully. Organizational investments play a key role in the productivity impact of ICT, Brynjolfsson and Hitt (2000) find. Conversely, organizational barriers can reduce the adoption of more efficient technologies due to misaligned incentives, as a study of the soccer ball industry in Pakistan shows (Atkin et al. 2017), examining the case of leather-cutting technologies.

The complementarity between organizational quality and knowledge is also clear in the context of Latin American countries. By merging granular employer-employee data with data on patenting and technology adoption in Brazil, we are able to look at the complementarity between knowledge management and organizational quality as measured by the number of hierarchies in firms.[9] Figure 2.17 plots the correlation between firm size and the probability of implementing two activities that require managing complex knowledge: technology adoption (summarized by a technology sophistication index, figure 2.17, panel a), and patenting (figure 2.17, panel b). As expected, the level of technology sophistication increases with firm size, but it is higher across the size spectrum for firms with four and five levels of hierarchy. The same is true for patents, although both level and slope increase as the number of hierarchies increases.

**FIGURE 2.17 The Level of Technology Sophistication and Patenting Activity of Firms in Brazil Increase with Firm Size and Number of Hierarchies**

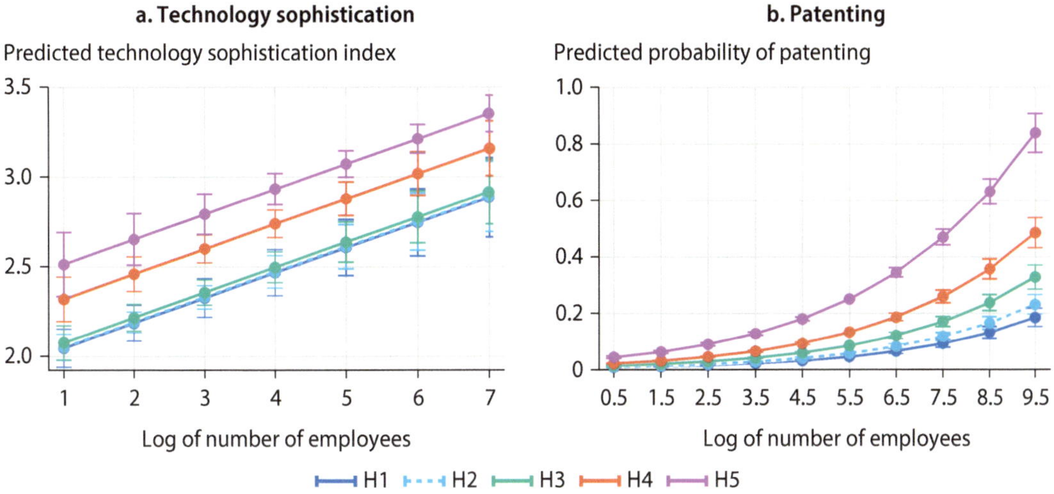

*Source:* Cirera, Cruz, and Martins-Neto, forthcoming.
*Note:* H1 through H5 indicate the five levels of firm hierarchies.

The relationship between technology and organizational quality also works in the other direction, suggesting a truly virtuous circle. Using FAT data merged with RAIS data, we find that the adoption of ERP technology in production planning and management processes translates into increases of hierarchies in Brazilian firms (figure 2.18). This is because it allows firms to increase information flows, reduce transaction costs, and integrate tasks more precisely in ways that make more organizational levels possible (Bloom et al. 2014a).

### *Expanding the Supply of Human Capital to Increase Organizational Capital*

Better-managed firms must recruit skilled professionals, which can pose significant challenges and costs, especially in countries with a shortage of college-educated workers. When companies struggle to find the right talent to expand their workforce, they may settle for organizational structures that do not fully utilize their existing knowledge pool. The growth of modern sectors in developing countries is hampered by the high relative cost of hiring managers, Hjort, Malmberg, and Schoellman (2022) find, which is often linked to lower educational levels and the migration of highly skilled workers to higher-income countries. As countries develop, the income disparity between managers and nonmanagers decreases, Esfahani (2019) observes.

**FIGURE 2.18 Adoption of ERP Increases the Number of Firm Hierarchies in Brazil**

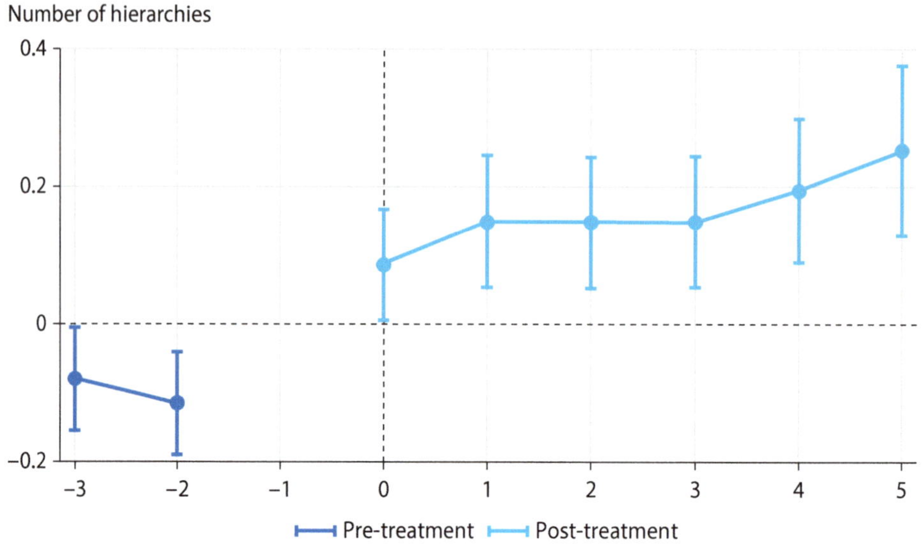

*Source:* Cirera, Cruz, and Martins-Neto, forthcoming.
*Note:* The x-axis indicates the years before and after ERP was adopted. Year t−1 is the base year. ERP = enterprise resource planning.

Policies that increase the availability of managers and other human capital can increase the organizational quality of firms. The sudden rise in China's college-educated workforce led to notably higher productivity increase in firms within industries that were more human capital–intensive, driven by accelerated technology adoption and a rise in the employment of highly skilled workers (Che and Zhang 2018). Viet Nam's expansion of its higher education system led to firms substituting noncollege workers with skill-biased capital and college-educated workers, leading to enhanced productivity (Vu and Vu-Thanh 2022).

Similarly, Brazil's university expansion between 2002 and 2012 (box 2.2) increased enrollment in higher education institutions and graduation rates in affected microregions. The increase in the supply of graduates resulted in a reduction in the relative cost of university graduates. This, in turn, increased the share of college-educated workers in firms in the microregions with new universities (figure 2.19). The expansion of universities resulted in increased intensity of the human capital of workers in firms.

## BOX 2.2 The Expansion of Federal Universities in Brazil

Between 2000 and 2012, Brazil embarked on an ambitious policy to expand access to tertiary education by implementing one of history's largest campus construction programs (map B2.2.1). The goal was to provide free-of-charge, on-site undergraduate programs to youth residing in areas with limited or no access to higher education institutions. Historically, federal universities were concentrated in the country's most populous and developed areas. The expansion program has led to the establishment of campuses in previously underserved regions, contributing to a more equitable distribution of higher education opportunities across Brazil. This expansion encompassed universities, university centers, colleges, and federal institutes of education, science, and technology, and greatly increased the skilled labor supply. Brazil's federal higher education network has grown significantly (for comprehensive information, refer to Conceição 2022). It currently comprises 63 federal universities, 40 federal institutes of education, science, and technology, 5 federal colleges, and 2 federal university centers (INEP 2020).

**Map B2.2.1 Higher-Education Programs Expanded Greatly across Microregions in Brazil between 2000 and 2012**

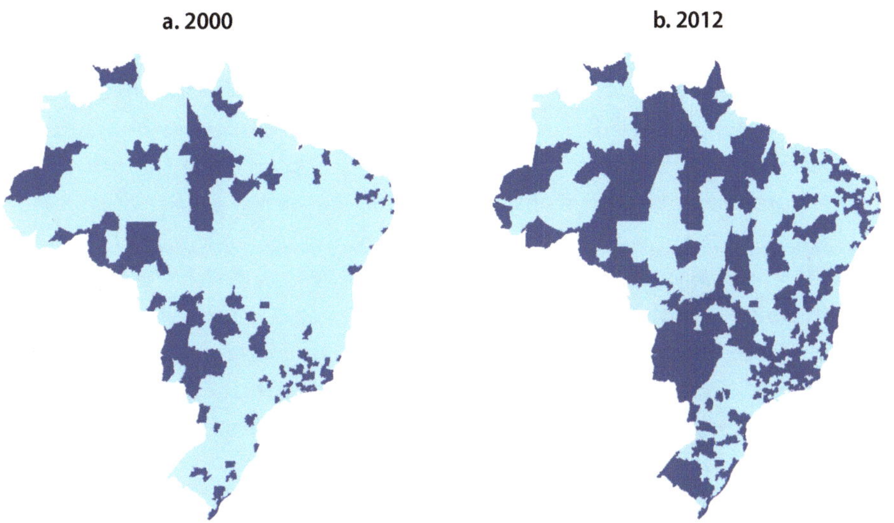


*Source:* Original map for this volume based on Brazilian Higher Education Census data.
*Note:* The dark blue areas in the maps display the microregions in Brazil with at least one campus offering courses in science, technology, engineering, and mathematics in 2000 and 2012.

**FIGURE 2.19 The Supply of College-Educated Workers Increased Following the Opening of New Universities in Brazil**

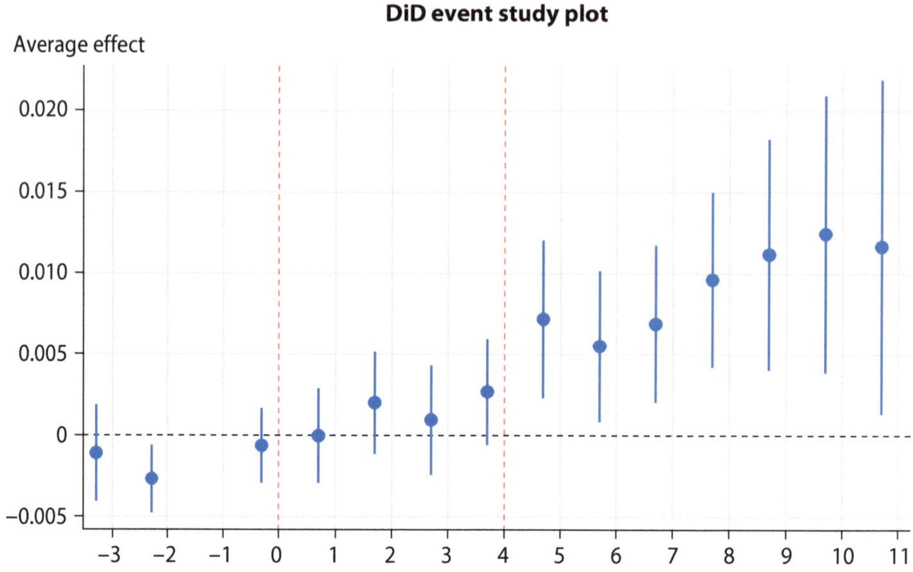

*Source:* Cirera, Cruz, and Martins-Neto, forthcoming.
*Note:* The figure shows the estimates of time-to-event dummies interacted with a treatment indicator from a regression including establishment and year fixed effects. The dependent variable is the share of college-educated workers. Year t–1 is the base year. Vertical bars show the estimated 95 percent confidence interval based on standard errors clustered at the individual level. DiD = difference-in-differences.

More importantly, Cirera, Cruz, and Martins-Neto (forthcoming) find a positive effect of this increase in higher education institutions in the number of hierarchies in firms, which as discussed in the previous section, is complementary to technology adoption (figure 2.20). With a significant lag of 6 years after the new higher education institutions were created, hierarchical depth increased in the microregions with the new universities. Recently, Dahlstrand et al. (2025) find that proximity to business schools increases the availability and matching of "leader" type chief executive officers who are responsible for higher productivity growth. These results suggest that there is an important component of management and organizational quality that has to do with the availability and costs of human capital.

A final important element is how this increase in organizational capital translates into improved performance. Given the limited firm-level information in RAIS, Cirera, Cruz, and Martins-Neto (forthcoming), following the methodology suggested by Imbert and Ulyssea (2023), use the wage premium of firms as a productivity measure. Firms that pay

**FIGURE 2.20 An Increase in Higher Education Institutions Increases the Average Number of Hierarchies in Firms**

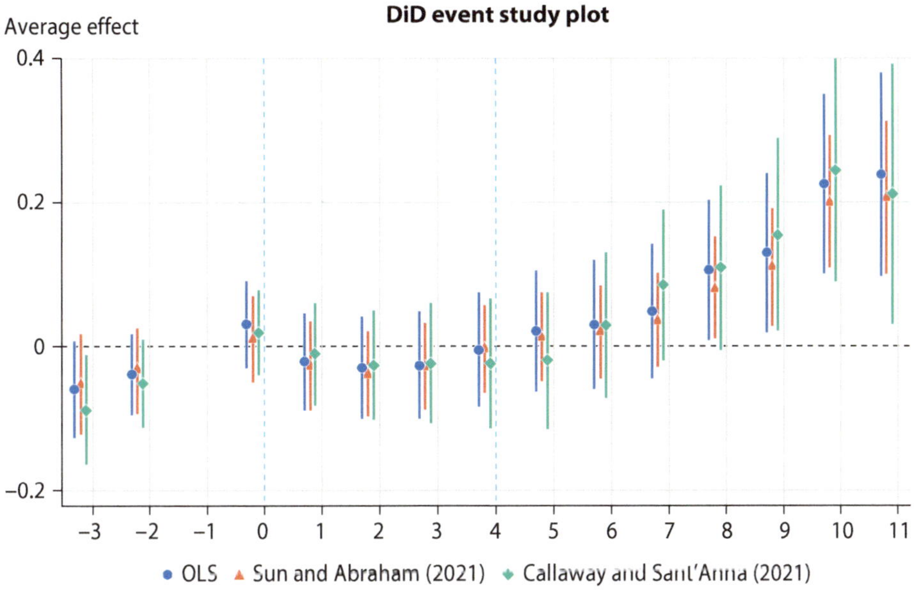

*Source:* Cirera, Cruz, and Martins-Neto, forthcoming.

*Note:* OLS based on OLS estimates; Callaway and Sant'Anna based on the difference-in-differences method in Callaway and Sant'Anna (2021); and Sun and Abraham based on the method described in Sun and Abraham (2021). The figure shows the estimates of time-to-event dummies interacted with a treatment indicator from a regression including establishment and year fixed effects. The dependent variable is the number of knowledge hierarchies. Year t–1 is the base year. Vertical bars show the estimated 95 percent confidence interval based on standard errors clustered at the individual level. DiD = difference-in-differences; OLS = ordinary least squares.

higher wages, beyond the premium associated with education and years of experience of workers, are also more productive, and this "excess" premium is a good measure of firm productivity. The authors find that the wage (productivity) premium firms pay to existing workers increases faster in firms in microregions where universities were established. This increase in organizational capital results in better performance and wages for workers. One channel of this improved performance is delegation. Hiring of more qualified workers and outside managers allows firms to expand to more and complex tasks that can be delegated to new managers. Lack of delegation can be costly. For instance, Akcigit, Alp, and Peters (2021) find that inefficiencies in delegation in plants account for as much as 11 percent of the income per capita difference between India and the United States and explain part of the size differences between Indian and US plants. Expansion of human capital allows for better organizational capital, including delegation, which results in improved performance.

## Barriers to Diffusion: Factors External to the Firm–The Enabling Environment and Incentives for Firm Demand for Knowledge

As discussed in chapter 1, the absence of critical factors of production or the existence of major distortions in markets can reduce the returns from investments in innovation, the most likely explanation of the innovation paradox. Clearly, an absence of skilled scientists can reduce the returns from R&D, and the absence of entrepreneurs who can take an idea to market breaks the link from investments to growth. But even if this were the case, barriers to expand or export, an inability to import necessary capital or intermediate goods, and/or an inability to finance and manage risk can deflate the most determined innovator. This section discusses a few select elements of the environment that interact with firms' capabilities in particular.

### Competition and Capabilities

There is no question that without competition, there is no incentive for firms to learn new capabilities and transfer technology. The manufacture of the Ford Falcon in Argentina is a classic example. Argentine manufacturers made few upgrades in 30 years of production and production continued a full two decades after manufacture ceased in the United States. Such blunting of innovation pressures is inevitable when there is no competition. Traditionally in Latin America, competition has been lower and markups higher than in other regions (figure 2.21), although markups have been converging as aggregate markups in other regions increase (Maloney et al. 2024).

**FIGURE 2.21 Mark-Ups Have Been Higher in Latin America than Other Regions but Are Converging**

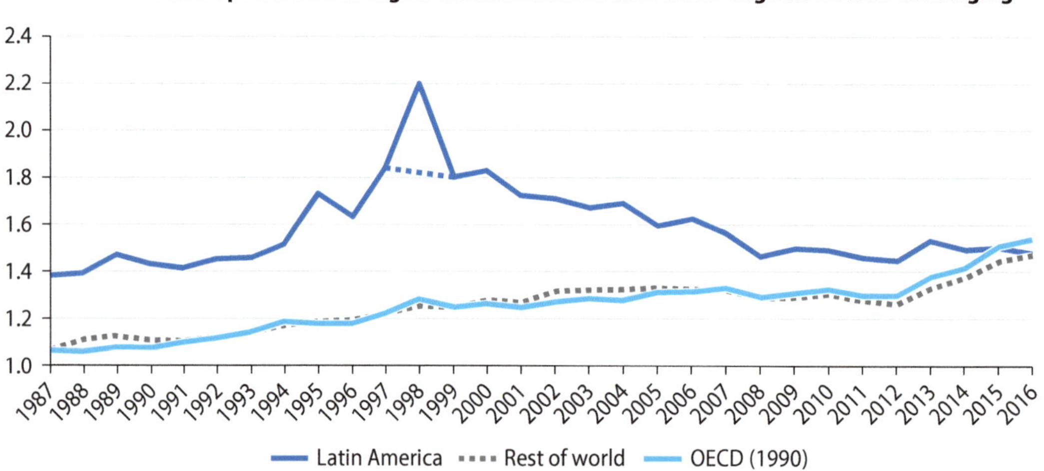


*Source:* Original figure for this volume based on De Loecker and Eeckhout 2018.
*Note:* OECD = Organisation for Economic Co-operation and Development. The y-axis presents a measure of markup (that is, price over marginal cost). For example, a value of 1.4 implies that on average firms charge prices that are 40 percent above costs.

A lack of a competitive environment acts as a disincentive to innovate. As highlighted in the *World Development Report 2024* on the middle-income trap (World Bank 2024), a central ingredient to accelerate the transition to a high-income country is to discipline incumbents so they have the pressure to innovate. This is reflected in the FAT data. When managers are asked about the main drivers for adopting a technology, most managers cite competition pressures as the most important factor. In Chile, competition is the perceived main driver of technology adoption for small and medium firms and is the third most important driver for large firms, after the need to reduce costs—which is closely related (figure 2.22). Some evidence for other countries confirms these survey results. In Peru, for instance, after the national competition authorities mandated the elimination of local entry barriers, productivity increased, Schiffbauer, Sampi, and Coronado (2025) find. More generally, pro-competition measures within the country tend to have positive effects on productivity, output, and employment in middle-income countries (World Bank 2024).

There is, however, an often-neglected complementarity between competition as a disciplining device and firm and country capabilities to respond to it, which was perhaps underemphasized by the so-called "Washington Consensus." Regardless of how undistorted the enabling environment,

**FIGURE 2.22 Competition Is a Very Important Driver of Technology Adoption in Chile**

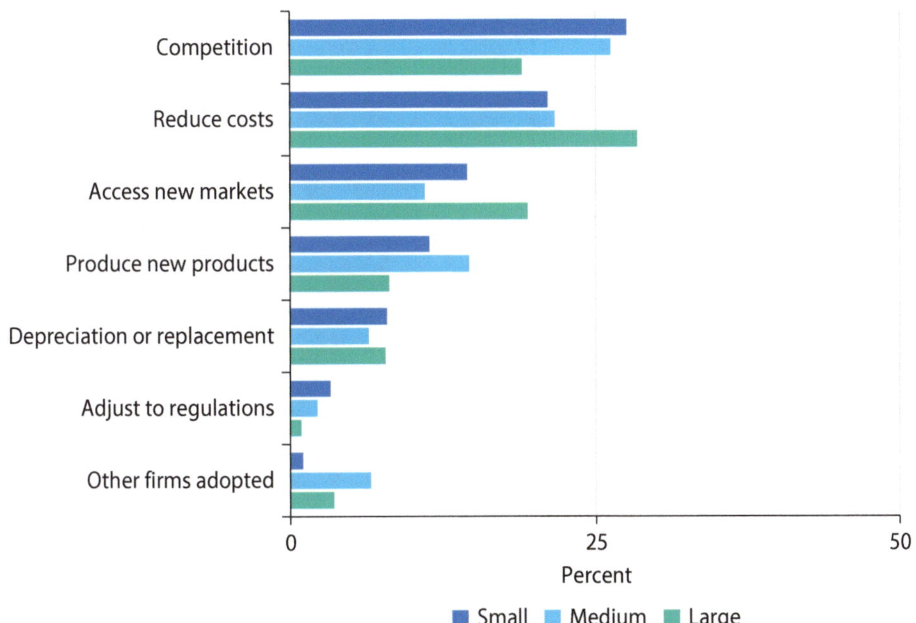


*Source:* Original figure for this volume based on the World Bank Firm-Level Adoption of Technology survey.
*Note:* The x-axis indicates the percent of firms citing a particular driver of technology adoption.

societies not populated with the necessary capabilities and structures will have difficulty constructively confronting frontier-level competition. This finding has slowly emerged from the literature in the tradition of Aghion et al. (2005), which postulates that industry leaders—those close to the frontier—will seek to escape new competition by innovating, while those further from the frontier may fail. As figure 2.23 shows, in a group of major advanced economies (France and the United Kingdom) and an emerging economy (China), 50 percent of firms are in the former category and seek to innovate, compared to only 7 percent in Chile (Maloney and Zambrano 2022). Having a lower share of leaders implies lower growth. Historically, faced with heightened competition arising from the new technologies of the Second Industrial Revolution, Latin America had very few global leaders and hence subcontracted entire industries (most critically, mining) to outsiders, or erected protective barriers, as discussed in chapter 1.

Similar results are found in the trade literature with respect to the "China shock." Bustos (2011) shows how tariff reductions in Argentina in the context of the trade deal between the European Union and the Mercosur trade bloc (Argentina, Brazil, Paraguay, Uruguay) incentivized firms to adopt new technologies given the larger scale and profits. This positive effect, however, was concentrated among firms at the top of the productivity

**FIGURE 2.23 Chile Has a Low Share of "Leaders"—Firms That Increase Innovation in the Face of Increased Competition**

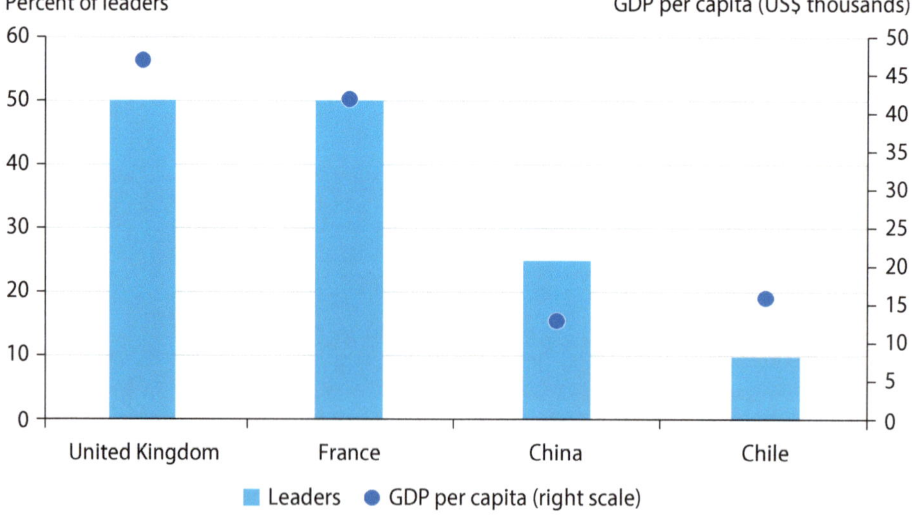


*Source:* Maloney and Zambrano 2022.

*Note:* United Kingdom data based on Aghion et al. (2009). France data based on Aghion et al. (2021). China data based on Bombardini, Li, and Wang (2017). Chile data based on Cusolito, Garcia, and Maloney (2023). GDP = gross domestic product.

distribution—those that were more capable. Similarly, Bas and Berthou (2016) find that during the trade liberalization process in the 1990s in India, only firms in the middle to upper deciles of productivity increased technology adoption and the import of capital goods following tariff cuts in intermediaries. This literature confirms the complementarities between competition and capabilities.

The causality, however, can also go the other way. Akcigit and Ates (2023) argue that the decline in competition and dynamism within the United States is precisely due to the decline in the diffusion of new technologies. When knowledge diffusion slows over time, market leaders are shielded from being copied, which helps them establish stronger market power. A decline in knowledge diffusion plausibly explains the widening productivity gap between frontier and laggard firms in the United States; Akcigit and Ates (2023) find that the resulting reduced competition accounts for more than 70 percent of declining business dynamism. They postulate that the decline in knowledge and diffusion spillovers results in an increasingly "technology-less" market, compounded by poor regulatory practices that cause lead firms to restrict knowledge flows.

The point remains, however, that competition and technical and firm capabilities cannot be treated as distinct realms of policy. Box 2.3 describes one example of a public policy instrument that recognizes this complementarity by attempting to increase competition via trade liberalization while trying to build capabilities to facilitate adjustment and transition to higher value-added activities. Latin America needs more competition, and knowledge capabilities are necessary both to generate it and guarantee positive growth effects.

### BOX 2.3 Argentina's Programa Nacional de Transformación Productiva

One example of public policy trying to address the complementarity between competition and capabilities is the short-lived Programa Nacional de Transformación Productiva (PNTP) program in Argentina. Created in 2016 within the Ministry of Production's Secretariat for Productive Transformation, the PNTP changed the traditional approach to trade adjustment assistance of subsidizing labor costs and re-skilling by supporting the transformation of uncompetitive firms (labeled "transformation firms") and the reallocation of production factors to "dynamic firms"

*(Continued on next page)*

**BOX 2.3 Argentina's Programa Nacional de Transformación Productiva *(continued)***

with competitive potential. For example, a company in a highly protected domestic market could either shut down when trade barriers were removed or apply to the PNTP with a transformation plan that would shift its business model, though typically with fewer workers.

**Program Benefits**

For displaced workers, the PNTP provided expanded unemployment insurance up to 2.5 times the minimum wage for up to 6 months (much more generous than standard unemployment insurance), assistance in finding new employment, and relocation benefits (though these were rarely used). For transformation firms, the program offered subsidized lending through interest rate subsidies and technical assistance in technological aspects via the National Institute of Industrial Technology (INTI).

**Program Implementation**

The PNTP implementation involved significant intergovernmental coordination. Identifying potential beneficiaries required program staff and labor officials to promote the program through business associations and labor unions. Union leaders generally viewed the program positively because it aided conflict resolution. The approval process engaged the Investment and Trade Promotion Agency to provide evaluation and technical assistance to firms that developed transformation or expansion strategies. Nine officials with graduate training and corporate experience assessed project viability and proposed solutions to improve them, and INTI provided technological extension services.

**Case Examples**

Several computer assembly firms successfully utilized the PNTP to manage their transformation. One prominent example involved a mid-size computer assembler from Córdoba that had employed approximately 500 workers. Through the PNTP, the company developed a transformation plan to become an authorized distributor for a major international brand while retaining technical service capabilities. The transformation required reducing the workforce to approximately 220 employees, but allowed the company to remain viable in the newly competitive environment. The PNTP provided extended unemployment benefits for displaced workers, financial

*(Continued on next page)*

**BOX 2.3 Argentina's Programa Nacional de Transformación Productiva *(continued)***

assistance through interest rate subsidies for the company to develop its new logistics infrastructure, and technical assistance from the Investment and Trade Promotion Agency to develop the new business model.

Another case featured a smaller computer assembly firm that pivoted entirely away from hardware, transforming into a software development company specializing in enterprise resource planning systems for small and medium businesses. This transformation maintained higher-skilled positions but required letting go of most assembly-line workers.

*Source:* Castro 2025.

## Finance and Capabilities: Managing the Risk of Innovation

The role of risk in technology adoption and innovation highlighted in figure 1.12 is supported by a substantial literature. For instance, Antràs and Helpman (2006) argue that weak domestic institutions that either exclude entrepreneurs, create additional uncertainty in the rules of the game, or make managing the implications of loss difficult (such as deficient bankruptcy laws) also cause poorer countries to specialize in less risky products. Doraszelski and Jaumandreu (2013) find that engaging in R&D roughly doubles the degree of uncertainty in the evolution of a producer's productivity level.

Risk and uncertainty are also present in firms' considerations to adopt existing technologies. Both adopters and non-adopters report in the FAT survey that lack or uncertainty about future demand is the third most important barrier, below lack of information, knowledge, or technical capacity; and cost (figure 2.24). Similarly, in Colombia, 84 percent of Colombian firms mention uncertainty around the demand for innovative goods and services to be a barrier to innovation.[10]

**FIGURE 2.24 Firms in Brazil and Chile Cite Risk and Uncertainty as the Third Main Barrier to Technology Adoption**

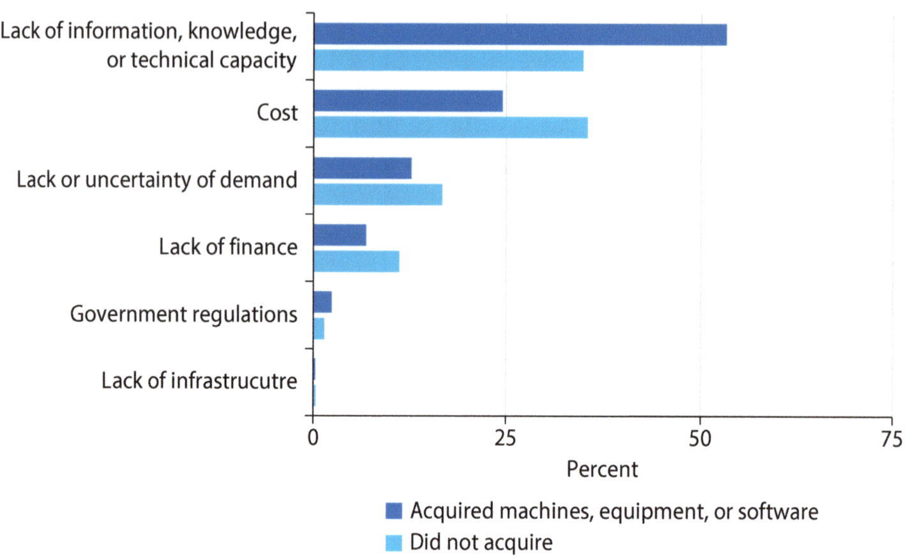


*Source:* Original figure for this volume based on the World Bank Firm-level Adoption of Technology survey.
*Note:* The x-axis reports the percent of firms citing a particular barrier to technology adoption.

There is substantial evidence that shallow financial markets prohibit the diffusion of risk.[11] "The incompleteness of insurance and credit availability play an important role in delaying the adoption of profitable new technologies," Foster and Rosenzweig (2010) argue, in the context of small-scale agriculture. Relatedly, Gorodnichenko and Schnitzer (2013) provide evidence that financial constraints affect the incentives of firms to innovate, which ultimately limits the ability of poor countries to catch up technologically with rich ones. Product quality growth is highly correlated with financial depth and exogenous shocks, such as the Asian financial crisis, as shown in figure 2.25 (Krishna et al. 2023). LAC's low levels of private credit are reflected in broader indexes of financial depth, where the region ranks second to last after Sub-Saharan Africa (figure 2.26).[12] Moreover, the region ranks only above Sub-Saharan Africa and East Asia and Pacific in terms of bank branches per 100,000 people at 11 branches, compared to 25 in North America.[13]

**FIGURE 2.25 Quality Growth Is Correlated with Financial Depth**

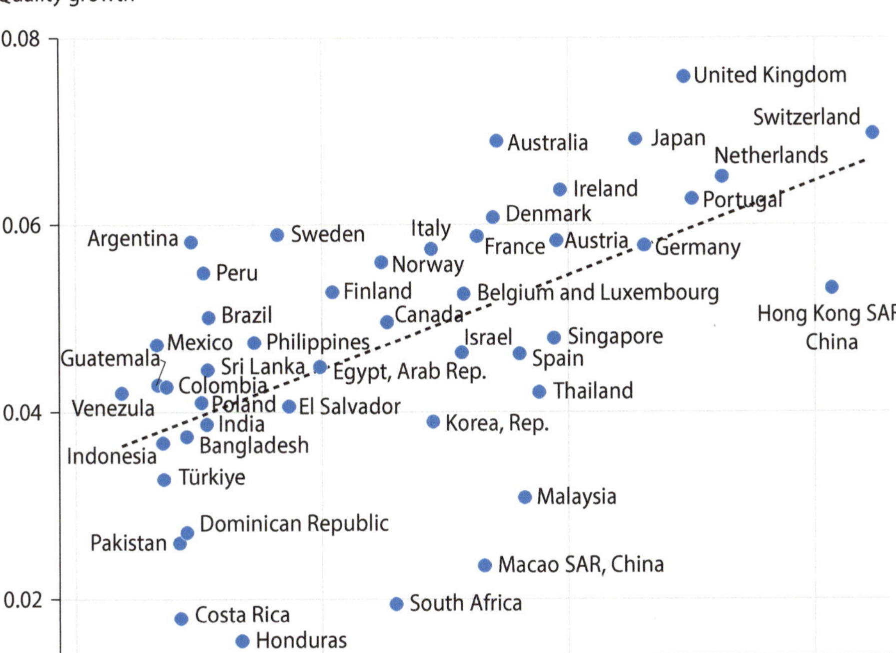


*Source:* Krishna et al. 2023.
*Note:* This figure shows the mean rate of quality growth (across products) against financial development for countries that export at least 50 HS10 products to the United States. Slope = 0.02 (t-statistic = 5.35). GDP = gross domestic product.

However, it is also the case that weak capacity (entrepreneurial capital) to evaluate and manage risk on the part of firms (as described in box 1.1 in chapter 1) is also driving LAC's low rate of risk-taking. Historically, those foreign entrepreneurs who drove industrialization were not characterized by greater accessibility to capital (Maloney and Zambrano 2022). For instance, Brazilian and Chilean firms rank "lack of finance" quite low on barriers to innovation in the FAT survey (figure 2.24). In Colombia, higher export quality is highly correlated with management quality, but financial access seems relatively unimportant. In practice, weak managerial capabilities—such as the inability to keep accounts or develop a business plan—can, in and of themselves, limit access to finance. And banks may also lack the capacity to evaluate the likely success of a proposed project.

**FIGURE 2.26 The Quality of LAC's Financial Markets Is Quite Low Compared to Other World Regions**

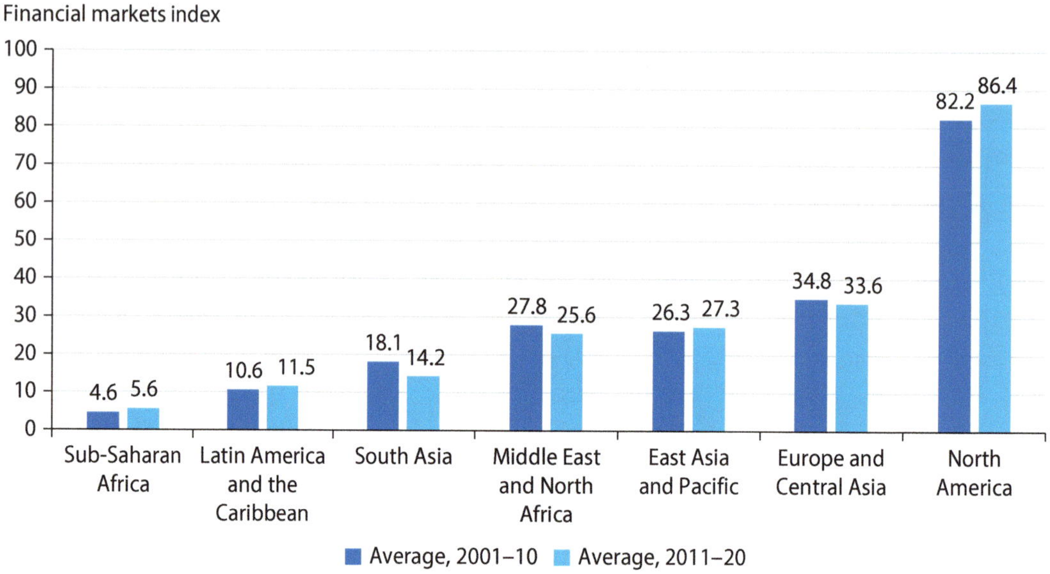

*Source:* Original figure for this volume based on the International Monetary Fund Financial Development Index Database.
*Note:* The Financial Markets Index is an aggregate of: (1) the Financial Markets Depth Index (which compiles data on stock market capitalization to GDP, stocks traded to GDP, international debt securities of government to GDP, and total debt securities of financial and nonfinancial corporations to GDP); (2) the Financial Markets Access Index (which compiles data on percent of market capitalization outside of top 10 largest companies and total number of issuers of debt—domestic and external, nonfinancial and financial corporations—per 100,000 adults); and (3) the Financial Markets Efficiency Index (which compiles data on stock market turnover ratio—stocks traded to capitalization). GDP = gross domestic product.

In sum, there is compelling evidence that both managerial capabilities and access to finance are interrelated, and both act as barriers to firms placing the bets that a new technology will improve their bottom line.

## Policies to Enable Innovation

Governments in the LAC region have a central role in facilitating an enabling environment for learning. As depicted in figure 1.12 in chapter 1, governments must oversee the overall functioning of the National Innovation System, as well as addressing market and systemic failures and coordination among various actors to expand and accumulate learning capabilities. While most countries in the region have expanded the innovation policy mix to include more policy instruments, the scope and depth of the policy mix is uneven across the region. Countries such as Brazil, Chile, and Colombia have a significant number of policies to support innovation in firms. Policies have evolved considerably in these countries to not only support the innovation of incumbents but also new innovative ventures and green innovation.

Chapter 5 provides a brief roadmap to transform industrial policies into learning policies for sustained growth. Despite the expansion of the policy mix in LAC countries, several problems remain in the realm of innovation and technology policies. First, government's role in innovation policies is not only to coordinate private actors but also to coordinate public actors and ministries, and innovation policies are still fragmented in the region. Part of the problem is related to the volatility of the innovation agenda and the lack of medium- to long-term strategy; indeed, strategy changes, often dramatically, with every change in government. In addition to the flux of the political cycle, there is lack of coordination among ministries and agencies, in a context in which governments need to eliminate barriers to investments and biases against external knowledge. Firms' use of external knowledge is often taxed in LAC. de Souza, Gaetani, and Mestieri (2024), using data for Brazil, find that tariffs can increase the flow of knowledge transfer because foreign firms may substitute investing in domestic production for exports or sell technology licenses to domestic firms. This implies that combining trade liberalization with subsidies to encourage technology transfer can increase welfare significantly. Incentivizing the use of external knowledge is central.

Second, LAC's innovation systems tend to be fragmented and poorly articulated; hence, incentives should be designed to enhance this articulation. Finland, for example, terminated tax exemptions for firms in favor of matching grants, which incentivized multiple parties to work together on a project, such as firms and universities. LAC still lags significantly in industry-university interactions (chapter 3).

Third, while countries have developed significant R&D tax incentives and subsidies that can be justified, they do not always focus on the key market failures or have the right set of incentives. Investments ranging from investment promotion tours abroad to R&D are all subject to the appropriation externality: other firms cannot be prevented from using the same knowledge, leading firms to underinvest. In addition, R&D spillovers are large, at least in high-income countries. Lucking, Bloom, and Van Reenen (2019) find that the ratio of social to private returns of R&D is a factor of four in the United States. R&D subsidies, tax credits, and patenting protection are all mechanisms designed to encourage firms to invest in knowledge to the social optimum. However, such mechanisms can be counterproductive if not well designed, or if firms are not capable of investing well, or are operating in an enabling environment where such investments will not lead to added knowledge. For instance, R&D subsidies may prolong the lifespan of firms that should exit the market (Acemoglu et al. 2018). Using data for Brazil, de Souza (2023) finds that innovation subsidies can lead to low-quality innovation and expansion directed to protected markets. In addition, Akcigit, Pearce, and Prato (2024) find that the impact of R&D subsidies is strengthened when combined with higher education policies. In developing countries, better education policies that build the pool of potential entrepreneurs and that can create better ventures are likely to produce higher public returns and more innovation in the long term. A better policy path for most countries in LAC is likely to first strengthen the quality of the talent pool and entrepreneurs, then to support the entry of innovative firms, and finally to subsidize R&D incumbents.

Finally, policies to enable innovation require targeting. Fiscal resources are strained in most LAC countries and not all firms can be supported. Trying to upgrade firms across the board is too expensive, and not all firms are ready to accumulate the capabilities needed to take risks. A gradual approach is needed. Low-cost untargeted measures that can provide information infrastructure to most SMEs in the region can act as a funnel to select firms (McKenzie 2021) that are more ready to undertake more expensive and complex interventions (Bloom et al. 2013) and can incentivize firms to engage in riskier activities and accumulation of technological capabilities.

## Conclusion

This chapter asked the question of what is preventing LAC firms from fully utilizing existing technologies. New data from the World Bank FAT survey for Brazil and Chile have refined the evidence on technology gaps and found that while diffusion has accelerated for some digital technologies, the region is still lagging in adoption of more complex technologies, and more importantly in the productive and intensive use of technologies adopted. Access and use of knowledge that is available to propel growth in the region is lagging.

The chapter also explored the question posed by the innovation paradox: what explains LAC's incomplete adoption of knowledge and technology when the returns should be very high. A key factor is the lack of capabilities internal to the firm, from human capital to managerial practices to organizational capital, which impedes the identification, implementation, and use of technologies, and the management of risks involved in innovation. This lack of capabilities combines with factors in the enabling environment that are external to the firm. Shallow financial markets, distorted factor and product markets, barriers to external trade and investment, and the absence of or too much competition effectively reduce the expected return or make it impossible to invest.

The next chapter focuses on the mission that universities in the region play in supporting the process of knowledge creation and diffusion, and how and why universities often fall short of delivering on that mission.

## ANNEX 2A: FAT Survey Data Used in Chapter 2

Chapter 2 uses data from the World Bank Firm-level Adoption of Technologies survey. The survey is a national or state representative survey stratified by firm size, group, region, and sector.

The survey first defines a set of business functions or tasks and, for each, asks firms about the technology they use. This chapter focuses only on general business functions (GBFs), which are business functions that are related to management and administrative functions and tasks that all firms, regardless of the sector activity, have to use. Figure 2A.1 shows the set of GBFs and the main technologies that can be used to perform the main tasks of the business function.

The survey also measures business function technologies for 15 sectors that are key for developing countries. Figure 2A.2 displays one example for business functions in the food sector. Most of the technologies in the figure can be ranked from 1 (manual technologies) to 5 (advanced technologies). This allows us to build a simple index of sophistication that averages across general business functions and sector-specific business functions. More importantly, the survey asks firms whether they have adopted each technology, and of the ones adopted, which technology is the more frequently or intensively used. This allows us to construct two measures of sophistication: an extensive measure based on adoption, and an intensive measure based on use. Finally, when an advanced technology is adopted, the survey asks the year of adoption, which allows us to plot the diffusion curves (Cirera, Comin, and Cruz 2022 for more details).

**FIGURE 2A.1 General Business Functions and Technologies**

**1. Administration (HR processes, finance, accounting)**
- Handwritten processes
- Computers with standard software (for example, Excel)
- Mobile apps or digital platforms
- ***Computers with specialized installed software***
- ***Enterprise resource planning or equivalent software integrated with other back office functions***

**2. Production or service operations planning**
- Handwritten processes
- Computers with standard software
- Mobile apps or digital platforms
- ***Specialized software for demand planning, demand forecast***
- ***Enterprise resource planning or equivalent software integrated with other back office functions***

**3. Sourcing and procurement**
- Manual search of suppliers without centralized database
- Computers with standard software
- Online social media, specialized apps, or digital platforms
- ***Supplier relation management not integrated with production planning***
- ***Supplier relation management integrated with production planning***

**4. Marketing/consumer information**
- Informal chat (face-to-face)
- Online chat (for example, WhatsApp or internet)
- Structured consumer surveys
- ***Costumer relationship management software***
- ***Big data analytics/artificial intelligence***

**5. Sales**
- Direct sales at the establishment
- Direct sales by phone or e-mail
- Sales through social media platforms or apps
- ***Online sales using external digital platforms (for example, Amazon, eBay, Alibaba)***
- ***Online sales (e-commerce) using its own website***
- ***Electronic orders integrated to specialized supply chain management systems***

**6. Payment methods**
- Exchange of goods
- Cash
- Check, voucher, or bank wire
- Prepaid, credit, or debit card
- ***Online or electronic payment***
- ***Online through platform***
- ***Virtual or cryptocurrency***

**7. Quality control**
- Manual, visual, or written processes without the support of digital technologies
- Manual, visual, or written processes with the support of digital technologies
- ***Statistical process control***
- ***Automated systems for inspection***

*Source:* Original figure for this volume based on the World Bank Firm-level Adoption of Technology survey.
*Note:* Technologies that are indicated in bold and italics denote the most advanced in the business function. HR = human resources.

**FIGURE 2A.2 Example of Sector-Specific Business Function Technologies—Food Processing**

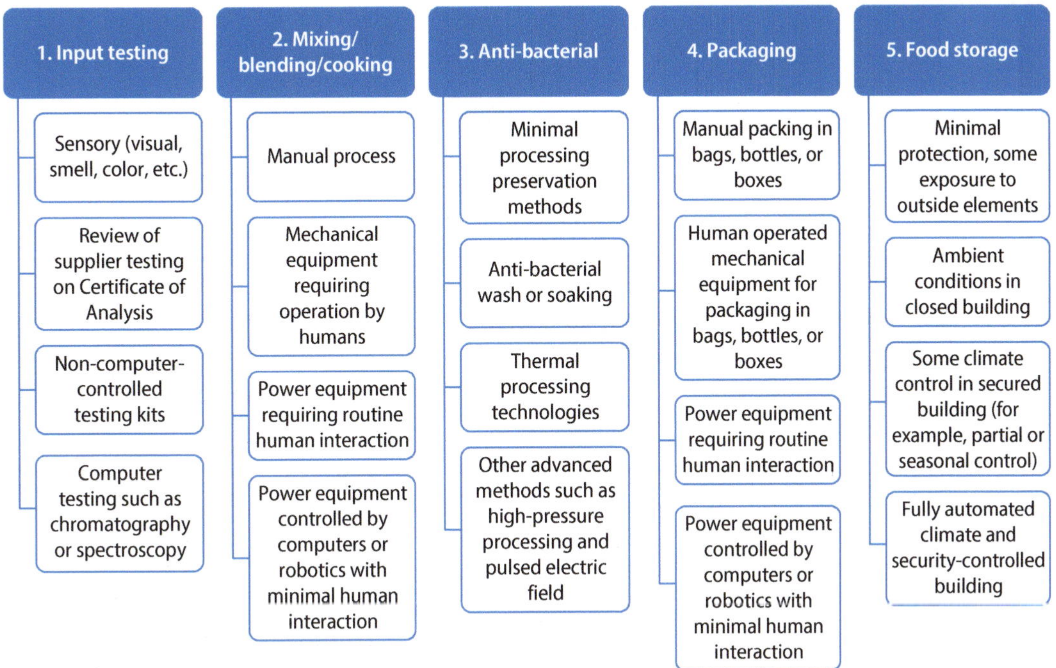


*Source:* Original figure for this volume based on the World Bank Firm-level Adoption of Technology survey.

## Samples of Surveyed Firms in LAC

The results reported for FAT surveys for Latin America and the Caribbean draw on surveys for two Latin American countries: Brazil and Chile.

### *FAT Survey Brazil*

The FAT survey in Brazil includes two states, Ceara and Parana. In Ceara, the survey was implemented in the second half of 2019 by the Industrial Federation of the state of Ceara, face to face, to a sample of 711 firms. In the state of Parana, a private contractor administered a phone survey to 609 firms in the last quarter of 2021 and first semester of 2022.

In total, the representative random sample includes 1,320 formal firms with five or more employees based on the 2018 and 2020 Brazilian employer-employee firm census from the Ministry of Labor. It also includes firms in agriculture, manufacturing, and services.

### *FAT Survey Chile*

In Chile, a private contractor administered a phone survey to 1,095 firms in the first semester of 2022. This nationally representative random sample of formal firms with five or more employees is based on firm-level data from the Servicio de Impuestos Internos. It also includes firms in agriculture, manufacturing, and services.

## Notes

1. The fictional patriarch and questor for knowledge José Arcadio Buendia observes this in the novel, *Cien años de soledad* [*One Hundred Years of Solitude*] (García Márquez 1967).
2. Technologies such as ERP and CRM are relatively inexpensive. There are cloud versions that have relatively inexpensive licenses, especially when they are adaptations of these types of technologies. In addition, in countries such as Brazil and Chile, there is a large market of technology solutions providers that can support small and medium enterprises in adopting some of these solutions. In the case of Brazil, for example, extension services such as SEBRAE and SENAI can provide training in the use of such technologies.
3. The wave of digitalization that ensued as a response to the COVID-19 pandemic (Avalos et al. 2024) has not become permanent for many businesses. For example, in an advanced country such as Australia, estimates suggest that about 60 percent of SMEs experienced bad digitalization (MYOB 2022); these are cases where there is a lack of integration between the digital technologies adopted and other systems and tasks in the firm. This can arise due to lack of skills and know-how or not having adequate organizational processes to fully implement the technologies. But as a result, some of these digital technologies are being abandoned or not fully utilized.
4. For instance, Atkin, Khandelwal, and Osman (2017) show how organizational barriers and labor incentives play a critical role as a barrier to adoption to a new technology to increase the efficiency in the production of soccer balls in Pakistan.
5. For more on RAIS, refer to their website: http://www.rais.gov.br.
6. These are the professions identified by Araújo, Cavalcante, and Alves (2009) as highly correlated with investments in R&D.
7. Firms' hierarchical and pyramid-shaped structures may also relate to incentive and information asymmetries. In an incentive-based theory, firms add new layers to increase monitoring and incentivize workers to exert more effort (Calvo and Wellisz 1978, 1979; Williamson 1967).
8. When experiencing significant growth, new exporters often reorganize by adding a management layer, adjusting wages across existing layers, and expanding employment within these layers to accommodate their expansion effectively. Conversely, firms with limited growth tend to focus on expanding within their existing layers by increasing the number of employees and average wages rather than undergoing reorganization (Caliendo, Monte, and Rossi-Hansberg 2017).
9. This analysis follows Cruz, Bussolo, and Iacovone (2018) and defines firms' "number of hierarchies" based on occupational categories as defined by the Brazilian Code of Occupations, which is composed of nine different categories (G1 through G9) according to similar levels of authority, skills, and competencies (https://cbo.mte.gov.br/cbosite/pages/home.jsf).
10. Original calculations based on OCyT (2022).
11. See, for instance, Greenwood and Jovanovic (1990), who argue that financial intermediaries encourage high-yield investments and growth by performing dual roles: pooling idiosyncratic investment risks, and eliminating ex ante downside uncertainty about rates of return. Beck (2002), Do and Levchenko (2007), Hausmann, Hwang, and Rodrik (2007), and Kletzer and Bardhan (1987), among others, explore the links between financial development and patterns of production specialization.

12. World Bank Open Data, Domestic Credit to Private Sector (percent of GDP), https://data.worldbank.org/indicator/FS.AST.PRVT.GD.ZS.
13. World Bank Open Data, Commercial Bank Branches (per 100,000 adults), https://data.worldbank.org/indicator/FB.CBK.BRCH.P5?locations=ZJ-Z7-XU-ZG-Z4-8S.

## References

Acemoglu, D., U. Akcigit, H. Alp, N. Bloom, and W. Kerr. 2018. "Innovation, Reallocation, and Growth." *American Economic Review* 108 (11): 3450–91.

Aghion, P., A. Bergeaud, M. Lequien, M. Melitz, and T. Zuber. 2021. "Opposing Firm-Level Responses to the China Shock: Horizontal Competition versus Vertical Relationships?" NBER Working Paper 29196, National Bureau of Economic Research, Cambridge, MA.

Aghion, P., N. Bloom, R. Blundell, R. Griffith, and P. Howitt. 2005. "Competition and Innovation: An Inverted-U Relationship." *Quarterly Journal of Economics* 120 (2): 701–28.

Aghion, P., R. Blundell, R. Griffith, P. Howitt, and S. Prantl. 2009. "The Effects of Entry on Incumbent Innovation and Productivity." *Review of Economics and Statistics* 91 (1): 20–32.

Akcigit, U., H. Alp, and M. Peters. 2021. "Lack of Selection and Limits to Delegation: Firm Dynamics in Developing Countries." *American Economic Review* 111 (1): 231–75.

Akcigit, U., and S. T. Ates. 2023. "What Happened to US Business Dynamism?" *Journal of Political Economy* 131 (8): 2059–124.

Akcigit, U., J. Pearce, and M. Prato. 2024. "Tapping into Talent: Coupling Education and Innovation Policies for Economic Growth." *Review of Economic Studies* 92 (2): 696–736. https://doi.org/10.1093/restud/rdae047.

Alfaro de Morán, M., and P. A. Amo. 2021. *Digital Entrepreneurship and Innovation in Central America.* Washington, DC: International Finance Corporation.

Alviarez, V., J. Cravino, and N. Ramondo. 2023. "Firm-Embedded Productivity and Cross-Country Income Differences." *Journal of Political Economy* 131 (9): 2289–327.

Antràs, P., and E. Helpman. 2006. "Contractual Frictions and Global Sourcing." NBER Working Paper 12747, National Bureau of Economic Research, Cambridge, MA.

Araújo, B. C. P. O. D., L. R. Cavalcante, and P. F. Alves. 2009. "Variáveis proxy para os gastos empresariais em inovação com base no pessoal ocupado técnico-científico disponível na Relação Anual de Informações Sociais (RAIS)." *Radar: tecnologia, produção e comércio exterior, Brasília* 5: 1–21.

Atkin, D., A. Chaudhry, S. Chaudry, A. K. Khandelwal, and E. Verhoogen. 2017. "Organizational Barriers to Technology Adoption: Evidence from Soccer-Ball Producers in Pakistan." *Quarterly Journal of Economics* 132 (3): 1101–64.

Atkin, D., A. K. Khandelwal, and A. Osman. 2017. "Exporting and Firm Performance: Evidence from a Randomized Experiment." *Quarterly Journal of Economics* 132 (2): 551–615.

Avalos, E., X. Cirera, M. Cruz, L. Iacovone, D. Medvedev, G. Nayyar, and S. Reyes Ortega. 2024. "Firms' Digitalization during the COVID-19 Pandemic: A Tale of Two Stories." *Science and Public Policy* 51 (6): 1241–56.

Bartel, A., C. Ichniowski, and K. Shaw. 2007. "How Does Information Technology Affect Productivity? Plant-Level Comparisons of Product Innovation, Process Improvement, and Worker Skills." *Quarterly Journal of Economics* 122 (4): 1721–58.

Bas, M., and A. Berthou. 2016. "Does Input-Trade Liberalization Affect Firms' Foreign Technology Choice?" Policy Research Working Paper 7883, World Bank, Washington, DC.

Beck, T. 2002. "Financial Development and International Trade: Is There a Link?" *Journal of International Economics* 57 (1): 107–31.

Bloom, N., B. Eifert, A. Mahajan, D. McKenzie, and J. Roberts. 2013. "Does Management Matter? Evidence from India." *Quarterly Journal of Economics* 128 (1): 1–51.

Bloom, N., L. Garicano, R. Sadun, and J. V. Reenen. 2014a. "The Distinct Effects of Information Technology and Communication Technology on Firm Organization." *Management Science* 60 (12): 2859–85.

Bloom, N., C. Genakos, R. Sadun, and J. V. Reenen 2012. "Management Practices across Firms and Countries." NBER Working Paper 17850, National Bureau of Economic Research, Cambridge, MA.

Bloom, N., R. Lemos, R. Sadun, D. Scur, and J. Van Reenen. 2014b. "JEEA-FBBVA Lecture 2013: The New Empirical Economics of Management." *Journal of the European Economic Association* 12 (4): 835–76.

Bloom, N., A. Mahajan, D. McKenzie, and J. Roberts. 2020. "Do Management Interventions Last? Evidence from India." *American Economic Journal: Applied Economics* 12 (2): 198–219.

Bloom, N., K. Manova, J. Van Reenen, S. T. Sun, and Z. Yu. 2021. "Trade and Management." *Review of Economics and Statistics* 103 (3): 443–60.

Bloom, N., R. Sadun, and J. Van Reenen. 2012. "Americans Do IT Better: US Multinationals and the Productivity Miracle." *American Economic Review* 102 (1): 167–201.

Bloom, N., and J. Van Reenen. 2007. "Measuring and Explaining Management Practices across Firms and Countries." *Quarterly Journal of Economics* 122 (4): 1351–408.

Bombardini, M., B. Li, and R. Wang. 2017. "Import Competition and Innovation: Evidence from China." https://www7.econ.hit-u.ac.jp/cces/trade_conference_2017/paper/matilde_bombardini.pdf.

Bresnahan, T. F., E. Brynjolfsson, and L. M. Hitt. 2002. "Information Technology, Workplace Organization, and the Demand for Skilled Labor: Firm-Level Evidence." *Quarterly Journal of Economics* 117 (1): 339–76.

Brynjolfsson, E., and L. M. Hitt. 2000. "Beyond Computation: Information Technology, Organizational Transformation and Business Performance." *Journal of Economic Perspectives* 14 (4): 23–48.

Brynjolfsson, E., L. M. Hitt, and S. Yang. 2002. "Intangible Assets: Computers and Organizational Capital." *Brookings Papers on Economic Activity* 2002 (1): 137–81.

Burstein, A. T., and A. Monge-Naranjo. 2009. "Foreign Know-How, Firm Control, and the Income of Developing Countries." *Quarterly Journal of Economics* 124 (1): 149–95.

Bustos, P. 2011. "Trade Liberalization, Exports, and Technology Upgrading: Evidence on the Impact of MERCOSUR on Argentinian Firms." *American Economic Review* 101 (1): 304–40.

Caliendo, L., G. Mion, L. D. Opromolla, and E. Rossi-Hansberg. 2020. "Productivity and Organization in Portuguese Firms." *Journal of Political Economy* 128 (11): 4211–57.

Caliendo, L., F. Monte, and E. Rossi-Hansberg. 2017. "Exporting and Organizational Change." NBER Working Paper 23630, National Bureau of Economic Research, Cambridge, MA.

Callaway, B., and P. H. C. Sant'Anna. 2021. "Difference-in-Differences with Multiple Time Periods." *Journal of Econometrics* 225 (2): 200–30.

Calvo, G. A., and S. Wellisz. 1978. "Supervision, Loss of Control, and the Optimum Size of the Firm." *Journal of Political Economy* 86 (5): 943–52.

Calvo, G. A. and S. Wellisz. 1979. "Hierarchy, Ability, and Income Distribution." *Journal of Political Economy* 87 (5): 991–1010.

Camerer, C., and D. Lovallo. 1999. "Overconfidence and Excess Entry: An Experimental Approach." *American Economic Review* 89 (1): 306–18.

Castro, L. 2025. "Trade Adjustment Programs in Developing Countries: An Insider's View." Unpublished.

Che, Y., and L. Zhang. 2018. "Human Capital, Technology Adoption and Firm Performance: Impacts of China's Higher Education Expansion in the Late 1990s." *Economic Journal* 128 (614): 2282–320.

Cirera, X., D. Comin, and M. Cruz. 2022. "Bridging the Technological Divide: Technology Adoption by Firms in Developing Countries." Overview booklet, World Bank, Washington, DC.

Cirera, X., M. Cruz, and A. Martins-Neto. Forthcoming. "Higher Education Expansion and Firms Organization."

Cirera, X., and W. F. Maloney. 2017. *The Innovation Paradox: Developing-Country Capabilities and the Unrealized Promise of Technological Catch-up*. Washington, DC: World Bank.

Cirera, X., W. F. Maloney, and M. Sarrias. 2017. "Management Quality and Innovation." Unpublished.

Comin, D. A., X. Cirera, and M. Cruz. 2025. "Technology Sophistication across Establishments," NBER Working Paper 33358, National Bureau of Economic Research, Cambridge, MA.

Comin, D., and M. Mestieri. 2018. "If Technology Has Arrived Everywhere, Why Has Income Diverged?" *American Economic Journal: Macroeconomics* 10 (3): 137–78.

Conceição, O. C. 2022. "Higher Education in Brazil: Evaluating the Impact of Recent Policies." Ph.D. thesis, Fundação Getulio Vargas, Escola de Economia de São Paulo (EESP).

Cruz, M., M. Bussolo, and L. Iacovone. 2018. "Organizing Knowledge to Compete: Impacts of Capacity Building Programs on Firm Organization." *Journal of International Economics* 111: 1–20.

Cusolito, A. P., A. Garcia, and W. F. Maloney. 2023. "Proximity to the Frontier, Markups, and the Response of Innovation to Foreign Competition: Evidence from Matched Production-Innovation Surveys in Chile." *American Economic Review: Insights* 5 (1): 35–54.

Dahlstrand, A., D. László, H. Schweiger, O. Bandiera, A. Prat, and R. Sadun. 2025. "CEO-Firm Matches and Productivity in 42 Countries." NBER Working Paper 33324, National Bureau of Economic Research, Cambridge, MA.

De Loecker, J., and J. Eeckhout. 2018. "Global Market Power." NBER Working Paper 24768, National Bureau of Economic Research, Cambridge, MA.

de Souza, G. 2023. "R&D Subsidy and Import Substitution: Growing in the Shadow of Protection." Federal Reserve Bank of Chicago Working Paper No. 2023-37.

de Souza, G., R. Gaetani, and M. Mestieri. 2024. "More Trade, Less Diffusion: Technology Transfers and the Dynamic Effects of Import Liberalization." Federal Reserve Bank of Chicago Working Paper No. 2024-20.

Deloitte. 2020. "Save-to-Transform as a Catalyst for Embracing Digital Disruption." Deloitte's Second Biennial Global Cost Survey: Cost Management Practices and Trends in Latin America. Deloitte. https://www2.deloitte.com/content/dam/Deloitte/us/Documents/process-and-operations/cost-management-practices-and-trends-in-latin-america.pdf.

Dixon, J., B. Hong, and L. Wu. 2021. "The Robot Revolution: Managerial and Employment Consequences for Firms." *Management Science* 67 (9): 5586–605.

Do, Q.-T., and A. A. Levchenko. 2007. "Comparative Advantage, Demand for External Finance, and Financial Development." *Journal of Financial Economics* 86 (3): 796–834.

Doraszelski, U., and J. Jaumandreu. 2013. "R&D and Productivity: Estimating Endogenous Productivity." *Review of Economic Studies* 80 (4): 1338–83.

Esfahani, M. 2019. "Investment in Skills, Managerial Quality, and Economic Development." Research Paper, Arizona State University Center for the Study of Economic Liberty.

Fernandez, J., L. Iacovone, and W. F. Maloney. Forthcoming, "Management Quality, Innovation, Risk and Export Performance: Evidence from a Matched-Production-Innovation-Export Transactions Data Set in Colombia."

Foster, A. D., and M. R. Rosenzweig. 2010. "Microeconomics of Technology Adoption." *Annual Review of Economics* 2 (1): 395–424.

García Márquez, G. 1967. *Cien Años de Soledad*. Buenos Aires: Editorial Sudamericana.

Garcia Sanchez, J. C. 2024. "Why Guadalajara Has Not Taken Off as a Generator of Innovative Entrepreneurship? An Extended Case Study." In *Emergent Ecosystems: Overcoming Systemic Obstacles for Technology Entrepreneurship*. Washington, DC: World Bank. Unpublished.

Garicano, L., and P. Heaton. 2010. "Information Technology, Organization, and Productivity in the Public Sector: Evidence from Police Departments." *Journal of Labor Economics* 28 (1): 167–201.

Garicano, L., and T. N. Hubbard. 2016. "The Returns to Knowledge Hierarchies." *Journal of Law, Economics, and Organization* 32 (4): 653–84.

Giorcelli, M. 2019. "The Long-Term Effects of Management and Technology Transfers." *American Economic Review* 109 (1): 121–52.

Giorcelli, M. 2021. "The Origin and Development of Firm Management." *Oxford Review of Economic Policy* 37 (2): 259–75.

Gorodnichenko, Y., and M. Schnitzer. 2013. "Financial Constraints and Innovation: Why Poor Countries Don't Catch Up." *Journal of the European Economic Association* 11 (5): 1115–52.

Greenwood, J., and B. Jovanovic. 1990. "Financial Development, Growth, and the Distribution of Income." *Journal of Political Economy* 98 (5): 1076–107.

Grover, A. G., and V. Karplus. 2021. "Coping with COVID-19: Does Management Make Firms More Resilient?" Policy Research Working Paper 9514, World Bank, Washington, DC.

Grover Goswami, A., D. Medvedev, and E. Olafsen. 2019. *High-Growth Firms: Facts, Fiction, and Policy Options for Emerging Economies.* Washington, DC: World Bank.

Hausmann, R., J. Hwang, and D. Rodrik. 2007. "What You Export Matters." *Journal of Economic Growth* 12 (1): 1–25.

Hjort, J., H. Malmberg, and T. Schoellman. 2022. "The Missing Middle Managers: Labor Costs, Firm Structure, and Development." NBER Working Paper 30592, National Bureau of Economic Research, Cambridge, MA.

Iacovone, L., W. F. Maloney, and D. McKenzie. 2022. "Improving Management with Individual and Group-Based Consulting: Results from a Randomized Experiment in Colombia." *Review of Economic Studies* 89 (1): 346–71.

Imbert, C., and G. Ulyssea. 2023. "Rural Migrants and Urban Informality: Evidence from Brazil." CEPR Discussion Paper No. 18160, Centre for Economic Policy Research (CEPR), London.

INEP (Instituto Nacional de Estudos e Pesquisas Educacionais Anísio Teixeira). 2020. *Resumo Técnico do Censo da Educação Superior 2020.* INEP.

Jiang, X. 2021. "Information and Communication Technology and Firm Geographic Expansion." CESifo Working Paper 10452, CESifo, Munich.

Kang, Y., and J. Suh. 2022. "Information Technology and the Spatial Reorganization of Firms." *Journal of Economics & Management Strategy* 31 (3): 674–92.

Kletzer, K., and P. Bardhan. 1987. "Credit Markets and Patterns of International Trade." *Journal of Development Economics* 27 (1–2): 57–70.

Krishna, P., A. A. Levchenko, L. Ma, and W. F. Maloney. 2023. "Growth and Risk: A View from International Trade." *Journal of International Economics* 142: 103755.

Kruger, J., and D. Dunning. 1999. "Unskilled and Unaware of It: How Difficulties in Recognizing One's Own Incompetence Lead to Inflated Self-Assessments." *Journal of Personality and Social Psychology* 77 (6): 1121–34.

Lucking, B., N. Bloom, and J. Van Reenen. 2019. "Have R&D Spillovers Declined in the 21st Century?" *Fiscal Studies* 40 (4): 561–90.

Maloney, W. F., M. Meléndez Arjona, P. Garriga, and R. Morales Lima. 2024. *Competition: The Missing Ingredient for Growth?* Latin America and Caribbean Economic Review, April 2024. Washington, DC: World Bank.

Maloney, W. F., and M. Sarrias. 2017. "Convergence to the Managerial Frontier." *Journal of Economic Behavior & Organization* 134 (C): 284–306.

Maloney, W. F., and A. Zambrano. 2022. "Learning to Learn: Experimentation, Entrepreneurial Capital, and Development." Documentos CEDE 19940, Universidad de los Andes, Facultad de Economía, CEDE.

Mariscal, A. 2018. "Firm Organization and Information Technology: Micro and Macro Implications." 2018 Meeting Papers 1076, Society for Economic Dynamics.

McKenzie, D. 2021. "Small Business Training to Improve Management Practices in Developing Countries: Re-assessing the Evidence for 'Training Doesn't Work'." *Oxford Review of Economic Policy* 37 (2): 276–301.

McKenzie, D. J., and C. M. Woodruff. 2015. "Business Practices in Small Firms in Developing Countries." Policy Research Working Paper 7405, World Bank, Washington, DC.

MYOB. 2022. *Australia's SMEs: A Snapshot.* MYOB Australia.

OCyT (Organización Colombiana para la Investigación Científica y Tecnológica). 2022. *Indicadores de Ciencia, Tecnología e Innovación 2021*. https://ocyt.org.co/wp-content/uploads/2023/06/Informe_indicadores_OCyT_2021.pdf.

Queiró, F. 2022. "Entrepreneurial Human Capital and Firm Dynamics." *Review of Economic Studies* 89 (4): 2061–100.

Schiffbauer, M., J. Sampi, and J. Coronado. 2025. "Competition and Productivity: Evidence from Peruvian Municipalities." *Review of Economics and Statistics* 107 (1): 95–108.

Spanos, G. 2016. "Organization and Export Performance." *Economics Letters* 146: 130–4.

Spanos, G. 2019. "Firm Organization and Productivity across Locations." *Journal of Urban Economics* 112: 152–68.

Sun, L., and S. Abraham. 2021. "Estimating Dynamic Treatment Effects in Event Studies with Heterogeneous Treatment Effects." *Journal of Econometrics* 225 (2): 175–99.

Verhoogen, E. 2023. "Firm-Level Upgrading in Developing Countries." *Journal of Economic Literature* 61 (4): 1410–64.

Vu, K., and T.-A. Vu-Thanh. 2022. "Higher Education Expansion, Labor Market, and Firm Productivity in Vietnam." Technical report, unpublished working paper.

Williamson, O. E. 1967. "Hierarchical Control and Optimum Firm Size." *Journal of Political Economy* 75 (2): 123–38.

World Bank. 2024. *World Development Report 2024: The Middle-Income Trap*. Washington, DC: World Bank.

# 3 The Role of Universities and Research Institutes in Learning Economies

*"The response of Britain [to German's industrial ascent] was inadequate because the Second Industrial Revolution rewarded those countries that could exploit the seemingly endless technological opportunities by producing an ever-increasing amount of science and engineering talent."*

—Johann Peter Murmann[1]

## Introduction

No country can adopt or develop new products or technologies without solid educational and research institutions in their National Innovation Systems. As the previous chapters discussed, creating or adopting products and technologies requires the human capital embodied in skilled individuals, such as professional and technical workers, researchers, and scientists. Innovative countries have educational systems that create that kind of human capital and strengthen knowledge exchange—the flow of people, ideas, and technologies.

Classic market failures particular to knowledge have given rise to government interventions and institutions, such as public universities and research institutes, to resolve them. In particular, the fact that knowledge is easily used by others implies that the individual or firm that invests in creating new technologies or in identifying existing technologies will not receive the full return from the investment. To offset this so-called appropriability externality, governments may subsidize research on the part of firms, grant patents giving temporary monopoly power over the exploitation of new ideas, or support institutions that undertake research relevant to a broad group of firms. In addition, some research tasks are simply too large or lumpy (requiring front-loaded high expenses) for individuals to undertake or require coordination among many actors. It may not make sense for every coffee grower to devise an antidote to new pests emerging due to climate change, or for every textile firm to engage in the constant monitoring of global trends to stay at the frontier, or for every firm in an emerging green energy cluster to carry out the fundamental research that would benefit many firms.

A substantial body of literature points to how the presence of such educational and research institutions advances growth, not only by making higher-order human capital available but also by diffusing and adapting information to the local context. The distribution of engineers across US states discussed in chapter 1, for instance, is highly correlated with the establishment of the land grant colleges that paired research with diffusion to farmers and emerging industry. These universities have also been critical incubators of new firms and indeed industries. The emblematic examples today are the interaction of the University of California (UC), Berkeley and Stanford University and the high-tech industry in Silicon Valley, and Harvard University and the Massachusetts Institute of Technology (MIT) in the Route 128 corridor near Boston. About half of US economic growth after 1945 has come from technologies that were created in universities, and university graduates head up the major companies that fuel US growth (Crawley et al. 2020). MIT alumni, for instance, contribute almost 10 percent of the US gross domestic product (GDP) (Crawley et al. 2020)—a GDP comparable to the size of the Indian or Russian economy.

Public research institutes (PRIs) have also been central players in resolving these market failures (box 3.1). Technological advances in the forestry sector in Scandinavia, for instance, have been driven by sector-specific research institutes. The Centros Technologicos in the Basque Country and Catalonia in Spain have been credited first with diffusion of best practices and then with sector-related research critical to moving up the manufacturing value chain. When paired with well-targeted public funding

## BOX 3.1 Self-Standing Research Institutes and Technology Transfer Organizations

Universities are not the only actors that can connect knowledge to industry. Public research institutes (PRIs) with some degree of public funding are also important actors in resolving market failures and linking to industry, although they generally do not undertake the role of building human capital (Link and Scott 2009). They are often created to perform some of the following functions:

1. *Advanced technical extension services.* PRIs can facilitate technology transfer in sectors such as light industry or agriculture when, for example, small firms face limited appropriability from their investments in new technologies that would provide large external benefits to the economy as a whole.
2. *Development of appropriate knowledge to transfer.* By developing technologies of industry-wide value, PRIs can facilitate technology transfer through their knowledge of the key technologies and working relationships with the industries supplying the technologies.
3. *Coordination of research efforts.* PRIs can serve as honest brokers, helping to facilitate cooperative efforts by industry, universities, and government in research that is subsidized by the government (Hall, Link, and Scott 2003). To play this role, the PRI needs to have its own capacity to conduct research.
4. *Bridge from basic to applied science.* PRIs can facilitate the diffusion of advances from research, such as in biotechnology, chemistry, materials science, and pharmaceuticals. In many cases, governments extend public funding to universities to develop the basic science because the ideas have a strong public good component, and there would not be sufficient incentive to develop them without government funding. Once the basic science is available, the knowledgeable PRI with both expertise in research and connections to industry can help to disseminate the information widely.
5. *Standards setting.* For more advanced countries, PRIs can participate in the development of standards, which helps reduce the risk associated with technology lock-in—difficulties in switching from out-of-date technologies—and facilitate the adoption of new technologies.

These functions are often not implemented in developing countries. A review of several PRIs in Latin America and the Caribbean revealed that not a single institution covered in the study seemed oriented to the outputs and outcomes from public research, therefore complicating the identification of a public good aspect to their

*(Continued on next page)*

**BOX 3.1 Self-Standing Research Institutes and Technology Transfer Organizations *(continued)***

research (Link and Scott 2009). Historical inertia from a period when PRIs in Eastern Europe served a preassigned client, such as a large state-owned enterprise, has made it difficult for some PRIs to evolve to support small and medium enterprises or start-ups. More profoundly, the tendency to import organizational charts can also lead to misalignment of mission with the sophistication of the economy.

Ensuring that PRIs promote growth also requires better performance contracts between PRIs and national and local governments. Clear mission orientation is needed, along with better performance metrics and business models that combine block grants with competitive grants and revenue from intellectual property and services provided to the private sector. The financing structure of these institutions is important to ensure alignment with the productive sector and research excellence, while underwriting the provisions of public goods. On one extreme, the full public financing of research centers can give them few incentives to interact with firms and produce research excellence. At the other extreme, heavy dependence on private financing ensures relevance to the private sector and high quality but underfunds public goods and the diffusion mission. For instance, the Crown Research Institutes in New Zealand received little block financing and as a result have functioned more like private consulting firms. The Finnish Technical Research Center (Valtion Teknillinen Tutkimuskeskus), as well as the Catapult Network in the United Kingdom and the Fraunhofer Institutes and research units in Germany, broadly follow a 1/3–1/3–1/3 model where one-third is block funding to cover public goods, one-third comes from matching grants, and one-third is from private sector contracts (Fedit 2021).

In addition, it is reasonable to ask whether a PRI is the right tool to remedy the failures that need to be addressed. If not linked to industry, PRIs can be expensive side-shows; if staff are not at the cutting edge, their advice can damage industry. In the case of the Meiji textile sector, for instance, official technology diffusion agencies diffused outdated technologies, and the truly productive diffusion was done privately by the dominant firms in the sector, as Braguinsky and Hounshell (2016) document. In the US land grant college system, extension systems were built into the academic environment, where they established quality control mechanisms for the promotion of technologies. The Spanish Centros Tecnologicos are largely private sector driven—which ensures relevance—but may also limit the public good dimension of knowledge diffusion and creation (Fedit 2021; Mas Verdú 2021).

of sufficient scale, government agencies such as the Defense Advanced Research Projects Agency in the United States have been instrumental in supporting and coordinating research institutions in introducing new technologies ranging from the internet and weather satellites to the creation of the antidote to the COVID-19 virus. In the context of Latin America and the Caribbean (LAC), government support through such a learning network of institutions could raise the level of sophistication within which the region exploits its current production basket and facilitates spin-offs to new sectors.

However, these institutions need to be well designed if they are to have a positive impact on growth. First and most obviously, the educational system needs to generate high-quality human capital relevant to the private sector across the entire skill spectrum. Second, there needs to be a clear and codified understanding that part of the mission of universities, and the unique mission of research institutes, is the resolution of the market failures surrounding knowledge and the provision of support to the private sector to realize the development of that knowledge. Meeting this mission, in turn, requires that the proper incentives be in place to ensure the quality of underlying research and its relevance to the private sector, as well as the cultivation of webs of interaction that guarantee a bidirectional flow of knowledge. In some countries, such as the United Kingdom, developing growth-supporting institutions has required an evolution from a more purely humanistic conception of the university to one incorporating elements of applied science, found in institutions like MIT, Stanford, and UC Berkeley.

In LAC, failures in the aspects listed above help explain why education and science and technology (S&T) outcomes in these countries are disappointing despite the adoption of seemingly good policies. The problem is not that these countries lack S&T or innovation systems. Rather, the problem is that these systems lack the strategic vision, continuity, incentives, scale—and, in some cases, resources—to enable them to become true networks of national learning that would permit firms and entrepreneurs to identify and exploit the technological opportunities latent in the global economy or embedded in foreign direct investment. At present, LAC's low human capital and weak institutions are not only short-circuiting the process by which its existing basket of goods would lead organically to a more dynamic and diversified economy, but also the benefits from deliberate attempts to enter new sectors.

## Outcomes Are Poor in the LAC Educational and S&T Systems

### Skills Are Missing in LAC's Workforce

LAC countries are missing skills critical to innovation. The region has relatively few skilled workers (figure 3.1). In the median LAC country, professionals, technicians, and managers account for 21 percent of the workforce. Not only is this share lower than in countries such as the United States and Germany (47 percent and 46 percent, respectively), but it is also lower than the share in LAC comparator countries such as Belarus and Malaysia (41 percent and 28 percent, respectively).

Researchers are also scarce in LAC, despite their critical role in knowledge production. The median LAC country has 347 researchers per million people, well below the median country in the Middle East and North Africa or East Asia and Pacific (708 and 1,688 researchers per million people, respectively).[2] Further, LAC holds the distinction of being the region where firms struggle the most to find qualified workers. A full 31 percent of firms in the median LAC country claim that the lack of qualified workers is a critical obstacle to their expansion.[3]

Even higher education graduates in LAC are less skilled than their counterparts in other countries. Only about half of higher education graduates in Ecuador and Peru and 72 percent in Mexico obtain minimum proficiency levels of numeracy, in contrast with 80–90 percent in the Russian Federation and Türkiye.[4]

### Research and Innovation Are Scarce and Do Not Have Much Impact

Research productivity in LAC is low (figure 3.2, panel a). Even the most productive countries (Chile, Uruguay, and Brazil) produce much less than Spain or the United States. Small countries rely on international collaboration for more than half of their output, whereas the larger countries of Argentina, Mexico, and Brazil have relatively less international collaboration than Spain or Portugal (figure 3.2, panel b).

**FIGURE 3.1 Skilled Workers Are Scarce in LAC**

Employment in knowledge-intensive service (% of workforce)

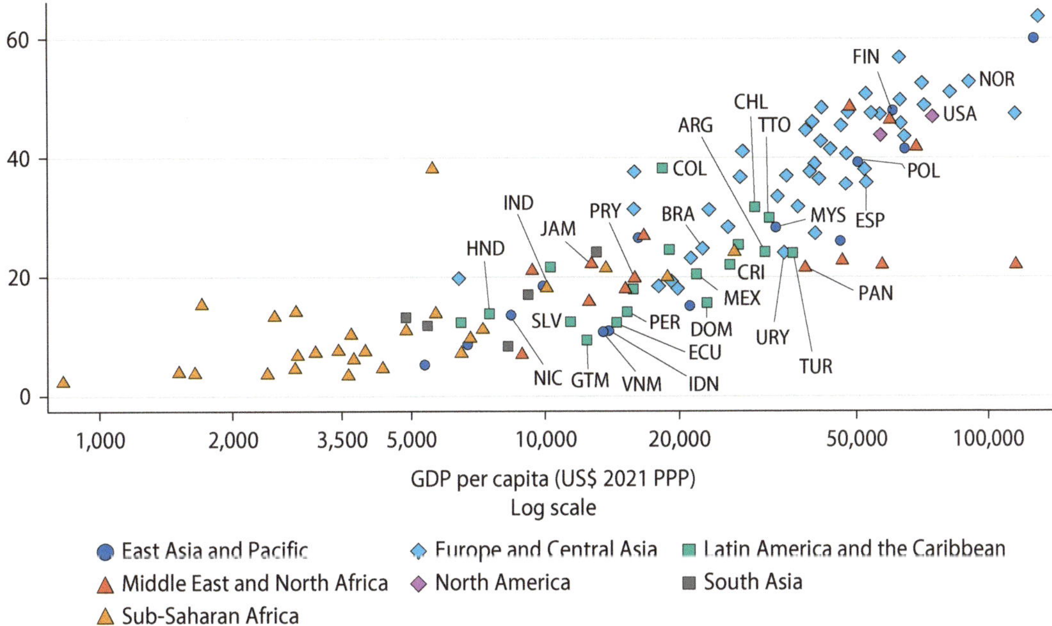


*Sources:* Original figure for this volume based on data from the International Labour Organization (ILO) ILOSTAT Database of Labour Statistics (https://ilostat.ilo.org) and World Bank World Development Indicators (https://databank.worldbank.org/source/world-development-indicators).

*Note:* For every country, the figure shows the workforce share employed in knowledge-intensive occupations, including managers, professionals, technicians, and associate professionals (categories 1–3 in the International Standard Classification of Occupations). Skilled workers' data for the last year available between 2011 and 2021. GDP per capita data are for circa 2022. The figure includes countries with more than 500,000 inhabitants. For country abbreviations, refer to International Organization for Standardization (ISO), https://www.iso.org/obp/ui/#search. GDP = gross domestic product; LAC = Latin America and the Caribbean; PPP = purchasing power parity.

Research in LAC is not only scarce but also has little impact. According to a measure of citations, the H-index, the median LAC country is third only to the median countries in East Asia and Pacific and Sub-Saharan Africa (figure 3.3, panel a).[5] The number of papers in the top 10 percent of citations in the corresponding field is much lower than that of Spain or Portugal (figure 3.3, panel b, blue and green bars). Not only are papers in LAC of little impact to other researchers, but they are also of little impact to industry, as evidenced by the number of papers cited in patents (figure 3.3, panel b, red diamonds).

**FIGURE 3.2 Research Is Scarce in LAC**

**a. Number of papers cited in Scopus (per 100,000 population)**

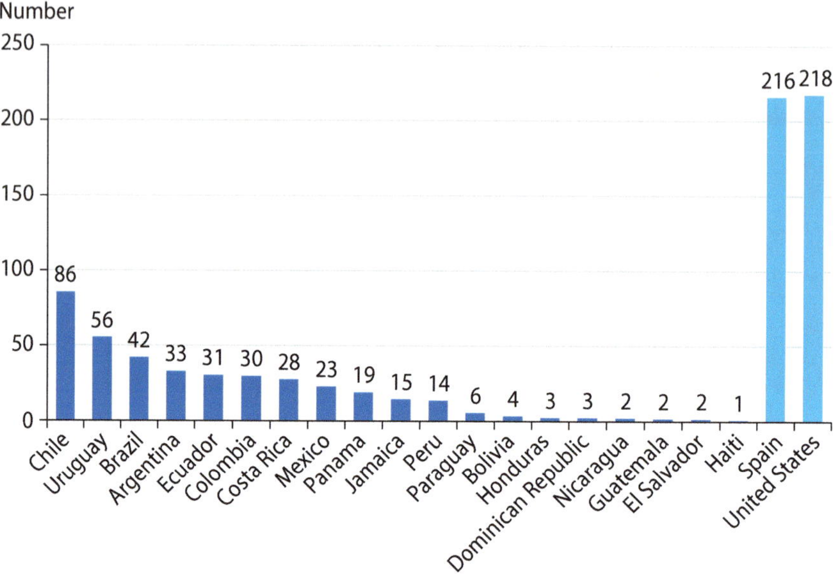


**b. Percent of papers produced in collaboration with foreign institutions**

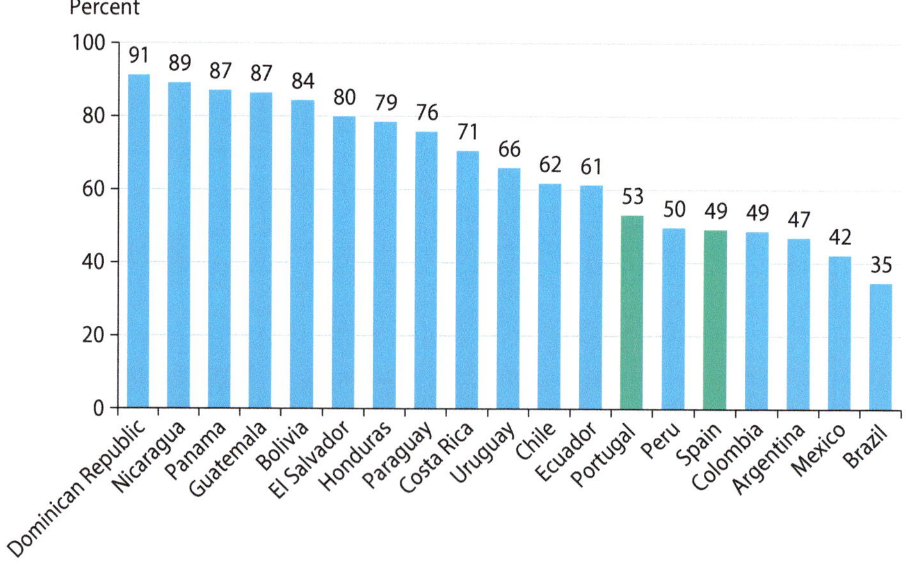


*Sources:* Original figure for this volume based on data from RICYT (http://www.ricyt.org/en/category/en/indicators/) based on Scopus (panel a) and SCImago IBER (https://www.scimagoiber.com/countries.php) (panel b).
*Note:* Panel a shows data for 2018 and 2019 (latest years available). Panel b shows data for 2017–21.

**FIGURE 3.3 Research Is of Little Consequence in LAC**

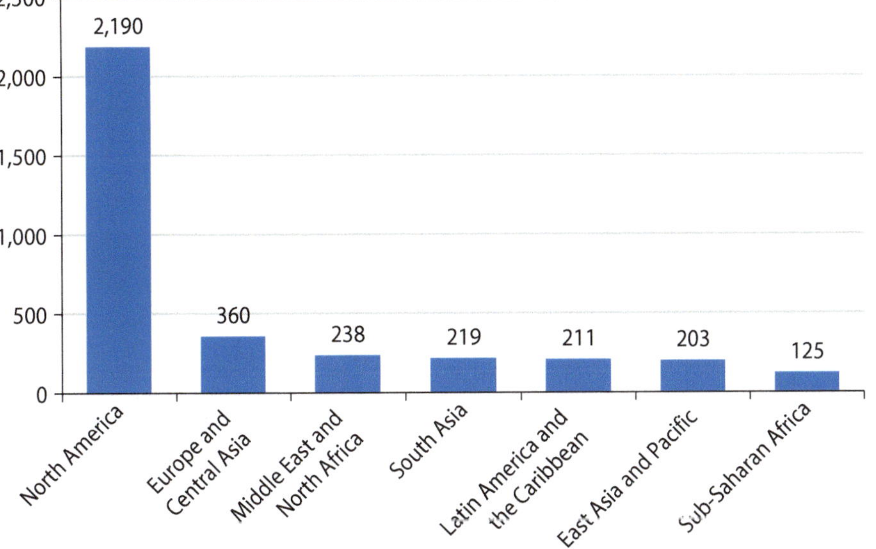


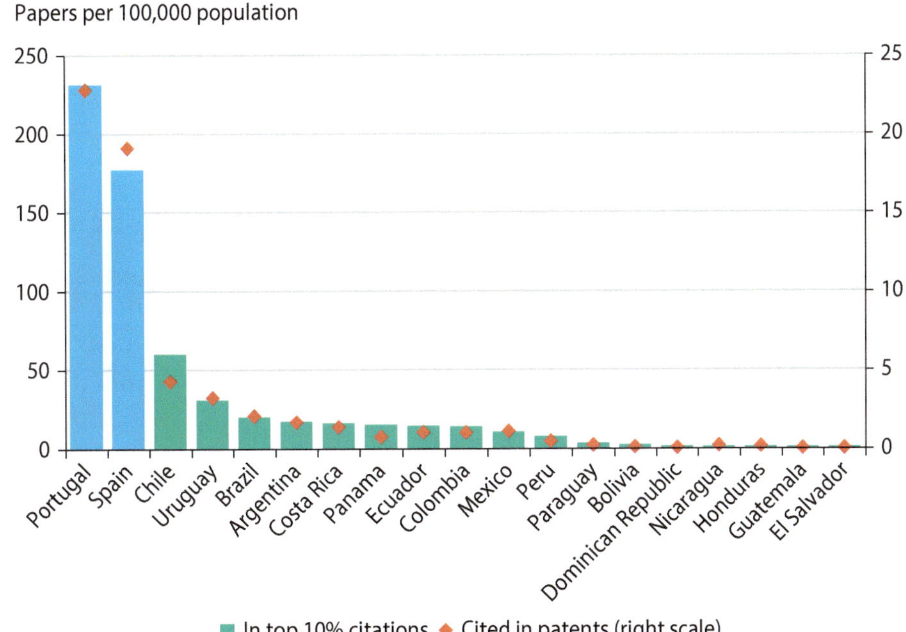


*Sources:* Original figure for this volume based on SCImago Country Rank (https://www.scimagojr.com/countryrank.php) (panel a) and SCImago IBER (https://www.scimagoiber.com/countries.php) (panel b).
*Note:* Panel a shows median H-index by region (median over countries); data are for 2022. For each indicator, panel b shows the 2017–21 total, divided by the 2023 population size. LAC = Latin America and the Caribbean.

More broadly, universities in LAC contribute little to innovation. To compare universities based on their innovation-related output, the SCImago Innovation Ranking gives equal weight to the number of patent applications, percent of publication output cited in patents (or technological impact), and number of publications cited in patents. In this ranking, LAC accounts for only 0.5 percent of the world's top 1,000 universities (figure 3.4). This percentage is second only to Sub-Saharan Africa's and is far below that of East Asia and Pacific (51 percent) and Europe and Central Asia (18.2 percent).

This modest contribution of universities to innovation also manifests in low invention in the economy. On average, LAC produces fewer patents than other regions. The median LAC country produces 0.5 patents per million people, well below the median country in North America (99.2), Europe and Central Asia (15), or East Asia and Pacific (1.8).[6] In addition, its patents are much less influential (figure 3.5). Most LAC countries accumulated about one highly cited patent per 100,000 people over the last four decades, less than comparable countries and far less than Spain (25) or the United States (152).[7]

Overall, LAC universities are falling short in providing the skills critical for innovation, and produce low-volume, low-impact research and development (R&D). This points to failures in the educational system—responsible for human capital development—and the S&T and innovation systems—responsible for knowledge production and exchange. It also points to these countries' struggle to retain or leverage their skilled human capital. The next section explores these issues.

**FIGURE 3.4 LAC Universities Are Not Innovative**

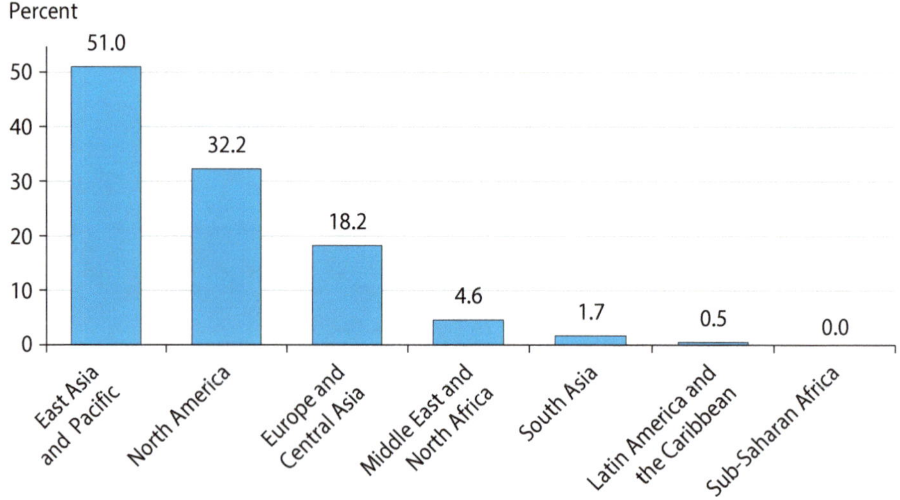


*Source:* Original figure for this volume based on SCImago Innovation Ranking data (https://www.scimagoir.com/rankings.php?ranking=Innovation).

*Note:* The figure shows the share of institutions by region in the top 1,000 universities according to the SCImago Institutions Rankings for innovation 2024. LAC = Latin America and the Caribbean.

**FIGURE 3.5 Innovations in LAC Have Little Impact**

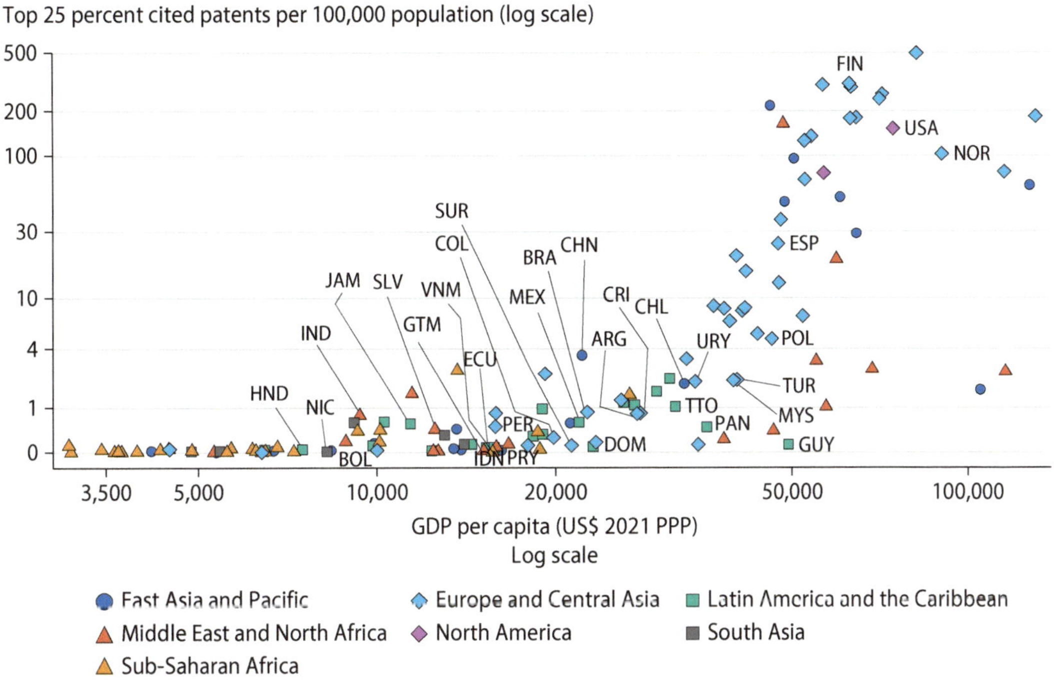

Top 25 percent cited patents per 100,000 population (log scale)

*Sources:* Original figure for this volume using OECD REGPAT Patent database (https://www.oecd.org/en/data/datasets/intellectual-property-statistics.html) based on EPO PATSTAT, and World Bank World Development Indicators (https://databank.worldbank.org/source/world-development-indicators).
*Note:* The figure shows the number of patents in the top 25 percent of citations during 1977–2016 scaled by population. GDP per capita data are for circa 2022. The figure includes countries with more than 500,000 inhabitants and GDP per capita above US$3,000 PPP. For country abbreviations, refer to International Organization for Standardization (ISO), https://www.iso.org/obp/ui/#search. GDP = gross domestic product; LAC = Latin America and the Caribbean; PPP = purchasing power parity.

## Outcomes Are Poor Because Policy Design and Implementation Are Poor

### The Educational System Fails to Create Foundational Skills

Foundational skills—including basic literacy, numeracy, critical thinking, and problem-solving—are usually developed in elementary and secondary school, yet LAC countries are failing their children in this regard. At the elementary level, learning proficiency (that is, the share of children 10–14 years old who can understand a text) in the median LAC country is 41 percent: only the level in Sub-Saharan Africa is lower (figure 3.6, panel a). Indeed, learning proficiency is lower for LAC countries than for others with comparable incomes (figure 3.6, panel b). China and Viet Nam, for instance, have learning proficiencies of about 80 percent.

**FIGURE 3.6 Few Children Can Read Well in LAC**

a. Learning proficiency by region

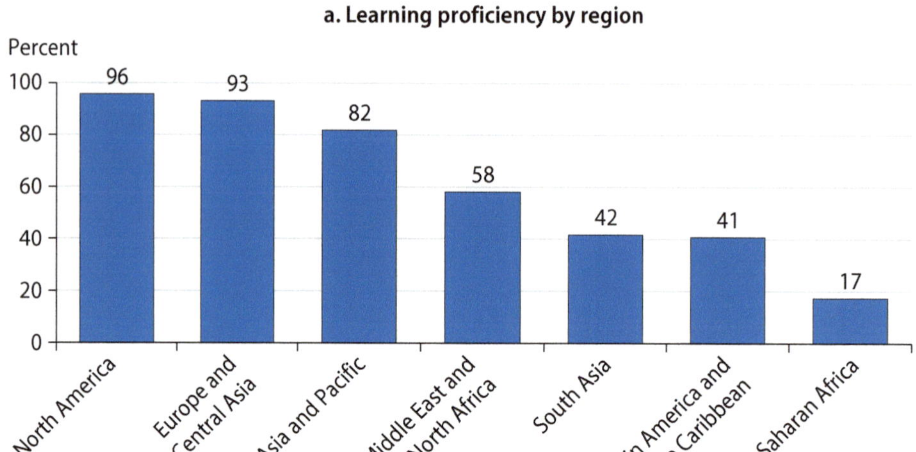


b. Learning proficiency and GDP per capita

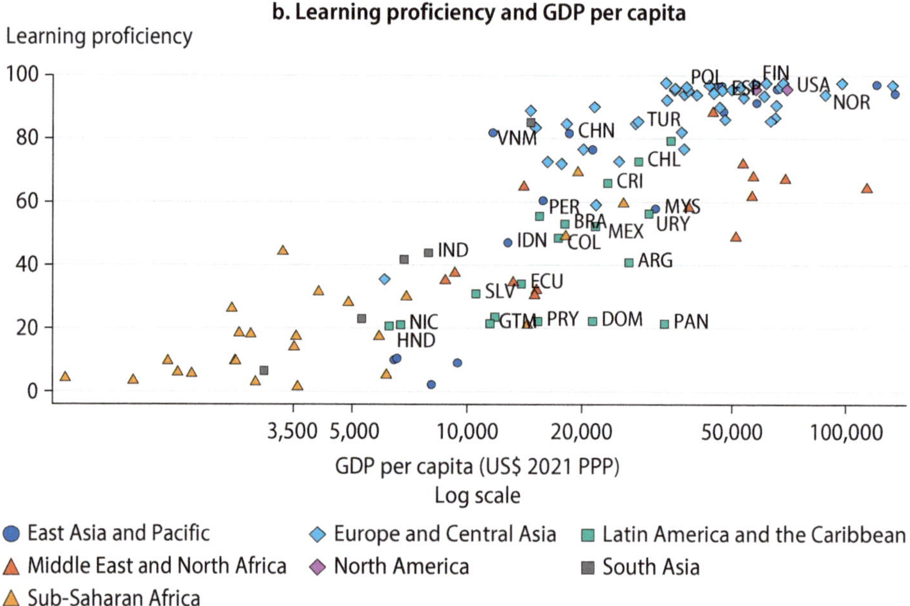


*Source:* Original figure for this volume based on UNESCO Learning Poverty Indicators (https://gaml.uis.unesco.org/learning-poverty/).

*Note:* A country's learning proficiency is calculated as the share of children at the end-of-primary age (10–14 years old) above minimum reading proficiency adjusted by out-of-school children. Panel a shows median across countries by region. For each country, the most recent year is used. Last year available is between 2001 and 2019. GDP per capita data are for 2019. For country abbreviations in panel b, refer to International Organization for Standardization (ISO), https://www.iso.org/obp/ui/#search. GDP = gross domestic product; LAC = Latin America and the Caribbean; PPP = purchasing power parity.

At the secondary level, the share of students who are proficient in math, science, and reading is alarmingly low as well. In the median LAC country, only 27 percent of students score above the minimum proficiency level in mathematics, well below all other regions.[8] The underperformance in math and science is particularly worrisome given the importance of science, technology, engineering, and mathematics (STEM) skills for innovation.

Not only is LAC failing to produce students with the minimum set of skills, but it is also failing to produce students with top skills (figure 3.7). Less than 0.5 percent of students in Argentina, Colombia, and Panama achieve at the top math level, and this percentage does not even exceed 1 percent in the best-performing countries, Uruguay and Chile. This contrasts with Türkiye, where more than 5 percent of students score at the top level, and Viet Nam, which has a higher share (5 percent) of top performers even though its income is lower than that at most of the LAC countries that participate in the Program of International Student Assessment.

**FIGURE 3.7 Few High School Students Are Top Performers in Math in LAC**

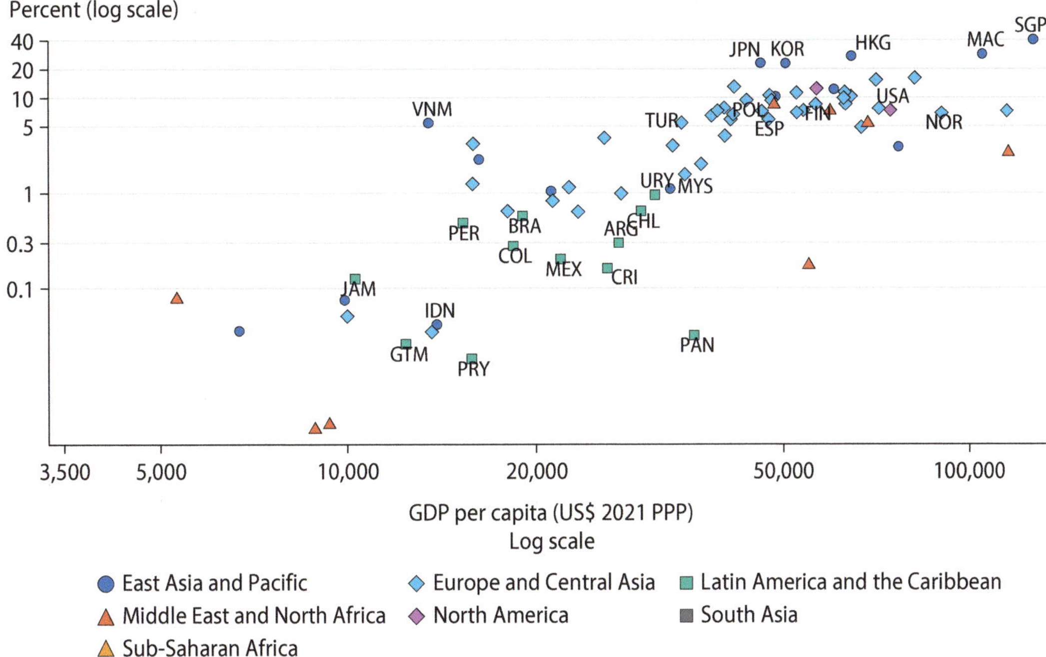


*Source:* Original figure for this volume based on OECD PISA 2022 Database (https://www.oecd.org/en/data/datasets/pisa-2022-database.html).

*Note:* The figure shows the percentage of 15-year-old students who meet the highest proficiency levels (levels 5 and 6) in the PISA mathematics assessment. GDP per capita data are for circa 2022. For country abbreviations, refer to International Organization for Standardization (ISO), https://www.iso.org/obp/ui/#search. GDP = gross domestic product; LAC = Latin America and the Caribbean; PISA = Program for International Student Assessment; PPP = purchasing power parity.

Similar to the importance of management quality to achieve firm outcomes reviewed in the previous chapter, recent literature also stresses the importance of better educational management to achieve student learning. In a study of eight countries, an increase of one standard deviation in the management score index of school principals is associated with an increase of 0.425 of a standard deviation in pupil achievement, as measured by test scores (Bloom et al. 2015). In this study, Brazil had an educational management score 25 percent below the average of Canada, Germany, Sweden, the United Kingdom, and the United States. The World Bank study *Managing for Learning: Measuring and Strengthening Education Management in Latin America and the Caribbean* confirms that Colombia, Haiti, and Mexico score even lower than Brazil in educational management quality, but that viable policies exist to redress shortfalls (Adelman and Lemos 2021).

### The Educational System Fails to Create Relevant Advanced Skills

Building on the foundational skills developed in elementary and secondary education, higher education systems provide advanced skills. LAC performs well in access to higher education, with a gross enrollment rate of 54 percent, second only to Europe and Central Asia with 74 percent and North America with 87 percent.[9] This high enrollment rate does not yield a commensurately high number of graduates: on average, about half of LAC higher education students do not graduate (Ferreyra et al. 2017).

While addressing dropout rates would increase the supply of advanced human capital, it would not be sufficient to improve innovation capabilities in LAC. In terms of advanced human capital, the region needs not only a greater quantity but also a greater "quality"—a better alignment of the skill supply with the productive and strategic needs of the economy. Currently only 17 percent of higher education graduates obtain a STEM degree in the median LAC country, a share that makes LAC and Sub-Saharan Africa tie for last place among regions (figure 3.8, panel a). When the focus is exclusively on science graduates, their share in LAC countries is a mere 2 percent, the lowest of all regions.[10]

Operating new technologies requires technical skills. These are typically developed in short-cycle higher education programs, which last 2–3 years and are often known as technical or technological programs. LAC has

**FIGURE 3.8 LAC Universities Produce Insufficient STEM or Short-Cycle Program Graduates**

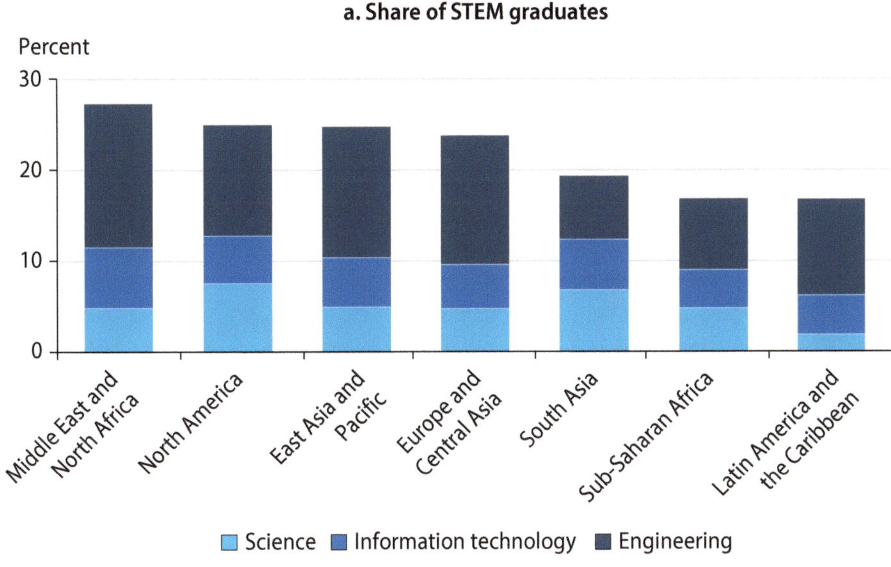


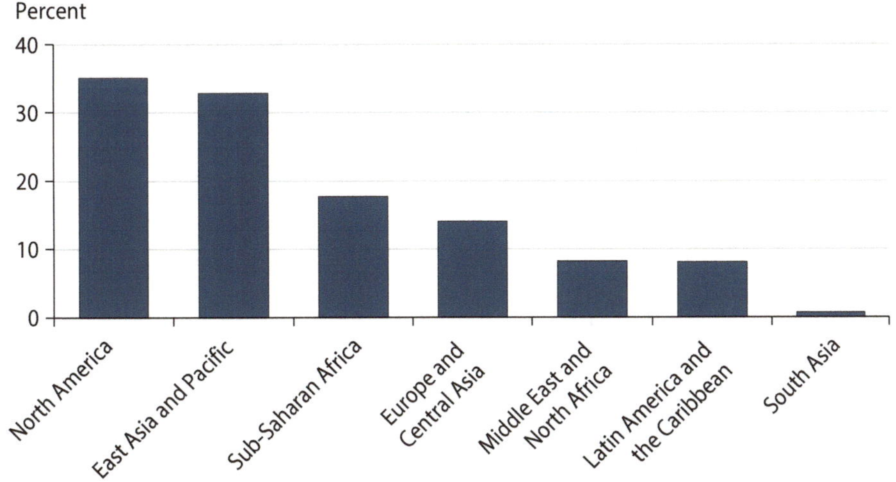


*Source:* Original figure for this volume based on UNESCO Institute of Statistics (http://data.uis.unesco.org).
*Note:* In panel a, for every region the figure shows the median field share over the countries in the last year available between 2000 and 2021. Science includes natural sciences, mathematics, and statistics. In panel b, the figure shows the weighted (by population) average of the share of higher education students enrolled in short-cycle programs across countries in each region for the last year available per country, computed as the ratio between the number of students enrolled in ISCED five programs and the number of students enrolled in all programs of higher education, expressed as a percentage. Short-cycle programs are technical or technological programs lasting 2–3 years. ISCED = International Standard Classification of Education; LAC = Latin America and the Caribbean; STEM = science, technology, engineering, and mathematics.

the second lowest share of higher education students enrolled in these programs (7.8 percent) across regions, only higher than that of South Asia and far below the share in North America and East Asia and Pacific (figure 3.8, panel b).[11]

At the top end of the skill distribution, few students are enrolled in highly selective PhD programs. The extent to which students are connected to the knowledge frontier is proxied by enrollment in US-based PhD and master's programs. Based on this metric, the countries most connected to the knowledge frontier are the Republic of Korea and Singapore (figure 3.9, panel a). While LAC countries are far less connected than Korea and Singapore, they vary in their connectedness. While the highest-income countries of the region (Costa Rica, Chile, Panama, Uruguay) are more connected than countries with comparable incomes outside the region (figure 3.9, panel b), the reverse is the case for the other LAC countries.

As with undergraduate students, the problem with top skills is not only quantity but also "quality" or composition. Although the number of graduates from master's programs from Chilean universities rose by 66 percent between 2007 and 2011, 71 percent of them obtain degrees in the social sciences rather than in fields relevant to Chile's productive structure or strategic needs. Among the Chilean students pursuing advanced degrees abroad with a Chilean government scholarship, 49 percent of master's students and 41 percent of PhD students are studying social sciences (Alvarez, Benavente, and Tejeda 2018). While just about 20 percent of the undergraduate and graduate students from Mexico, Colombia, and Brazil who are studying in the United States pursue STEM programs, this share exceeds 60 percent among students from India and the Islamic Republic of Iran (figure 3.10). To make matters worse, not only do LAC countries have few researchers (as discussed later), but most researchers are outside the private sector—where they could develop new products—and exclusively inside universities and research institutes.

This compositional issue is evident even among Nobel Laureates. The region boasts 17 Nobel Laureates. However, only five were honored for their work in the sciences (two received the chemistry award and three the physiology or medicine award).[12] Among these five scientists, three were from the same country (Argentina) and, perhaps more disappointingly, they all received their awards before the year 2000.

**FIGURE 3.9** **LAC Trains Fewer Graduate Students in the United States Than Its Peers**

**a. Full sample**

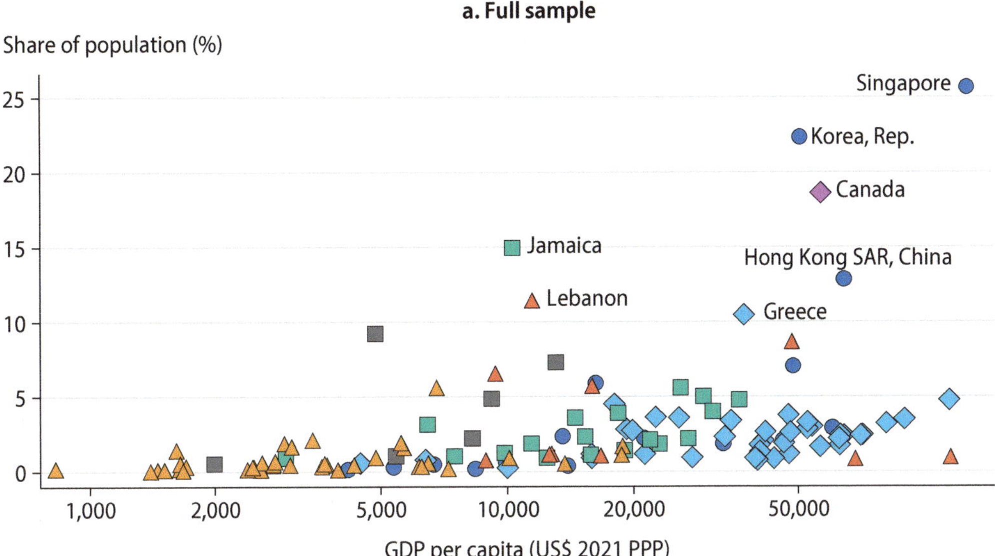


**b. Close-up view (less than 0.1 percent)**

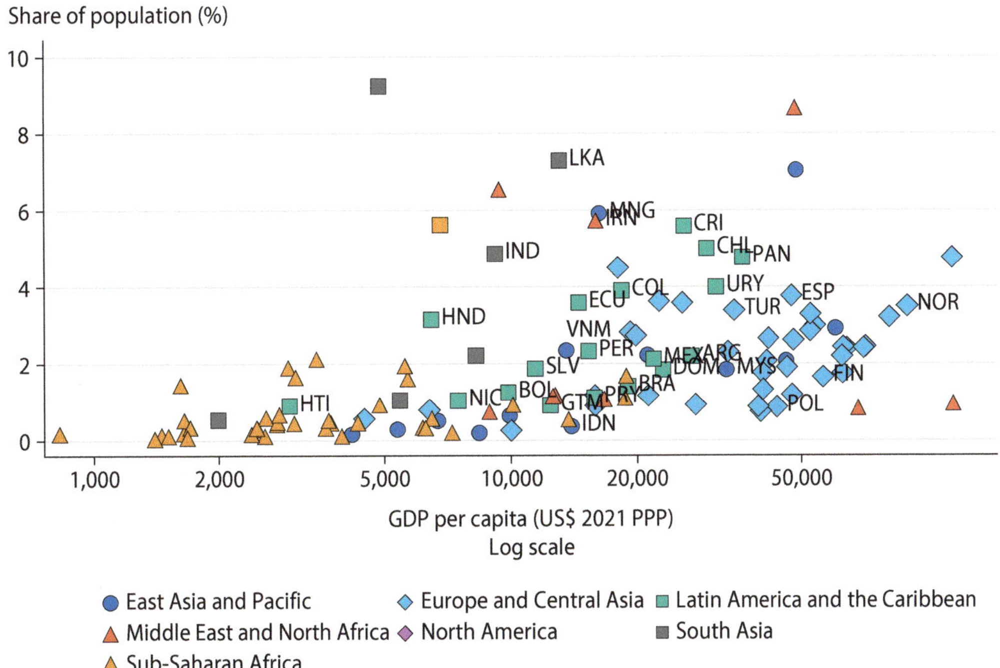


*Sources:* Original figure for this volume based on Open Doors data (https://opendoorsdata.org/) and World Bank World Development Indicators (https://databank.worldbank.org/source/world-development-indicators).

*Note:* For each country, the figure shows the number of students enrolled in US universities in graduate programs (master's or PhD programs) as a percentage of the country's population in the 24–34 age group. Panel a shows the full sample. Panel b truncates the y-axis scale at 0.1 percent. Data are for 2019. GDP per capita data are for circa 2022. For country abbreviations, refer to International Organization for Standardization (ISO), https://www.iso.org/obp/ui/#search. GDP = gross domestic product; LAC = Latin America and the Caribbean; PPP = purchasing power parity.

**FIGURE 3.10 Few LAC Students Receive World-Class Training in STEM**

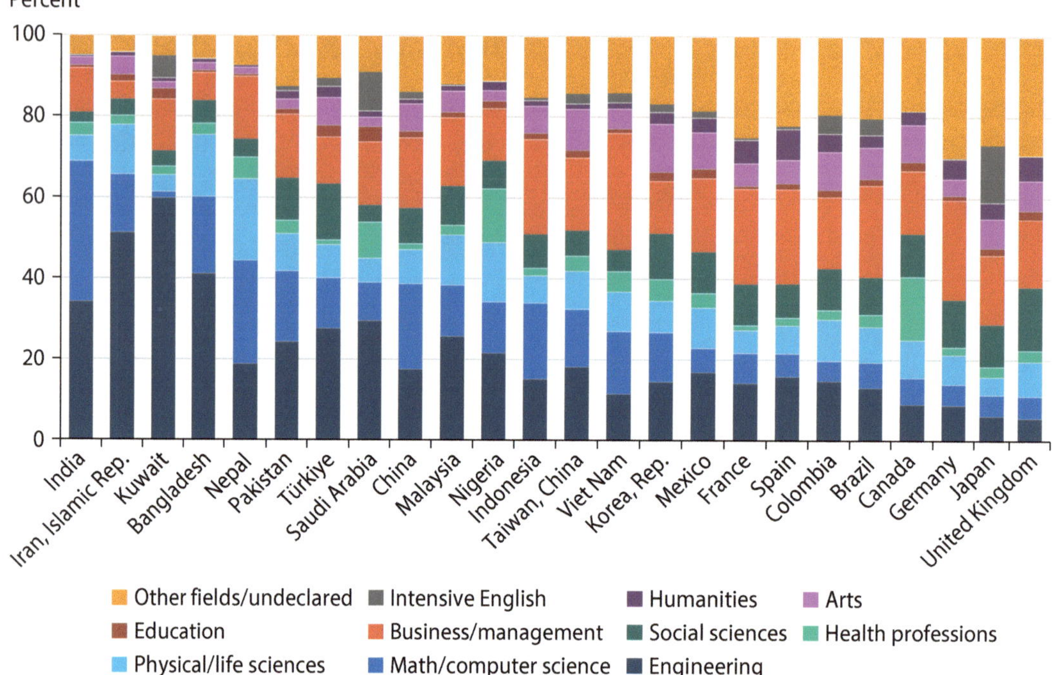


*Source:* Original figure for this volume based on Open Doors data (https://opendoorsdata.org/).
*Note:* For each country, the figure shows the distribution of students enrolled in US universities in undergraduates or graduate programs across fields of study. Data are for 2019. LAC = Latin America and the Caribbean; STEM = science, technology, engineering, and mathematics.

## Inequitable Access Shrinks the Talent Pool Needed for Innovation

Even though LAC needs a large and deep talent pool, inequitable access to higher education prevents many talented individuals from furthering their skills and thereby limits the size of the talent pool for professionals, technicians, scientists, managers, and entrepreneurs. The share of students ages 25–29 who completed at least 2 years of higher education is 55 percent among those from the top wealth quintile but only 6 percent for those from the bottom wealth quintile. If this gap were closed, the share of individuals from that age range completing at least 2 years of higher education would rise by about 130 percent.[13]

Students are best positioned to pursue STEM in college when they have received a solid academic preparation in high school. In Colombia, students who score in the top quintile of the mandatory high school exit exam—whose score can be viewed as a measure of college academic readiness—are more likely than others to enroll in STEM fields (figure 3.11, panel a). College academic readiness, however, varies greatly among students and is highly correlated with family income (figure 3.11, panel b).[14] As a result,

**FIGURE 3.11 In Colombia, Few Students Are Prepared to Major in STEM Fields**

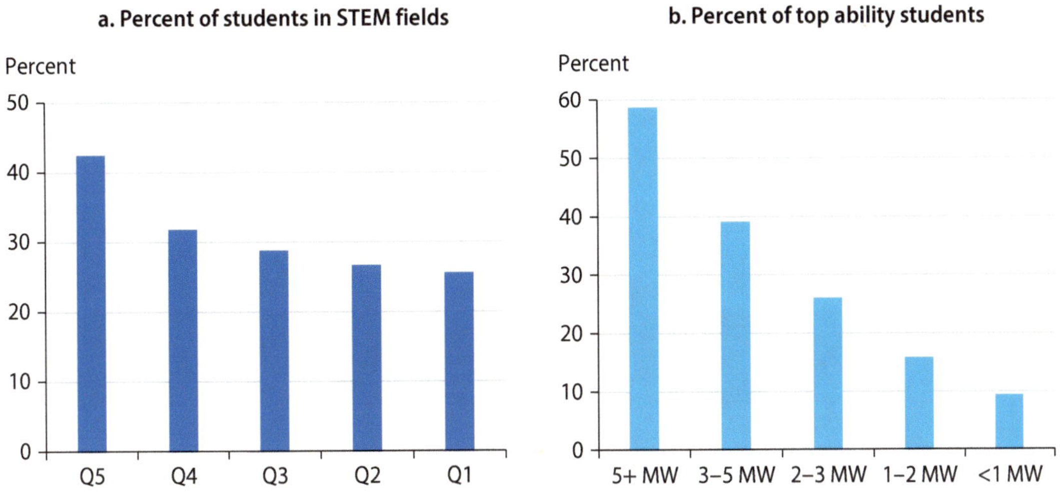

*Sources:* Original figure for this volume based on data from Saber 11 and SPADIES from Colombia's Ministry of Education for the student cohort that took Saber 11 in 2009.

*Note:* Panel a shows the percentage of college students from each ability quintile that began a STEM program within 5 years of taking Saber 11, a high school exit examination administered annually in grade 11 in Colombian high schools. Data correspond to students enrolled in bachelor's programs. Q = quintile; Q5 is the highest. Panel b shows the percentage of students from each income bracket (measured in terms of minimum wage, MW) who scored in the top quintile of Saber 11 ("top ability" students). Ability quintiles are built based on the standardized distribution of total Saber 11 scores. STEM = science, technology, engineering, and mathematics.

very few low- and middle-income students are eligible for STEM majors. Inequitable access to quality secondary schooling therefore hampers the development of the very talent needed for innovation.

## Poor Funding Does Not Fully Explain Poor Educational Outcomes

Are LAC's poor educational outcomes due to poor funding? Relative to countries with similar incomes, most LAC countries devote comparable resources to education (figure 3.12). The median LAC country spends 4.5 percent of its GDP on education, slightly below the median country in Europe and Central Asia (5 percent) and above the median country in East Asia and Pacific (3.2 percent). Several LAC countries (Haiti, Trinidad and Tobago, Guatemala, Paraguay, Ecuador, the Dominican Republic, Panama, Peru) spend less than 4 percent of their GDP on education, yet most countries in the region exceed this threshold. Hence, while some LAC countries may need to raise their education spending, poor funding may not be the leading explanation for the region's poor educational outcomes.[15]

**FIGURE 3.12 In Most LAC Countries, Education Spending Is on Par with Spending in Other Countries**

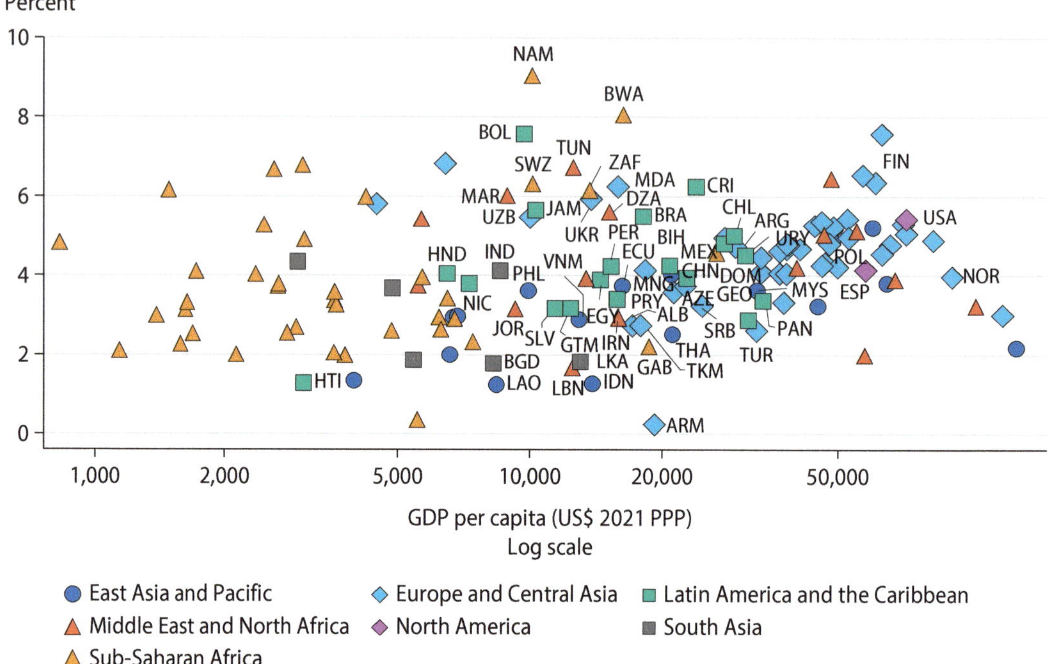


*Sources:* Original figure for this volume based on UNESCO Institute for Statistics (https://uis.unesco.org/) and World Bank World Development Indicators (https://databank.worldbank.org/source/world-development-indicators).
*Note:* Data correspond to the most recent year with available data between 2013 and 2022 and includes spending in elementary, secondary, and tertiary education. For country abbreviations, refer to International Organization for Standardization (ISO), https://www.iso.org/obp/ui/#search. GDP = gross domestic product; LAC = Latin America and the Caribbean; PPP = purchasing power parity.

## R&D Spending Is Low and Is Not Geared to Bring Innovation to Markets

Most LAC countries invest little in R&D, even relative to countries with similar income (refer to chapter 1). As a result, their S&T systems are underfunded and overstretched among too many projects. Because cutting-edge research—particularly in the sciences—can be expensive, this limits the region's ability to conduct world-class research. Except for Brazil, no country in the region compares to Spain in R&D funding—and no country at all compares to the United States (refer to the bar heights in figure 3.13, panel a). As a result, LAC scientists often report having substandard levels of laboratory infrastructure and equipment, having limited funding for reagents (typically imported and subject to import tariffs, which raise their cost), and not having access to international journals. In addition, their salaries—virtually the only type of R&D expense covered by public funding in the region—are low relative to those in other occupations (Ciocca and Delgado 2017).

A stark difference between the United States and LAC countries is the low participation of the business sector in R&D. While most R&D is funded by industry in the United States, it is not in LAC (figure 3.13, panel a), where most of it is publicly funded and channeled through universities. Brazil is again the exception, with a share of business-funded R&D comparable to Spain's. And, while about 40 percent of researchers work in the private sector in the median country in East Asia and Pacific or Europe and Central Asia, this share drops to 7 percent in the median LAC country.[16] Experimental research (for example, developing new prototypes and models) is usually carried out by the private sector and captures more than 60 percent of R&D spending in the United States, relative to 30 percent or less in most of LAC.[17] In other words, little R&D in LAC is channeled to new product development.

Further, R&D in LAC is not geared toward solving specific local problems (such as Dengue infections or Chagas disease). This is because universities typically reward researchers for the prestige of their academic publications, not the social impact of their research findings (Ciocca and Delgado 2017). Moreover, the funding necessary to conduct this type of research is scarce because S&T systems lack strategic priorities to allocate public R&D funding and are not always focused on specific local problems. Relative to total R&D funding, the share captured by STEM in countries such as Argentina, Chile, and Mexico is above 40 percent (similar to that of Spain and the United States) but is only 20 percent for Central American countries (figure 3.13, panel b). What is common across LAC countries, however, is the relatively high share of R&D funding devoted to social sciences—much higher than in the United States.

## Some Research Funding in LAC Prioritizes Research Careers, Often Due to Low Wages in the Sector

To fund research, generally S&T systems can finance research projects, research careers, or researchers' training. Table 3A.1 in annex 3A describes the S&T agencies in Argentina, Brazil, Chile, Colombia, Costa Rica, Ecuador, Mexico, and Peru. Of the 12 agencies included in the table, all but one provide funding for research projects, two provide funding for research careers, and nine provide funding for researchers' training. Funding for research projects is awarded via competitive grants, with proposals reviewed by expert committees. Projects are typically funded for 1–3 or 3–5 years. Funding for research careers, in turn, rests on a competitive process whereby researchers are selected for entry into the career and then earn a monthly stipend contingent on passing periodic evaluations.

**FIGURE 3.13 R&D Spending in LAC Is Low and Not Geared toward Innovation**

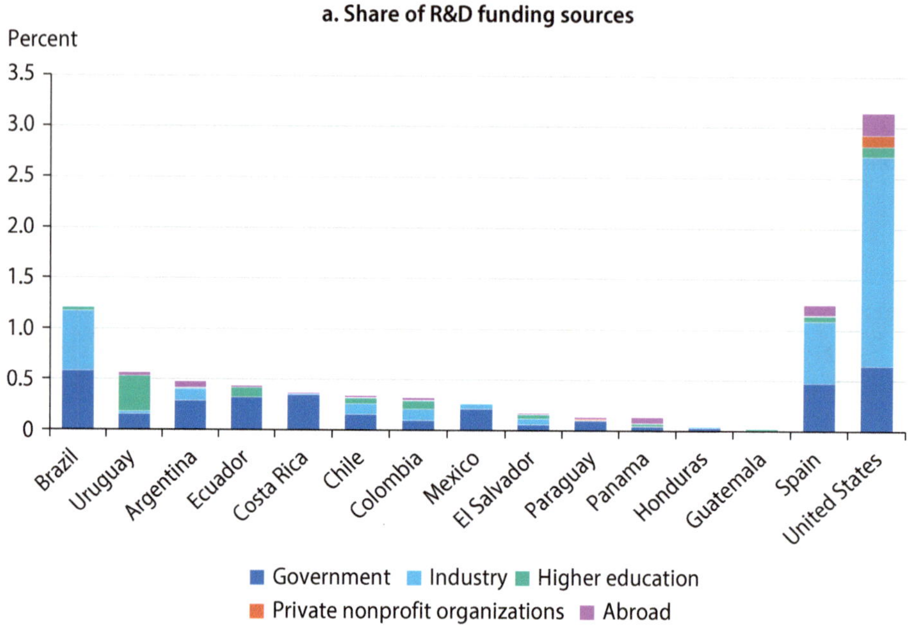

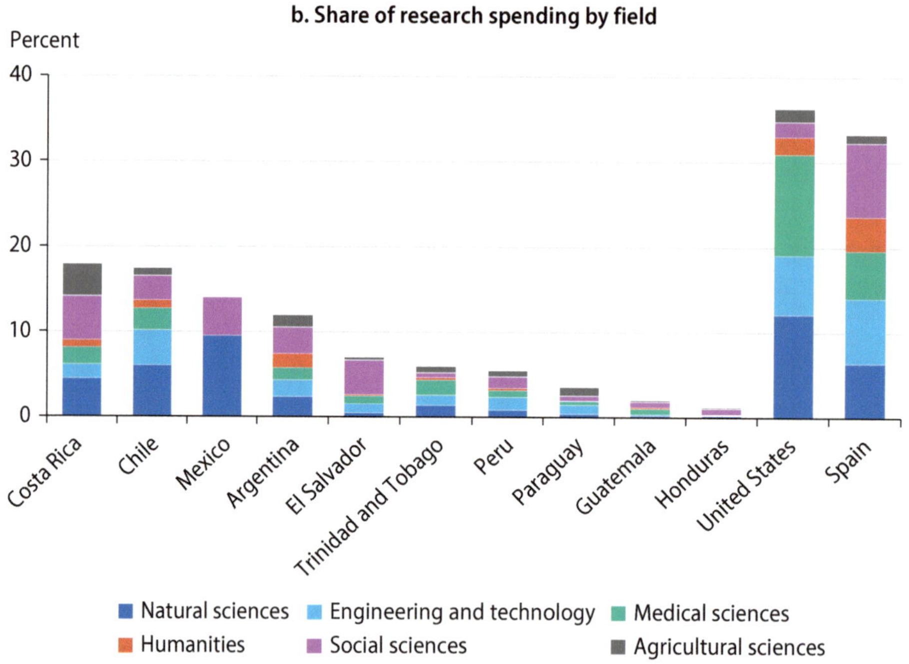

*Source:* Original figure for this volume based on RICYT data (http://www.ricyt.org/en/category/en/indicators/).
*Note:* Panel a shows total research and development (R&D) spending as a percentage of GDP, disaggregated by funding source. Panel b shows the spending share by field relative to the research conducted at higher education institutions. Only two fields are reported for Mexico. GDP = gross domestic product; LAC = Latin America and the Caribbean.

There are trade-offs between funding research projects and funding research careers. Because project-based funding is shorter term than career-based funding, it may provide greater incentives for researchers to increase and improve their efforts by inducing them to compete periodically for funding. At the same time, it may not encourage the kind of long-term, ambitious projects that can lead to breakthrough innovations.[18] Despite its potential to aid such discoveries, career funding in LAC has become an implicit salary subsidy to the universities that employ career researchers, while the remaining faculty in the country conduct very little research.[19] While admission to research careers is selective, the allocation of slots among fields of study does not seem to follow any kind of strategic prioritization—a clear instance of inefficiency for countries with limited fiscal resources.[20]

## Higher Education Is Not Connected to Firms: The Absent Third Mission

Through its triple missions, higher education can play a key role in innovation. First, it can develop skills by educating students and forming professionals, managers, and technicians who will adopt or produce innovations. Second, it can produce new knowledge—the bedrock of innovation—through research. Third, it can exchange knowledge with industry to innovate and develop new products and production methods.

These missions are successfully accomplished when higher education institutions are closely connected to enterprises and employers—to gauge the demand for skills in the labor market and for knowledge in the business sector, and to collaborate in the production of such skills and knowledge.

The link between higher education and industry, however, is weak in LAC. Firms in LAC do not view university graduates' skills as relevant to their needs, with the average firm in the median LAC country scoring the relevance of those skills at 4.4 out of 7.[21]

Firms in LAC report less interaction with industry on R&D activities than those in other regions—the least among all regions (figure 3.14, panel a). On average, only 2 percent of all the publications produced in the region are coauthored by researchers engaged in university–industry collaboration,[22] while the corresponding figure is 4.3 percent in the United States (THE 2020). When universities are ranked based on their industry income (which is obtained from industry contracts and serves to measure knowledge exchange), only 1 percent of the top 500 higher education institutions in the world are from LAC—the lowest share among all regions (figure 3.14, panel b). The volume of patents filed jointly by higher education institutions and firms—another metric of university–industry interaction—is also low in LAC (figure 3.15). While LAC countries have produced less than 0.5 joint patents per 100,000 people in the past 50 years, the corresponding figure is close to 8 for Spain and the United States. On average, only 2.1 percent of all patents produced in the region are the fruit of university–industry collaboration.

**FIGURE 3.14 University–Industry Interaction Is Rare in LAC**

**a. University–industry R&D collaboration**

Score
6
5
4
3
2
1
0

North America
East Asia and Pacific
Europe and Central Asia
South Asia
Middle East and North Africa
Sub-Saharan Africa
Latin America and the Caribbean

**b. Share of universities in the top 500 according to the industry-income ranking**

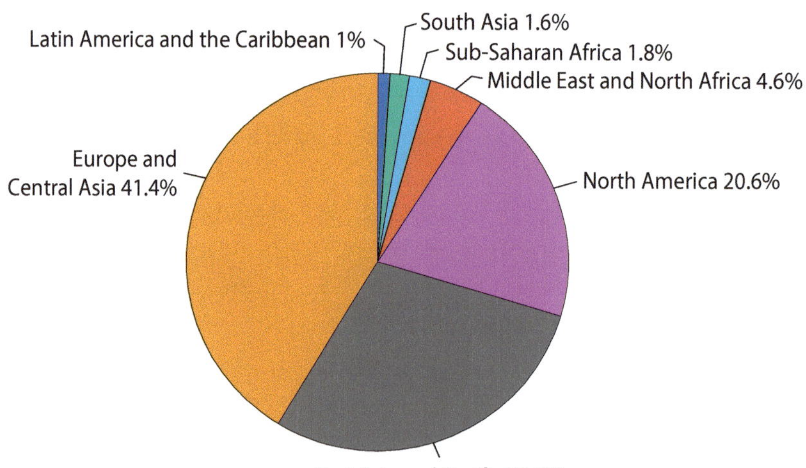


*Sources:* Original figure for this volume based on World Bank World Development Indicators (https://databank.worldbank.org/source/world-development-indicators) and World Intellectual Property Organization based on World Economic Forum, Executive Opinion Survey 2021 (panel a); and Times Higher Education World University Rankings report 2023 (panel b).

*Note:* Data on university–industry research and development (R&D) collaboration are from 2014 to 2021, and are the average answer to the following survey question: In your country, to what extent do businesses and universities collaborate on R&D? [1 = not at all; 7 = to a great extent]. Panel b shows the percentage of universities from each region that are included in the top 500 Times Higher Education industry income ranking. Industry income is the income that an institution earns from industry contracts. LAC = Latin America and the Caribbean; R&D = research and development.

**FIGURE 3.15 Joint University–Industry Innovation Is Scarce in LAC**

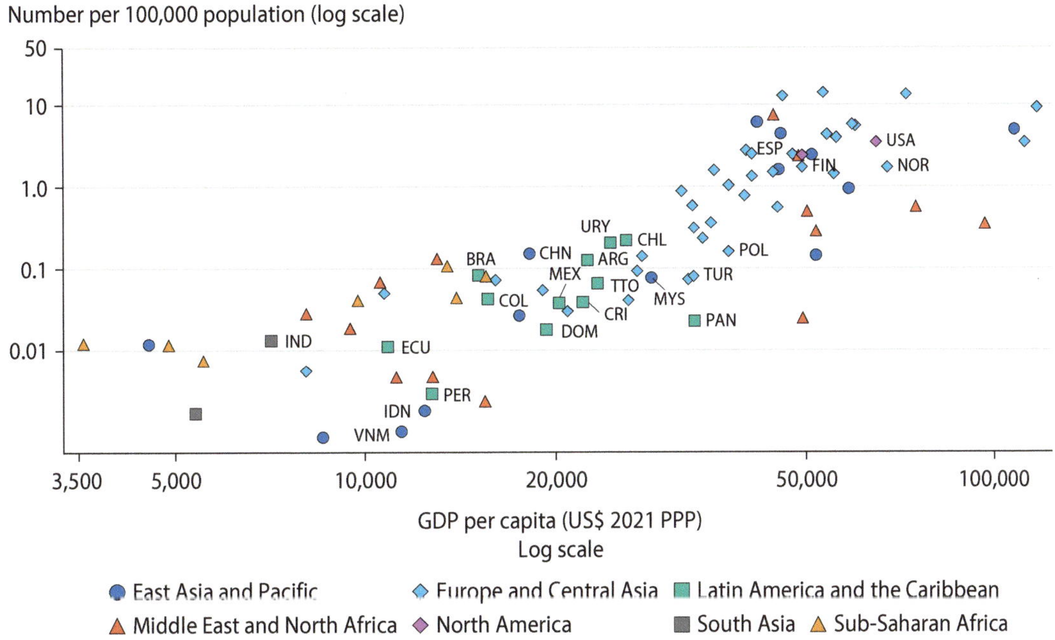

Number per 100,000 population (log scale)
50
10
1.0
0.1
0.01
USA
NOR
ESP
FIN
POL
TUR
MYS
PAN
URY
CHL
ARG
CHN
BRA
MEX
TTO
COL
CRI
DOM
IND
ECU
PER
IDN
VNM
3,500
5,000
10,000
20,000
50,000
100,000
GDP per capita (US$ 2021 PPP)
Log scale

East Asia and Pacific
Europe and Central Asia
Latin America and the Caribbean
Middle East and North Africa
North America
South Asia
Sub-Saharan Africa

*Sources:* Original figure for this volume using OECD Patent Database (https://www.oecd.org/en/data/datasets/intellectual-property-statistics.html) based on EPO PATSTAT, and World Bank World Development Indicators (https://databank.worldbank.org/source/world-development-indicators).

*Note:* The figure shows the number of patents from university–industry collaborations per 100,000 population by country of inventor using whole counts (that is, the patent is counted fully for each country when it has inventors from multiple countries). To be counted as a joint university–industry product, a patent's filers must include at least one higher education or research institution and one non-higher education or research institution. Data on patents range from 1969 to 2021. GDP per capita data are for circa 2022. The figure includes countries with more than 500,000 inhabitants and GDP per capita above US$3,000 PPP. For country abbreviations, refer to International Organization for Standardization (ISO), https://www.iso.org/obp/ui/#search. GDP = gross domestic product; LAC = Latin America and the Caribbean; PPP = purchasing power parity.

Several factors may account for the lack of university–industry R&D interaction in LAC. Perception is one of them: if firms view universities as weak in research, they might not seek to collaborate in R&D. Figure 3.16 presents some evidence in favor of this hypothesis. Conditional on GDP per capita, university–industry interaction (as reported by the firms) is lower in countries where the perceived quality of research institutions is lower. Further, most LAC countries are below average in both dimensions; only Costa Rica, Guatemala, Honduras, Mexico, and Trinidad and Tobago are above average in both dimensions. And, while Argentina and Chile are above average in terms of perceived quality of research institutions, they are below average in university–industry interaction, indicating that other factors might hinder collaboration. This finding also holds when measuring university–industry interaction through the number of joint patents—and when measuring university quality through research output rather than firms' perception of research quality (annex 3B).

**FIGURE 3.16 University–Industry Collaboration in R&D Is Low Where Perceived Quality of Scientific Research Institutions Is Low**

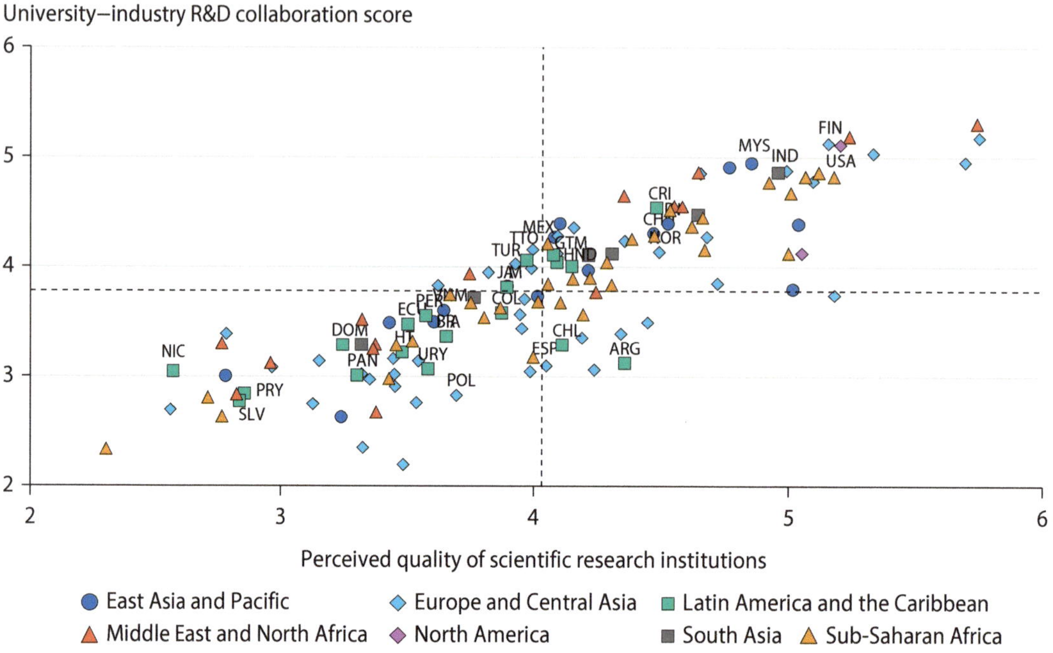
University–industry R&D collaboration score
6
5
4
3
2
2
3
4
5
6
Perceived quality of scientific research institutions
NIC
PRY
SLV
DOM
PAN
URY
POL
JAM
TUR
MEX
GTM
COL
CHL
ESP
ARG
CRI
MYS
IND
FIN
USA
East Asia and Pacific
Europe and Central Asia
Latin America and the Caribbean
Middle East and North Africa
North America
South Asia
Sub-Saharan Africa

*Sources:* Original figure for this volume using World Economic Forum 2017 based on World Economic Forum Executive Opinion Survey, and World Bank World Development Indicators (https://databank.worldbank.org/source/world-development-indicators).
*Note:* Data are conditional on GDP per capita. Each variable is residualized by log GDP per capita (2022) in US$ PPP and recentered at the raw mean. Data on university–industry R&D collaboration are the 2016–17 weighted average answer to the survey question: In your country, to what extent do businesses and universities collaborate on research and development (R&D)? [1 = not at all; 7 = to a great extent]. Quality of scientific research institutions is the 2016–17 weighted average answer to the survey question: In your country, how do you assess the quality of scientific research institutions? [1 = extremely poor—among the worst in the world; 7 = extremely good—among the best in the world]. Dashed lines denote sample averages. For country abbreviations, refer to International Organization for Standardization (ISO), https://www.iso.org/obp/ui/#search. GDP = gross domestic product; PPP = purchasing power parity; R&D = research and development.

In addition to firms' perception of university research quality, institutional incentives may explain the lack of university–industry interaction. In LAC, faculty are mostly rewarded for their publication record, not their interaction with industry (CINDA 2015). Further, this interaction is often frowned upon in academic circles. Legal obstacles (at the national or institutional level) sometimes prevent universities from owning intellectual property or shares in spin-off firms. The dynamism and speed required to interact with industry are not typical of universities, whose decision-making process is often slow and cumbersome.

History offers an additional explanation for the lack of university–industry interaction in LAC.[23] Most universities in the region were founded with one clear mission—undergraduate teaching—and only later, as research became more widespread, did they begin to offer graduate training. Between the 1950s and the 1980s, several countries adopted top-down, supply-based science policies that included the creation of several PRIs, many of them focused on supporting the sectors viewed as relevant by the policy makers (nuclear technology in Argentina; aeronautics and oil in Brazil; coffee in Costa Rica; oil in Mexico; and agriculture in most countries). Thus, while universities and PRIs interacted with society and the economy during that period, they responded to government directives rather than industry's own demand. And, since large swaths of private industry were protected from import competition at the time, they had little need for sophisticated knowledge. Over time, these factors may have contributed to local firms' disregard for universities and research institutes.

In contrast, over the last two or three decades governments in the developed world have steadily encouraged university–industry interaction and have made it a centerpiece of their innovation systems (see, for instance, Cirera et al. 2020; Guimón and Paunov 2019). Today, those countries often give grants for joint university–industry R&D, innovation vouchers to firms to purchase services from universities, tax incentives for firms to conduct joint R&D, financial support for academic spin-offs, and innovation loans for joint university–industry projects. They also facilitate the creation of university or technology parks—for example, by providing space in public universities for the establishment of enterprises that interact with the university community, or by allocating competitive funding for the establishment of technology parks in university campuses. While developing countries such as such as China, India, and Malaysia have vigorously followed in this trend (Larsen et al. 2016; Lee 2014), LAC countries have been less active. The ensuing lack of interaction between university and industry is a major point of departure from developed countries (box 3.2).

### BOX 3.2 University–Industry Interaction in the United States

In the United States, the Industrial Revolution created a demand for industry-related skills (MacLeod and Urquiola 2021). Then-new universities, such as Johns Hopkins and Cornell, responded by offering business and engineering programs, while incumbents such as Harvard imitated the new entrants by adding those offerings to their existing offerings. Additional institutions entered this competition, including private ones (Stanford University, University of Chicago) and public ones (Massachusetts Institute of Technology, MIT; University of California, Berkeley).

*(Continued on next page)*

**BOX 3.2 University–Industry Interaction in the United States *(continued)***

Some sought to attract researchers, whose performance they began to measure based on the journals recently launched by professional and scientific associations. While some institutions launched their research activities based on private resources (such as Stanford), others have always relied on a combination of public and private funding (such as MIT). Over time, the share of federal funding in research has become increasingly important across the board.

Today, universities interact with industry in several kinds of research and development activities, such as joint research, sponsored research (providing industry income), and knowledge transfer in science and technology (S&T) parks and start-ups.[a] A prominent example of research collaboration is the case of Caltech (California Institute of Technology), which has developed a strong collaboration with industry in terms of coauthorships. It averaged about 118 coauthored publications per year in 2015–19 with global companies such as Hoffmann La Roche, IBM, and Siemens (THE 2020). In terms of sponsored research, Stanford University is among the top US universities, with an average industry research income of US$107,000 per academic staff member. Stanford has also been a leader in knowledge transfer by facilitating the birth and growth of Silicon Valley companies such as Google, which began in the 1990s as a graduate project of two Stanford students, Sergey Brin and Larry Page.

a. This paragraph is based on THE (2020).

## LAC Countries Struggle to Retain or Engage Highly Skilled Individuals

In most LAC countries, individuals who emigrate are, on average, more highly educated than those who stay in the country (this is shown in figure 3.17, where most LAC countries are above the 45-degree line.) The ensuing potential for brain drain is particularly large for Caribbean countries such as Barbados, Trinidad and Tobago, and Jamaica, where 35–40 percent of emigrants are highly educated. The scale of migration is so high that it is probably best to think of how brain drain can be converted into a "skills export" industry where the countries make a net profit by fully recouping training costs (World Bank 2023). Among larger countries, the brain drain potential is high for Argentina and Brazil—where the share of skilled emigrants is also 35–40 percent—but less so for Chile and Mexico, where the share of skilled emigrants is less than 10 percent, even though the share of skilled domestic workers is the same as Argentina's.

**FIGURE 3.17 Many LAC Countries Lose Highly Skilled Individuals**

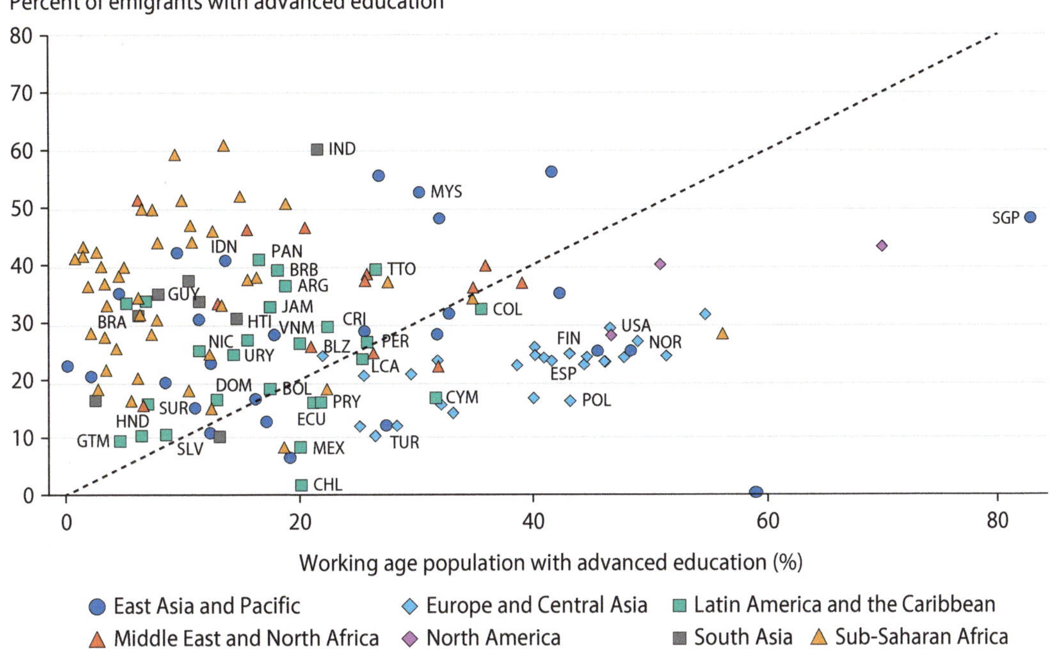


*Sources:* Original figure for this volume based on the Database on Immigrants in OECD Countries (DIOC) 2015/16 (https://www.oecd.org/en/data/datasets/database-on-immigrants-in-oecd-and-non-oecd-countries.html) and ILO Statistics (https://ilostat.ilo.org/topics/population-and-labour-force/).

*Note:* For each country, the vertical axis shows the share of emigrants to OECD countries with higher education (ICSED levels 5+), and the horizontal axis shows the country's share of working-age population with higher education. Working-age population is 15+ years old. For country abbreviations, refer to International Organization for Standardization (ISO), https://www.iso.org/obp/ui/#search. LAC = Latin America and the Caribbean.

To summarize, policies in LAC countries fall short at developing human capital, encouraging innovative research, and stimulating university–industry interaction. To further understand why these S&T systems underperform, the next section conducts a deep dive for five large countries in the region.

## Why Are LAC's Knowledge Institutions Weak Partners for Industry?

Argentina, Brazil, Chile, Colombia, and Mexico account for about 70 percent of LAC's researchers,[24] 85 percent of research output, and more than 95 percent of patent applications.[25] Hence, understanding what is not working there gives insight into the region's overall performance. Despite differences in specific policies, these countries' S&T and university–industry interaction policies share several traits.

### S&T Funding Is Often Low, Unfocused, Fragmented, and Volatile

S&T funding is usually provided through competitive grants administered by S&T agencies (listed in annex table 3C.1 in annex 3C). The maximum annual awards range from a low of US$51,000 in Mexico and US$59,000 in Argentina to a high of US$180,000 in Colombia and US$772,000 in São Paulo (in purchasing power parity dollars). Only grants in Brazil are comparable to those in the United States, where average awards at the National Science Foundation (NSF) and National Institutes of Health (NIH) are US$237,600 and US$592,600 per year, respectively.[26] One element associated with award sizes is selectivity—if selectivity is high, relatively few projects are funded at high levels. Several of the agencies in LAC apply relatively low standards and fund many projects at low levels, as they seek to maximize the number of beneficiaries and the participation of underrepresented groups of researchers.

Most of the research funded by these programs is driven by investigators' interests and curiosity rather than national strategic goals. The funding is short-term (usually 2–4 years), which is comparable to the average from NSF average (3 years) but is lower than that from NIH (5 years) or the European Research Council (5–7 years).[27] This prevents researchers—particularly those in the sciences—from engaging in long-term projects requiring large investments in equipment, teams, and infrastructure. In some countries (Argentina, Brazil, and Mexico), the total volume of research funding has fluctuated greatly in recent years, reflecting countries' fiscal constraints and the shifting priorities of successive administrations, and further preventing the development of ambitious, long-term agendas.

To some extent, these negative S&T funding features have persisted because the programs have rarely been evaluated in a rigorous fashion. Countries often conduct result "evaluations" merely by examining the program's outcomes—for example, the number of papers published by researchers who gained access to the corresponding funding—without considering whether those outcomes might have been accomplished anyway, even without the funding. A rigorous impact evaluation, in contrast, would compare the program's outcomes with those from the appropriate counterfactual (such as the absence of the program). The few existing impact evaluations of S&T programs show that researchers who obtained S&T grants in Argentina and Chile published more, and produced more influential papers, than researchers who applied for the grants but did not obtain them. Positive effects were more likely in geographic areas with greater research capabilities and in STEM projects (Benavente et al. 2012 for Chile; Cliodinámica 2021 for Chile; Ghezan and Pereira 2016 for Argentina).

### University–Industry Grants Are Relatively Large but Poorly Monitored

Pioneered by Brazil and Chile, most of these countries have implemented programs (listed in annex table 3C.2 in annex 3C) to promote university–industry collaboration in long-term innovation projects, generally under the supervision of S&T or innovation agencies.[28] The most common instrument is competitive grants for research partnerships (consortia) of universities, enterprises, and public research labs. Argentina, Chile, and Colombia have also implemented matching grants, where the match is provided by the enterprise partner. Brazil stands out in terms of incentives for university–industry collaboration. In addition to research grants, Brazil provides subsidized loans for high-risk innovation projects, and the state of São Paulo provides funding for applied research centers at universities and for university researchers' work inside companies. Meanwhile, currently Mexico has no programs to promote university–industry collaboration.

Relative to S&T grants, innovation grants are longer term (up to 10 or 15 years in Brazil and Chile, although only up to 3 or 5 years in Argentina and Colombia). They are also more generous. Most research grants exceed US$400,000, and matching grants in Argentina and Chile can be as high as US$7.4 million (in purchasing power parity dollars). From the point of view of government agencies, it is easier to monitor the traditional recipients of S&T funds (academic institutions) than the recipients of innovation grants (which include enterprises) (Tello et al. 2022).

Perhaps for this reason, few innovation grant programs have been adequately evaluated—which is particularly troublesome, given the size and duration of these grants. Nonetheless, the existing impact evaluations for these programs have uncovered positive impacts on the exports of Chilean firms (relative to firms that applied to the program but did not receive the grant) (Dornelles, Pertuzé, and Epstein 2018) and on the innovation spending, employment, and exports of Argentine firms (relative to firms that applied to the program to work on their own, without a university partner) (Gurcanlar et al. 2021).

One downside of innovation grants is that they have not promoted the formation of new partnerships but have rather favored existing ones. From the point of view of applicants, obtaining and managing these large, long-term grants is easier for existing partnerships—which already have experience in joint work—than for new ones.[29] From the point of view of the funding agency, it is less risky to fund an existing partnership than a new one.

The question of why, with the highest R&D spending in LAC by far, Brazil grows at similar rates to other countries in the region may find an answer in how those resources are used. For instance, the relative shares of R&D going to universities versus directly supporting technology is 69.5 percent and 22.6 percent, compared to 30.5 percent and 77.4 percent, respectively, in Korea. If the linkages to the private sector are weak, R&D impact may also be weak. An additional explanation may be that R&D subsidies have flowed to highly protected sectors, effectively permitting Brazilian firms to gain market share despite evident productivity gains (de Souza 2023).

### Universities Engage in Few Commercialization Efforts Despite Favorable Laws

Following Argentina's pioneering legislation in 1990, most countries in LAC have enacted laws to create Technology Transfer Offices (TTOs) inside universities.[30] TTOs manage the intellectual property (IP) aspects of knowledge exchange: they file for IP protection; handle IP marketing and licensing; manage the creation of spin-offs; and maintain IP assets. In practice, the role of TTOs is quite limited in many cases, as universities usually set up separate offices—for instance, foundations—to handle the administrative and logistical aspects of university–industry interactions and therefore bypass the slow and burdensome university bureaucracy.

Over the last 30 years, Argentina, Brazil, and Chile have passed legislation—inspired by the Bayh-Dole Act passed in 1980 in the United States—that gives universities ownership of the inventions made under federally funded research and allows the sharing of royalties between the university, the corresponding department or college, and the inventors.[31] They have also sought to develop an institutional framework to promote the creation of spin-offs, start-ups, business accelerators, incubators, and collaboration networks with industry.

Despite this favorable legal framework, low patenting on the part of universities is pervasive in the region, and IP management is the least frequent mode of university–industry interaction. Obtaining patents is expensive for universities; the average cost of applying for a patent at the US Patent and Trademark Office, for example, ranges between US$8,500 and US$15,400.[32] Even when they obtain patents, universities often refrain from licensing them to third parties for commercialization.[33] Maintaining patents is costly as well, which further disincentivizes patenting activity.

Countries have also passed laws to facilitate the creation of technology-based enterprises in universities—for example, by granting leave to faculty interested in creating those firms, giving faculty greater firm ownership, or making firm-related and academic activities compatible. Despite these national laws, the environment to create technology-based enterprises is ultimately determined by university-specific policies. Although most universities have a TTO, few engage in actual innovation. As a result, the most frequent mode of university–industry interaction is one in which universities provide services such as consulting, technical assistance, and testing and experimentation. Much less common are joint R&D projects or commercial endeavors such as patenting or creating technology-based enterprises.

### There Are Some Good Models in LAC to Emulate

Notwithstanding this landscape, there are several exemplary cases of university–industry interaction in the region. These include National Universities of Litoral, San Martin, and Quilmes in Argentina; the State University of Campinas (Unicamp), the University of São Paulo, and the Federal University of Minas Gerais in Brazil; the University of Concepcion in Chile; the University of Antioquia, the Industrial University of Santander, and the Manizales University System in Colombia;[34] and the Autonomous University of Nueva Leon and the Monterrey Institute of Technology and Higher Education in Mexico.

These success stories share common elements. First, these universities made a strategic decision to pursue interaction with industry and assigned a high priority to this goal—either because this mission was part of their charter or because they deliberately embraced it—even before the national legislative framework was available. Second, they favored a combination of research and entrepreneurship—rather than research alone—on the part of some faculty. Third, they provided physical infrastructure for joint projects with industry—especially to develop incubators. Fourth, they are located in geographic regions with high productive and technological capabilities, where interactions with industry are more likely to take place and succeed. Fifth, they have experimented with alternative arrangements and designed their own policies based on that experience. Box 3.3 discusses three successful cases.

## BOX 3.3 Successful Examples of Knowledge Exchange in LAC

In Argentina, National University of Litoral (UNL) created its Technology Transfer Office (TTO) in 1994, and in 2001 founded the Litoral Centro technological park to incubate technology-based enterprises. Over the last 30 years, many biotechnological companies associated with UNL have been created, including Biosynaptica, Biotecnofe, Celint, Cellargen Biotech, Infira, and Zelltek. Today, the park hosts 25 companies.

These start-ups opened before any institutional framework had been established, as the university produced its own guidelines for the creation of spin-offs only in 2021. According to the guidelines, the UNL can own equity in the companies, as can university researchers—except for those who occupy leadership positions in the institution. In contrast to UNL, another Argentine university, National University of San Martin, does not own equity from its spin-offs and only obtains revenues from intellectual property. Currently, UNL and National University of Buenos Aires hold the largest number of patent families in the country.

In Brazil, the University of Campinas (Unicamp), located in the state of São Paulo, was founded in 1966 as a modern research university. Clarity in this identity, as well as the full administrative autonomy granted by the state of São Paulo to its universities in 1989, have been essential to Unicamp's fast rise from a new university to a top 500 university in the world, according to the Times Higher Education ranking. Unicamp is part of a local ecosystem of innovation and has a strong collaboration with the National Synchrotron Light Laboratory, also located in Campinas and home to the only particle accelerator in South America.

In the late 1990s, Unicamp started developing the model for an innovation agency on campus that would be charged with promoting university–industry interaction. In 2003, Inova was created. Since its inception, Inova has covered three domains: intellectual property; industry partnerships and agreements; and parks and incubators. Its governance is different from that of the rest of the university—its director, for instance, typically comes from the business sector and not academia. Just a few years after its creation, Inova was already a model for other Brazilian universities seeking to innovate under the 2004 Innovation Law's framework and went on to train more than 300 institutions.

The number of patents obtained each year by Inova has risen steadily over time, from 8 in 2010 to 62 in 2015, and 129 in 2021. In 2021, Unicamp's overall patent portfolio

*(Continued on next page)*

**BOX 3.3 Successful Examples of Knowledge Exchange in LAC *(continued)***

reached a peak of 1,276 active patents. Unicamp is currently pursuing projects in the automotive, biotechnology, oil and gas, energy, pharmaceutical, agricultural machinery, chemistry, and health sectors. Most of the funding for these projects comes from tax incentives and benefits, such as the federal Rota 2030 program. As of 2021, Inova alumni had founded 1,131 companies, including unicorns such as Movile.

In Mexico, the Monterrey Institute of Technology and Higher Education (Tecnológico de Monterrey, or Tec) is a private, not-for-profit university founded in 1943. Initially established in Monterrey, it now has 26 campuses across Mexico. While it was founded by a group of local entrepreneurs to expand technological education, it now plays a central role in entrepreneurship, innovation, and knowledge transfer in the country.

Tec operates four technology parks that function as innovation hubs, attracting entrepreneurs, small and medium enterprises, investors, and government institutions, and which have supported about 300 start-ups. Through a deliberate knowledge transfer strategy, Tec helps researchers and entrepreneurs commercialize their technologies, offers incubation services, and provides continuous education and consulting to enhance innovation. For example, Tec has "extension faculty" who work directly with companies to support research and education. Each campus is designed to meet the needs of local companies, such as technology transfer for the tech industry in the Mexico City campus and support to the aerospace cluster in the Queretaro campus. Currently, Tec is developing DistritoTec, a project aimed at transforming the 20-kilometer radius around the Monterrey campus into a high-tech innovation district by integrating academia, industry, and government efforts.

*Sources:* Barletta and Pereira 2024; Ewers 2018; Inova Unicamp Innovation Agency 2022; Knobel and Pedrosa 2016; OECD /IDB 2022; Serrano et al. 2023; www.timeshighereducation.com; for Tec, https://tec.mx/en.

To summarize, over the last 30 years, Argentina, Brazil, Chile, Colombia, and Mexico have developed S&T grants for scientific research, innovation grants for university–industry interaction, and a legal framework for universities to manage intellectual property. They have not, however, designed these grants to promote research excellence or innovation in strategic areas, and have not always evaluated them rigorously. Except for a few cases, most universities continue to reward academic production almost exclusively and discourage faculty members from engaging in knowledge exchange with universities, while maintaining structures and procedures that are ill-suited to innovation and entrepreneurship.

While state funding or regulation could have further encouraged universities to interact with industry, this has not been the case in these countries. Absent such incentives and immersed in a professorial culture that only values research and looks uneasily at the private sector, universities remain separate from industry and innovation, with only a handful of entrepreneurial universities succeeding in this endeavor. Yet even these universities have found an obstacle that towers above all others—the lack of industry demand for their knowledge and services. In other words, companies show no need for what universities can offer. While this might be due to firms' low perception of the quality of university research (as previously described), it might also be due to the underlying patterns of economic activity in these countries—focused on sectors with low value added and little productivity growth.

## Making Education and Science, Technology, and Innovation Policies in LAC More Conducive to Innovation

### Focus on the Desired Skills and Outcomes of Education

The indispensable condition to build innovation capabilities is the presence of educational systems that can effectively produce skills at all levels and for all students.[35] First, these systems must succeed at teaching foundational skills—a student who cannot read or multiply cannot possibly reach the knowledge frontier. While some LAC countries may need to raise their education spending, they all must spend efficiently. For elementary and secondary education, recent evidence indicates that interventions such as structured curriculum and teaching at the right level are not only effective in terms of learning outcomes but are also cost-effective (Akyeampong et al. 2023; Angrist et al. 2023).

Second, countries need higher education systems that are tightly connected with firms to develop skills, produce relevant research, and exchange knowledge with industry. In terms of skills development, higher education institutions must be attuned to industry skills needs and teach not only coded knowledge (such as calculus or economic models) but also cognitive and noncognitive skills such as critical thinking and teamwork. This requires changing what is taught and how it is taught. Innovative engineering schools are providing a blueprint for these changes (box 3.4). Further, countries must choose strategically which skills to promote—countries with a large mining sector, for instance, may want to promote the training of mining engineers and technical workers.

When searching for a job, recent higher education graduates often face the obstacle of their lack of work experience. Lack of experience prevents them from finding a job, which in turn prevents them from accumulating experience—and a vicious circle ensues. One way of breaking this circle—and of teaching valuable skills for the labor market—is to insert outside work into the curriculum. Dual training and co-ops provide useful models to integrate classroom-based and work-based experience. Dual training splits the apprentice's time between the higher education institution and a firm, while co-ops alternate study and work periods. INA's Dual Education (Costa Rica), Formados Corporation (Ecuador), and the Dual Formation Program (Guatemala) provide dual training in LAC. Northeastern University and the University of Cincinnati—among others—provide co-ops in the United States.

LAC countries can promote short-cycle programs, which produce the technical skills required by firms and are a desirable choice for individuals who seek practical, short training.[36] In LAC, labor market outcomes are better for graduates from short-cycle programs that engage more closely with industry and with students' job search (Dinarte-Diaz et al. 2023; Ferreyra et al. 2021).

### BOX 3.4 Innovative Engineering Training in Advanced Economies

In recent decades, various actors in the United States—including the National Science Foundation, engineering schools, and firms—have advocated for changes in engineers' education, arguing that it should include hands-on learning and research opportunities, teamwork and communication skills, and business and managerial training. Changes are underway in individual institutions and across the field of engineering.

For instance, noting that changes had been slow at existing universities, the F. W. Olin Foundation responded by launching a new engineering school in 2002. Located in Needham, Massachusetts, in the tech-heavy Route 128 corridor outside Boston, the Olin College of Engineering has been an active innovator. Olin focuses on hands-on engineering, allowing students to learn as they work on real-world projects, in classes that emphasize team- and project-based work. Thanks to Olin's partnerships with industry, students interact with firms during their studies through semester-long lab projects, industry-sponsored research, and their senior capstone project. Perhaps as a result, almost 40 percent of Olin alumni have been involved in a start-up venture.

*(Continued on next page)*

**BOX 3.4 Innovative Engineering Training in Advanced Economies *(continued)***

Efforts are also occurring around the world. Leading engineering schools in Africa, Asia, Canada, Europe, New Zealand, the United Kingdom, and the United States have responded to the gap between engineering education and the real-world demands on engineers by participating in the Conceive, Design, Implement, and Operate (CDIO) Initiative. CDIO rests on the premise that engineers should be able to CDIO complex engineering systems in team-based environments. It advocates for a rigorous curriculum that includes "CDIO opportunities" whereby students learn to design, build, and test systems.

The CDIO Initiative was developed as a collaborative with input from academics, industry, engineers, and students, and is available for all engineering schools in the world. The collaborative develops syllabi and materials to share among themselves and others. Currently, CDIO is being used in aerospace, applied physics, electrical engineering, and mechanical engineering departments. About 200 universities worldwide are currently participating in CDIO, with Latin America and the Caribbean accounting for about 10 percent of them.

*Sources:* Olin College of Engineering (https://www.olin.edu) and CDIO Initiative (www.cdio.org).

## Build a Pipeline for Top Talent

Several LAC countries devote some of their S&T funds to train top students and researchers. As important as this is, developing top talent must start much earlier—in elementary education—by identifying students with unusual potential and providing them with opportunities to develop their talents, such as attending advanced classes and enrichment activities.[37] Particularly for students of limited means, selective public high schools can provide access to top-quality education and raise the odds of admission into selective higher education institutions, as the experience of the previously selective public high schools in Chile demonstrates.[38] Top elementary and secondary education cannot promote top talent, however, when financial constraints prevent low-income, high-ability students from attending college—a situation that any LAC country seeking to form a large and deep talent pool should clearly avoid. Programs such as the University for All Program (ProUni) in Brazil seek to address this issue through scholarships for low-income students in private higher education institutions. In Colombia, Ser Pilo Paga was a financial aid program targeting high-ability, low-income students.[39] Partnerships between private philanthropists and public institutions can help build the top talent pipeline as well. In Colombia and Peru, the VelezReyes+ Foundation provides scholarships for low-income, high-ability students to study software engineering at top public and private universities and, together with leading tech companies, has developed a tech fellowship and apprenticeship program.[40]

## Shape Education through Information, Funding, and Regulation

To steer the educational system in the direction described, three policy tools can be useful. The first is collecting information and measurement on student outcomes as well as university research and innovation. When society—including parents—see the poor learning outcomes of their schools and children, they are more likely to demand change. When through a public portal a student sees the return to every higher education program offered in her country, she is more likely to choose a high-paying major such as a STEM field. And, when society sees public information on universities' research output, it gains a better sense of their contributions to society and demands accountability. Perhaps two of the most important education reforms enacted in Chile over the last 50 years has been the adoption of test-based assessments for basic education, which began during the 1980s and are still in use today (Fontaine and Urzúa 2018), and the creation of a higher education portal to report academic and labor market outcomes for every program offered in the country.[41]

The second policy tool is funding. First, funding for skills development must be equitable. Higher education funding in LAC is regressive because it favors advantaged individuals to the detriment of others. It also provides higher per student funding to students in bachelor's programs than short-cycle programs—even though students in bachelor's programs have less need of funding because they are more advantaged, on average (Ferreyra et al. 2021). Moreover, quality short-cycle programs often require costly technology. Funding for skills development and research must be strategically allocated to fields of importance to the country's growth.

The third policy tool is regulation. By tapping into the first tool—information and measurement—policy makers can gauge the performance of the educational system and establish outcome-based accountability; based on these outcomes, it can allocate funding and make decisions to open, expand, or close programs. For instance, universities in Denmark sign a performance contract with the central government establishing their objectives and the pay associated with fulfilling them and base their academic offerings on the skill needs of the local business community.[42] This type of system rewards the most effective institutions, which can then grow and serve larger segments of the market. An agile regulator is critical—one that does not stifle innovation by imposing unduly heavy burdens on institutions but encourages innovation and rewards success.

### Promote Research Excellence and University–Industry Interaction

While LAC countries have adopted competitive research grants, these must be more selective and subject to national strategic interests. By defining areas of strategic importance, countries can increase the resources available to areas of national interest. By increasing selectivity, they can make more resources available for large-scale projects. Critically, countries must resist the temptation of using S&T funding as a mechanism to provide basic funding to as many researchers as possible; they must view it, instead, as a mechanism to foster excellence in research. In LAC, a successful example of grants for research excellence was the Millennium Science Initiative (box 3.5).

**BOX 3.5 Creating High-Quality Research Networks in LAC: The Millennium Science Initiative**

In the late-1990s, an initiative began in Chile that quickly spread to other countries: the Millennium Science Initiative (MSI).[a] The MSI is a group of projects, partially funded by World Bank loans, that have sought to promote science and technology (S&T) capacity in several countries by creating competitive grant programs for research. These programs included two tiers. The first awarded short-term, relatively small grants extending over 3–5 years to promising research groups ("nuclei"). The second tier awarded longer-term, larger grants to international-level groups or centers of excellence ("institutes"). With these mechanisms, MSI programs aimed at replicating successful features of the S&T systems in developed countries while funding a limited number of deserving researchers at levels comparable to those in the developed world.

The MSI had its origins at a June 1998 meeting of high-level researchers, government officials, and science policy experts in Santiago, where Chile's then-President Frei helped create the concept. Within a few years, the World Bank had engaged with Brazil, Chile, Mexico, and the República Bolivariana de Venezuela to develop MSI projects. Chile committed to continue the project even after closing the corresponding World

*(Continued on next page)*

**BOX 3.5 Creating High-Quality Research Networks in LAC: The Millennium Science Initiative *(continued)***

Bank loan in 2002; today, it provides funding for 17 institutes and 36 nuclei. These include the Millennium Institutes of Astrophysics, Oceanography, Green Ammonias Energy, Genome Regulation, and Integrative Biology; and the Millennium Nucleii of Invasive Salmonides, Nano Biophysics, and Super Adaptable Plants.[b] Between 2009 and 2014, the MSI in Chile witnessed an increase in research quantity and quality, the training of young researchers, and the development of research networks (Innovos 2015).[c] In Brazil, the MSI lasted until 2008, when it was superseded by a program to support national S&T institutes (World Bank 2005a). In the República Bolivariana de Venezuela, the MSI program had the additional goal of building S&T leadership capacity (World Bank 2005b). In Mexico, the MSI was financed exclusively with public funds that supported four competitively selected institutes until 2004 (Science Initiative Group 2019). A few years after its inception, demand for the MSI had reached Africa; between 2007 and 2013, Uganda ran an MSI program as part of its strategy to strengthen S&T capacity (World Bank 2016).

*Sources:* https://www.iniciativamilenio.cl/en/home_en/; Crawford et al. 2006; Innovos 2015; Science Initiative Group 2019; World Bank 2002, 2005a, 2005b, 2016.

a. This paragraph is based on World Bank (2002).

b. https://www.iniciativamilenio.cl/en/home_en/.

c. Today, the MSI is overseen by ANID (Agencia Nacional de Investigación y Desarrollo de Chile).

Similar considerations apply to the funding of researchers. Lifelong funding to a researcher—akin to granting her tenure—can have detrimental effects on the motivation and effort of researchers. If such a privilege is granted, it should be limited to researchers who have demonstrated superior skills over a reasonable period of time. And, as a previous World Bank report has emphasized (Salmi 2009), a key consideration when pursuing research excellence is the need to be strategic—focusing efforts and resources on excellence in one field or activity rather than aiming at being excellent at everything.

Although several LAC countries have adopted funding incentives to promote university–industry interaction (mostly through innovation grants), these incentives have not fostered new partnerships beyond existing ones. Making those programs more easily accessible to new partnerships is therefore critical. This might require the creation of grants that are smaller and shorter term than the current ones. For countries that do not have them yet, solid intellectual property regulations—establishing, for example, who owns the products developed by universities under public funding—is a priority, as well. Property rights were highlighted in a recent study that examines the experience of 11 universities supporting entrepreneurs in Argentina, Brazil, Chile, Colombia, Mexico, and Uruguay (OECD/IDB 2022). According to the study, those institutions have embedded entrepreneurship in multiple aspects of their operations, including curricula; incentives for faculty, staff, and students; and industry interaction. They teach entrepreneurship to multiple audiences, including science and engineering students, and students seeking to create start-ups or spin-offs. Several of these institutions host accelerators, incubators, and innovation centers; several were attracted to specific locations by local governments seeking to promote entrepreneurship. Still, one challenge facing many of these institutions is that of ambiguous or unfavorable intellectual property regulations at the university or national level.

Financial and regulatory incentives are key to induce universities to participate in the innovation ecosystem. So long as university funding is mostly linked to enrollment, universities will have little incentive to interact with industry. The experience of Finland—where the share of basic funding has declined over time in favor of results-based funding, including knowledge exchange results—is highly instructive in this regard (box 3.6).

### BOX 3.6 Incentives for Increasing University or Private Sector Collaboration in Finland

Though Finland possessed strong social capital as a Nordic country, its innovation reforms in the 1980s focused heavily on shifting the incentives to ensure collaboration with industry. Motivated by the desire to catch up with western Europe, in the 1980s Finland undertook a reform of its science and technology system as part of a comprehensive economic reform aimed at building a more modern, competitive, and dynamic economy. The Science and Technology Policy Council introduced the concept of the National Innovation System and undertook the coordination of multiple policies related to innovation, including those in education, science, and regional development. In addition, it coordinated policies with other areas of government. The Technology Development Center (now the National Technology Agency, Tekes) and the first technology centers (science parks) were established.

University research acquired the specific role of supporting the development of internationally competitive industries. To this end, more funding was channeled

(Continued on next page)

**BOX 3.6 Incentives for Increasing University or Private Sector Collaboration in Finland *(continued)***

to joint university–industry research projects. The new policies clearly established that universities would no longer function in isolation but as an integral part of the National Innovation System and implemented incentives and management practices to ensure it occurred.

In the 1990s, Finland deepened these reforms by adopting the "new public management" policies. These introduced competitive mechanisms, productivity measurement, and performance-based accountability, all toward the goal of enhancing university performance in national innovation. Line-item budgeting (detailing specific expenses such as staff salaries and facilities maintenance) was replaced by lump sum budgeting (assigning total funds rather than their specific allocation), with an emphasis on targeted, competitive, and program-based funding and on multiyear budgeting.

Public resources were increasingly channeled through competitive funding, as opposed to block financing (grants), with a premium placed on cooperation with other universities or industry. In 1993, the government launched a competitive program to identify research centers of excellence, which were then awarded extra financial support. Since 1994, the operational budget for universities has consisted of three blocks (basic, result-based, and project funding). Result-based funding is based on a performance contract that is annually negotiated by the Ministry of Education with individual universities. Over time, the share of block funding has declined while the share of results-based funding has grown.

*Source:* Nieminen and Kaukonen 2001.

## Form Research and Knowledge Exchange Partnerships

In today's world, it is unthinkable for single universities in developing countries to conduct ambitious, large-scale research on their own, though research partnerships—both with domestic and international institutions—can make it possible. In Colombia, the Scientific Ecosystems project (partly financed by the World Bank) provided funding for research consortia as long as these included multiple Colombian universities—of various sizes, prestige levels, and geographic locations—and partner institutions abroad.

In Chile, UC Davis Chile hosts the Life Sciences Innovation Center, established by UC Davis with CORFO's assistance (UC Davis Chile Life Sciences Innovation Center, no date). When it started in 2015, UC Davis Chile was focused on the wine industry. Following an initial trip by representatives of the Chilean government, universities, and industry to UC Davis to learn about the latter's work in viticulture and enology in California, a close relationship was established between UC Davis and a group of Chilean universities and research institutes (Andres Bello University, Development University, Federico Santa Maria University, the Institute of Agricultural Research, Talca University, and Tarapaca University) and private companies. The partnership quickly expanded beyond the wine industry to include agriculture, food supply, and the environment, and has yielded outcomes as varied as new plant disease control mechanisms, improved irrigation management, and successful extension programs. Today, the partnership is exploring issues such as how to promote the adoption of electric and hydrogen vehicles, and how to improve lighting technology.

In many cases, the groundwork for partnerships such as UC Davis Chile may already be in place. The connection between UC Davis and Chile, for instance, started in the mid-1960s, when an agreement was signed to send students and professors from the University of Chile to train at UC Davis. In the short term, this agreement was key to the development of the fruit and wine industry in Chile; in the medium term, it laid the foundation for today's successful partnership at UC Davis Chile.

### Tap the Diaspora

LAC countries have a wealth of human capital embodied in their diaspora, and leveraging the diaspora must be a key ingredient of their growth strategies (World Bank 2024). Tapping the diaspora has been critical to innovation in East Asia and the Pacific countries. In China, the Thousand Talent program has brought back researchers for permanent employment or short-term visits,[43] providing them with salaries and resources comparable to those they would obtain at top foreign universities. Starting in 1994, Malaysia implemented several "brain gain" programs to attract the diaspora and foreign experts with a focus on high-tech industries, including semiconductors and biotechnology (Rasiah, Lin, and Muniratha 2015).

For LAC, the most instructive example from East Asia and the Pacific is probably that of Taiwan, China. Since the 1950s, Taiwan, China attempted several strategies to attract emigrees with skills in strategic industries such as semiconductors, computers, and telecommunications. Providing living accommodations, grants, and professional opportunities had limited success, but a series of actions undertaken since the early 1980s were met with greater success. In the mid-80s, the government of Taiwan, China recruited Morris Chang, VP at Texas Instruments (TI) and responsible for TI's worldwide semiconductor business, as the chairman and president of the Taiwanese industrial research organization, the Industrial Technology Research Institute, which went on to play a key role in the Taiwanese semiconductor industry. Meanwhile, the Technology Advisory Committee, consisting of a Taiwanese diaspora with experience in multinational corporations, was formed to advise the government on global technology trends, and the Hsinchu Science Industrial Park was established in 1980 to incentivize the return of entrepreneurs, including those working in Silicon Valley. Over time, Hsinchu became a globally connected innovation hub; by 1996, more than 2,500 engineers and scientists had returned to work there and had founded 40 percent of the park's companies. While initially focused on entrepreneurship, returnees later became involved in institutional matters and provided policy advice, which the government implemented despite strong local resistance (Kuznetsov 2013; Rasiah, Lin, and Muniratha 2015).

Several LAC countries have adopted diaspora talent programs but very few have sustained them for more than 5 years. Two programs that are still active are Mexico's Talent Network and Argentina's RAICES, which were first implemented in 1991 and 2003, respectively. RAICES seeks to promote the return of Argentine expatriate scientists and covers transportation and moving expenses for the scientist and her family. It also finances short academic visits abroad and promotes scientific networks for Argentine scientists. Although these programs have not been formally evaluated, RAICES is credited with the return of about 1,500 scientists; the extension of research networks; and scientists' assistance in the formulation of S&T policies. Meanwhile, the Talent Network program is credited with the return of about 3,700 scientists to Mexico as of 2017.[44] Unlike RAICES, which does not guarantee a job, Mexico's Talent Network provides returnees with a research position.

Recent diaspora talent programs have been implemented in Peru and Brazil. In Peru, a World Bank operation approved in 2017 to strengthen science, technology, and innovation has sought to expand the pool of scientists by attracting international researchers and Peruvian returnees through generous research grants and research stipends, and by incentivizing them to conduct research in areas of strategic importance.[45] In 2024, Brazil launched the Brazil Saber program to repatriate 1,000 scientists (about 35,000 Brazilian scientists currently work abroad). The program will include research stipends, funding for research infrastructure, and work opportunities to promote research and knowledge exchange.

Through their talent diaspora programs, LAC countries have learned that repatriating or retaining scientists is costly, and that attempting to sustain large-scale, ambitious talent diaspora programs over time often gives rise to "living dead" programs that, while nominally active, are ineffective (Kuznetsov 2006, 2013). Instead, LAC countries may experience greater success by adopting light-touch programs that seek to engage their talent diaspora for specific and well-defined tasks, such as providing guidance on domestic academic or business projects, mentoring faculty and students, and contributing to the discussion of national science, technology, and innovation policies.

Countries can also engage their diaspora indirectly—without specific programs—through the provision of enabling conditions for productive collaborations with the diaspora. India offers an instructive example in this regard. Although India did not have a deliberate diaspora policy in the 1990s, many highly skilled expatriates—including graduates from the Indian Institutes of Technology and the Indian Institutes of Management, in which India had been investing since the 1960s—returned or begun collaborating remotely with locals following the 1990s liberalization of the Indian economy, particularly in the rising IT sector (Kuznetsov 2013; Rasiah, Lin, and Muniratha 2015).

Diasporas do not need to be large to produce an impact. In 1997, Dr. Ramon Garcia, a Chilean applied geneticist and co-founder and chief executive officer of a US-based biotechnology company contacted the Chile Foundation, a private-public entity charged with technology transfer on renewable resources, to explore potential collaborations.[46] These materialized in the founding of three new, co-owned companies to undertake long-term R&D projects and transfer key technology to Chile's rapidly growing agribusiness sector. In 2005, Global Chile, a network of approximately 100 individuals like Dr. Garcia, was established to channel their contributions to Chile's innovation system by providing, for example, mentoring for innovation start-ups and connections with successful Chilean entrepreneurs abroad. Through concrete steps, these diaspora initiatives can grow and eventually transform an entire economic or geographic sector.

Ultimately, the LAC region needs to revamp its educational and S&T systems in ways that are more aligned with the needs of society and industry—an agenda that is as clear today as it was in 2009, when the World Bank first articulated it (Salmi 2009). Box 3.7 explores concrete steps that universities, in particular, might be able to take in that direction.

### BOX 3.7 Seeking Practical Ways to Transform Universities into Engines of Growth

A recent study, *Universities as Engines of Economic Development* (Crawley et al. 2020), offers 11 practices in education, research, and catalyzing innovation to strengthen knowledge exchange between universities and their partners. The practices represent both the goals and needs of the universities and their external partners.

In the case of education, graduates are the biggest driver of knowledge exchange, but political and commercial stakeholders require the right talent that can help them create more jobs and economic prosperity. To make this exchange more efficient and powerful, universities around the world are adapting their educational practices to anticipate and train this talent. For instance, at Aalborg University in Denmark, students routinely split their time between projects and coursework. Mexico's Monterrey Institute of Technology and Higher Education educational model has emphasized real-world problems and skills competency since 2013.

Research is also reimagined under the 11 practices. One practice stresses the importance of collaborative research within and across scientific disciplines—or even rejecting the idea of a discipline as an organizing principle for university research, in favor of solving problems.

Catalyzing innovation is the newest and perhaps most challenging role of universities. Under this role, universities move beyond research to create technologies, business models, health care systems, and other products. The Massachusetts Institute of Technology (MIT) Industrial Liaison Program is one example of catalyzing innovation to guide and share university products with commercial partners. Even at MIT, the appropriateness of the university's role in catalyzing innovation information is challenged by some faculty, although it is precisely the start-ups, patents, new companies, and other impacts of this type of program that has driven regional and national growth.

The 11 practices offer a road map to recreate responsive and effective universities. These, in turn, can be supported by specific practices to transform the university's values and culture; change faculty development, facilities, and governance; and reach out to external partners. The World Bank is currently working with the MIT team to distill the practices into concrete protocols that universities can use to effect change.

*Source:* Crawley et al. 2020.

# ANNEX 3A: Science and Technology Agencies in Latin American and Caribbean Countries

**TABLE 3A.1 Public Government Science and Technology Agencies in Latin America and the Caribbean**

| | | Funding model | | | | | |
|---|---|---|---|---|---|---|---|
| Country | Agency | Projects | Researchers | Education or Training | Groups or Alliances | Description | Website |
| Argentina | CONICET (Consejo Nacional de Investigaciones Científicas y Técnicas) | x | x | x | — | CONICET finances research careers. It selects individuals to become researchers; those who choose a research career receive a monthly stipend and usually work at a university. The career has several rungs, and promotion is based on performance.<br><br>CONICET also finances research projects. To apply for funding, at least one member of the research team must be affiliated with CONICET. CONICET issues calls for Oriented Research Projects (PIO), Projects of Executing Units (PUE), and Multiannual Research Projects (PIP), lasting 2, 5, and 3 years, respectively.<br><br>CONICET offers doctoral and postdoctoral scholarships for Argentine and foreign students. | https://proyectosinv.conicet.gov.ar/ |
| | Agencia I+D+i | x | — | x | x | Agencia I+D+i (previously known as ANPCyT) is an agency within the Ministry of Science, Technology, and Innovation. Its goal is to promote scientific research and productive innovation. Agencia I+D+i runs three funds: the Scientific and Technological Research Fund (FONCYT), aimed at research groups; the Argentine Sectorial Fund (FONARSEC), to strengthen university–industry links; and the Argentine Technology Fund (FONTAR), aimed at companies and research institutions focused on the productive sector. | https://www.argentina.gob.ar/ciencia/agencia |

(Continued on next page)

**TABLE 3A.1 Public Government Science and Technology Agencies in Latin America and the Caribbean *(continued)***

| Country | Agency | Funding model | | | | Description | Website |
|---|---|---|---|---|---|---|---|
| | | Projects | Researchers | Education or Training | Groups or Alliances | | |
| Brazil | CNPq (Conselho Nacional de Desenvolvimento Científico e Tecnológico) | x | — | x | — | CNPq is the country's longest-standing agency promoting science and operates under the umbrella of the Ministry of Science, Technology, Innovation and Communication (MCTIC). It provides funding for scientific and technological research, and for the development of research networks.<br><br>CNPq also provides a range of scholarships, ranging from Junior Scientific Initiation for high school students to Productivity Scholarships in Research for outstanding researchers. It also provides dissertation funding and postdoctoral funding for students and researchers in science and technology. | https://www.gov.br/cnpq/pt-br |
| | FINEP (Financiadora de Estudos e Projetos) | x | — | — | x | FINEP fosters the promotion of science, technology, and innovation in companies, universities, technology institutes, and other public or private institutions. It works under the umbrella of the Ministry of Science, Technology, Innovation and Communication (MCTIC).<br><br>FINEP runs programs for specific regions of Brazil, in conjunction with the regional development banks and state research foundations. It provides subsidies for science, technology, and innovation projects, and subsidized loans. FINEP runs 15 sectoral funds for sectors such as health, biotechnology, agribusiness, petroleum, energy, minerals, aeronautics, space, transport, water, and information technology. It also runs funds that are not sector-specific, including the Green-Yellow Fund, which focuses on university–company interaction, and the Infrastructure Fund, to support and improve infrastructure at technological institutions and companies. | http://www.finep.gov.br/ |

*(Continued on next page)*

**TABLE 3A.1 Public Government Science and Technology Agencies in Latin America and the Caribbean *(continued)***

| Country | Agency | Funding model | | | | Description | Website |
|---|---|---|---|---|---|---|---|
| | | Projects | Researchers | Education or Training | Groups or Alliances | | |
| | CAPES (Coordenação de Aperfeiçoamento de Pessoal de Nível Superior) | — | — | x | — | CAPES operates under the umbrella of the Ministry of Education. Its goal is to expand access to higher education and graduate studies. It finances study and research scholarships in Brazilian and foreign institutions, conference travel, and international collaboration. Most of the funding for graduate programs is devoted to agrarian sciences, administration and accounting, biodiversity, dentistry, engineering, and education. CAPES also fosters the initial and continuing education of basic education teachers. | https://www.gov.br/capes/pt-br |
| Chile | ANID (Agencia Nacional de Investigación y Desarrollo de Chile) | x | — | x | x | ANID (previously CONICIT) finances individual scientific-technological research of researchers with residence in Chile. It also supports students with permanent residence in the country through postgraduate scholarships to study in Chile and abroad. | https://www.conicyt.cl/fondecyt/category/concursos/fondecyt-regular/ |
| | CORFO (Corporación de Fomento de la Producción) | x | — | — | x | CORFO is a public institution responsible for supporting entrepreneurship, innovation, and competitiveness, and strengthening human capital and technological capabilities. | https://www.corfo.cl/sites/cpp/sobrecorfo |
| Colombia | MINCIENCIAS (Ministerio de Ciencia, Tecnología e Innovación) | x | — | x | x | MINCIENCIAS offers financial support through calls for applications to specific research projects, and for the creation and development of research groups.<br><br>It also offers scholarships for PhD studies (including abroad) and postdoctoral positions. | https://minciencias.gov.co/oferta_institucional/programas_proyectos_ctei |

*(Continued on next page)*

**TABLE 3A.1 Public Government Science and Technology Agencies in Latin America and the Caribbean *(continued)***

| Country | Agency | Funding model: Projects | Funding model: Researchers | Funding model: Education or Training | Funding model: Groups or Alliances | Description | Website |
|---|---|---|---|---|---|---|---|
| Costa Rica | CONICIT (Consejo Nacional para Investigaciones Científicas y Tecnológicas) | x | — | x | — | CONICIT seeks to create capabilities in science and technology. It provides funding for a wide array of activities, including graduate and postdoctoral training; basic and applied research projects; experimental or technological development; infrastructure and equipment for centers of scientific excellence; short-term training of researchers; and participation in national and international events, research centers, and research projects. | http://www.conicit.go.cr/ |
| Ecuador | SENESCYT (Secretaria de Educación Superior, Ciencia, Tecnología, e Innovación) | x | — | — | x | SENESCYT provides financial support to research projects through the INÉDITA (Programa Nacional de Financiamiento para la Investigación y Desarrollo Tecnológico) program. It offers funding for programs of multiple durations. | https://www.educacionsuperior.gob.ec/<br>https://www.gob.ec/senescyt<br>https://www.undp.org/es/ecuador/publicaciones/programa-inedita-proyectos-2018-2023 |

*(Continued on next page)*

**TABLE 3A.1 Public Government Science and Technology Agencies in Latin America and the Caribbean *(continued)***

| Country | Agency | Funding model | | | | Description | Website |
|---|---|---|---|---|---|---|---|
| | | Projects | Researchers | Education or Training | Groups or Alliances | | |
| Mexico | CONAHCYT (Consejo Nacional de Humanidades, Ciencia y Tecnología) | x | x | x | x | CONAHCYT supports research careers through the National Researchers System and Researchers for Mexico programs, which provide financial support and an affiliation after a selection process.<br><br>CONAHCYT offers funding for research projects in specific areas through its PRONACES (National Strategic Programs) office, which coordinates the National Research and Advocacy Projects (Pronaii). This funding is available to any researcher, including those not affiliated with CONAHCYT.<br><br>CONAHCYT offers scholarships for PhD and postdoctoral studies. | https://conahcyt.mx/conahcyt/areas-del-conahcyt/desarrollo-cientifico/ |
| Peru | CONCYTEC (Consejo Nacional de Ciencia, Tecnología, e Innovación) | x | — | x | x | CONCYTEC seeks to promote science, technology, and innovation. It is in charge of the Innovation, Science and Technology Fund (FINCyT) and other programs such as ProInnóvate and Prociencia.<br><br>FINCyT was established through the cooperation of the Peruvian government and the Inter-American Development Bank. Its goals are to generate scientific and technological knowledge, promote innovation in companies, strengthen technological research capabilities, and strengthen the national innovation system. | https://www2.proinnovate.gob.pe/<br><br>https://www.proinnovate.gob.pe/noticias/noticias/item/2963-proinnovate-y-prociencia-presentan-programas-de-fondos-para-promover-y-mejorar-la-ciencia-e-innovacion-en-el-pais |

*Source:* Original table for this volume based on agencies' websites (last accessed February 2024).
*Note:* In the "researchers" column, agencies that finance researchers' careers are indicated. "Education or training" refers to funding for scholarships, fellowships, internships, or postdoctoral studies. "Groups or Alliances" refers to groups for joint university–industry research or innovation.

## ANNEX 3B: Robustness Checks for the Association between University Research Quality and University–Industry Interaction Support for R&D

This annex explores whether the positive association between firms' perception of university quality and their research and development (R&D) interaction with firms is robust to the use of alternative measures of university quality (such as research output) and university–industry interaction (such as joint patents). Because this relationship could be driven by GDP per capita, the two figures that follow are conditional on GDP per capita.

The robustness checks find that the positive association continues to hold when using an alternative measure of university–industry R&D interaction—namely, joint university–industry patents. The number of joint patents is indeed lower in countries where the perceived quality of research institutions is lower (figure 3B.1). In LAC, only Brazil, Chile, and Uruguay are (slightly) above average in the number of joint patents; the remaining countries are at or below average. In other words, LAC firms might refrain from interacting with universities out of a sense that the latter have little to contribute due to their low research quality.

Are LAC firms being too negative in their assessment of research quality or the extent of university–industry interaction? If so, the use of self-reported data might exaggerate the negative relationship between research quality and university–industry interaction. Using alternative indicators both for university research quality and university–industry R&D interaction continues to yield a positive association between university research quality and university–industry interaction. Figure 3B.2 shows that, conditional on GDP per capita, countries with higher research quality (as measured by the number of citable documents) have above-average university–industry interaction (as measured by the number of joint university–industry patents). Only one LAC country—Chile—is (slightly) above average in the two dimensions; the remaining LAC countries are clustered in the lower left side of the figure, with relatively low research quality and university–research interaction. This contrasts with other regions, whose countries are more evenly spread around the average, and especially with Sub-Saharan Africa, whose countries are above average in at least one dimension.

**FIGURE 3B.1 The Number of Joint Patents Is Lower in Countries Where the Perceived Quality of Research Institutions Is Low**

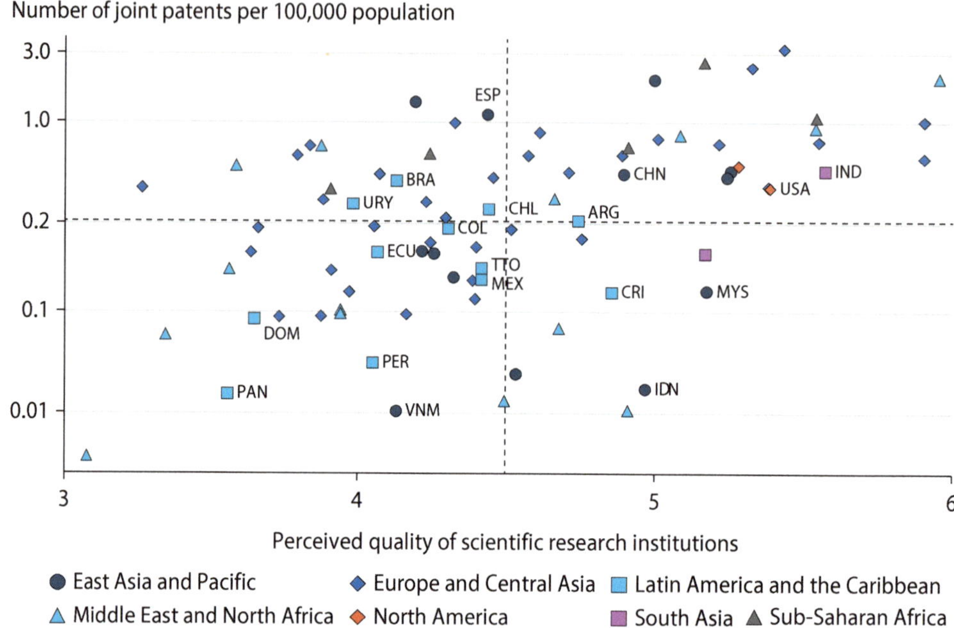


*Sources:* Original figure for this volume using the OECD Patent database based on EPO PATSTAT (https://www.oecd.org/en/data/datasets/intellectual-property-statistics.html), and *The Global Competitiveness Report 2017–2018* (World Economic Forum 2017), based on World Economic Forum Executive Opinion Survey.

*Note:* Each variable is residualized by log GDP per capita (2022) in US$ PPP and recentered at the raw mean. The figure shows the number of patents from university–industry collaborations per 100,000 population by country of inventor using whole counts: that is, the patent is counted fully for each country when it has inventors from multiple countries and the quality of scientific research institutions. Data on patents range from 1969 to 2021. Quality of scientific research institutions is the 2016–17 weighted average answer to the survey question: "In your country, how do you assess the quality of scientific research institutions? [1 = extremely poor—among the worst in the world; 7 = extremely good—among the best in the world]." For country abbreviations, refer to International Organization for Standardization (ISO), https://www.iso.org/obp/ui/#search. GDP = gross domestic product; PPP = purchasing power parity.

**FIGURE 3B.2 Countries with Higher Research Quality Have Above-Average University–Industry Interaction**

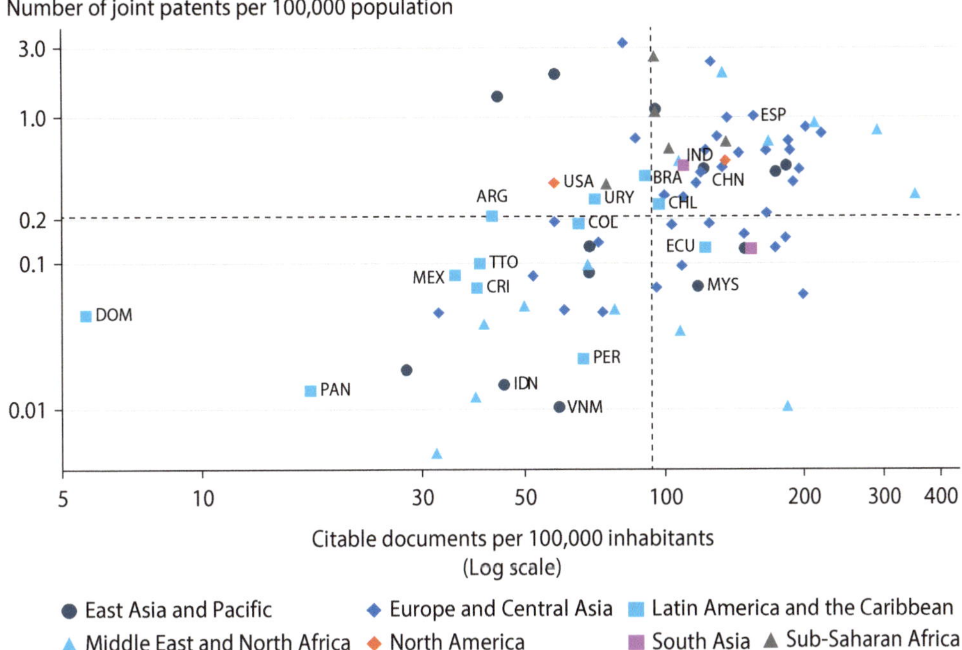


*Sources:* Original figure for this volume using the OECD Patent database based on EPO PATSTAT (https://www.oecd.org/en/data/datasets/intellectual-property-statistics.html), and SCImago Journal Rank (https://www.scimagojr.com/).
*Note:* Each variable is residualized by log GDP per capita (2022) in US$ PPP and recentered at the raw mean. The figure shows the number of patents from university–industry collaborations per 100,000 population by country of inventor using whole counts: that is, the patent is counted fully for each country when it has inventors from multiple countries and the number of citable documents per 100,000 inhabitants. Data on patents range from 1969 to 2021. The figure includes countries with more than 500,000 inhabitants and GDP per capita above US$3,000 PPP. Citable documents correspond to the number of articles, reviews, and conference papers by a country per 100,000 population in 2022. Dashed lines denote sample averages. For country abbreviations, refer to International Organization for Standardization (ISO), https://www.iso.org/obp/ui/#search. GDP = gross domestic product; PPP = purchasing power parity.

## ANNEX 3C: Research Funding and Funding for University–Industry Collaboration from Science and Technology Institutions in Latin America

The two tables that follow, based on original research for this volume, present information on research funding (annex table 3C.1) and funding for university–industry collaboration (annex table 3C.2) from science and technology institutions in selected Latin American countries.

**TABLE 3C.1 Research Funding from S&T Institutions in Latin America, Selected Countries**

| | Research funding—Main program | | | | | |
|---|---|---|---|---|---|---|
| **Country** | **Funding agency** | **Name** | **Annual funding per project (PPP dollars)[a]** | **Duration** | **STEM share of the budget** | **Impact evaluations** |
| Argentina | Agencia I+D+i | FONCYT-PICT | US$59,000 | 2–4 years | 68% | Ghezan and Pereira (2016) |
| Brazil | CNPq (Conselho Nacional de Desenvolvimento Científico e Tecnológico) | Auxilio a Pesquisa—Grupos Emergentes or Grupos Consolidados | US$63,000–US$106,000 | 2–3 years | n/a | n/a |
| | FAPESP (Fundação de Amparo à Pesquisa do Estado de São Paulo)[b] | Projetos Regular and Projetos Temáticos[b] | US$77,000–US$772,000 | 2–5 years | 36% | n/a |
| Chile | ANID (Agencia Nacional de Investigación y Desarrollo de Chile) | FONDECYT | US$121,000 | 2–4 years | 40% | Benavente et al. (2012); Cliodinámica (2021) |
| Colombia | MINCIENCIAS (Ministerio de Ciencia, Tecnología e Innovación) | Investigación Fundamental | US$180,000 | 3 years | n/a | n/a |
| Mexico | CONAHCYT (Consejo Nacional de Humanidades, Ciencia y Tecnología) | Ciencia Basica y de Frontera | US$51,000 | 3 years | 48% | n/a |

*Source:* Barletta and Pereira 2024, based on web sites and interviews.

*Note:* Funding per project corresponds to the maximum value (or range of maximum values, if multiple grant programs are offered) available for research grants. Figures are based on the terms and conditions of the latest call as of March 2024. S&T = science and technology; STEM = science, technology, engineering, and mathematics. n/a = not available; FAPESP = Fundação de Amparo à Pesquisa do Estado de São Paulo.

a. All dollar amounts are in purchasing power parity (PPP) dollars. To make PPP calculations for Argentina, a nominal exchange rate of 1,000 Argentine pesos per dollar was used, as well as the projected 2024 implied PPP conversion rate (the 2023 implied PPP conversion rate was used for the other countries).

b. FAPESP has two programs for funding scientific research; both are included in the table because they are equally valued by the scientific community, and each captures a substantial share of FAPESP's budget. The main difference between them is the projects they focus on: the regular programs (Projetos Regular) focus on curiosity-driven research, while the thematic programs (Projetos Temáticos) focus on topics defined by FAPESP.

**TABLE 3C.2 Funding for University–Industry Collaboration from Science and Technology Institutions in Latin America, Selected Countries**

| Country | Institution | Main program | Description | Funded unit | Modality | Total funding per project (PPP dollars) | Duration |
|---|---|---|---|---|---|---|---|
| Argentina | Agencia I+D+i | Fondos Estratégicos en Alta Tecnología | The program supports partnerships to generate, adapt, and transfer knowledge with high potential impact on the productive sector by enabling public-private collaborative research. | Public-private associative consortium (AC), composed of scientific research institutions and enterprises. | Enterprises provide matching funds | US$7,400,000 (maximum) | 5 years |
| Brazil | FINEP (Financiadora de Estudos e Projetos) | FINEP Conecta | The program aims to bridge the gap between industry and academia by providing subsidized loans for risky but highly innovative projects. Loan terms (such as interest rates, grace period, and loan maturity) depend partly on firm size. | Firm | Subsidized loan | US$1,900,000 | 10–16 years |
| | FAPESP (Fundação de Amparo à Pesquisa do Estado de São Paulo) | PITE (Programa de Apoio à Pesquisa em Parceria para Inovação Tecnológica) | Created in 1995, PITE funds research projects in academic institutions or research institutes, developed in cooperation with researchers from companies and co-financed by these companies. | University or research institution | Research grant | US$965,000 (maximum) | 5 years |
| | | PIPE (Programa Pesquisa Inovativa em Pequenas Empresas) | Created in 1997 and modeled after the Small Business Innovation Research (SBIR) program in the United States, PIPE seeks to finance high-potential research conducted at small companies. | Firm | Research grant | US$384,000 (maximum) | 1–2 years |

*(Continued on next page)*

**TABLE 3C.2 Funding for University–Industry Collaboration from Science and Technology Institutions in Latin America, Selected Countries *(continued)***

| Country | Institution | Main program | Description | Funded unit | Modality | Total funding per project (PPP dollars) | Duration |
|---|---|---|---|---|---|---|---|
| | | Engineering or applied research centers | The program finances engineering research centers (ERCs), or applied research centers, which conduct research in areas of strategic importance to the technological development of the state of São Paulo. ERCs are funded by FAPESP and a partner company for up to 10 years. Each ERC is hosted by a university or research institution. Projects are selected in public calls for proposals issued by FAPESP and partner companies. Partner companies are strongly motivated to help define the research agenda, participate in research, and apply the research findings. | University or research institution | Research grant | US$1,900,000 (maximum) | 10 years |
| Chile | ANID (Agencia Nacional de Investigación y Desarrollo de Chile) | FONDEF | Created in 1991, FONDEF seeks to increase the competitiveness of the national economy by promoting linkages among research institutions, companies, and other entities to conduct applied research and technological development projects of interest to firms and society. Between one and three companies must participate in every project. These business partners must provide funding for at least 30 percent of the grant requested from FONDEF. | University or research institution | Research grant | US$425,000 (maximum) | 2 years |

*(Continued on next page)*

**TABLE 3C.2 Funding for University–Industry Collaboration from Science and Technology Institutions in Latin America, Selected Countries *(continued)***

| Country | Institution | Main program | Description | Funded unit | Modality | Total funding per project (PPP dollars) | Duration |
|---|---|---|---|---|---|---|---|
| | CORFO (Corporación de Fomento de la Producción) | Crea y Valida Colaborativo | The program supports the development of new or improved technology-based products, processes, and/or services. It accompanies the process of validating prototypes at industrial and commercial scale. It creates linkages among the collaborating entities and companies and facilitates knowledge and technology exchanges. | Firm | Matching grant | US$467,000 (maximum) | 2–3 years |
| | | Consorcios Tecnológicos Estratégicos | The program seeks to create alliances for the transfer of knowledge and technology to end-users in small and medium-size enterprises; to build a portfolio of technology development projects that are fully demand-driven; and to promote lines of applied research with a business focus. Technology consortia are collaborative initiatives organized by a specific productive and/or economic sector; they search for technological solutions for their sectors. | Associative consortium (AC) composed of scientific research institutions and companies. Roles within the AC are (1) technology manager (receives the funds); (2) co-executor (at least two); and (3) associates (at least two) that co-finance the project. | Matching grant | US$7,400,000 (average) | 10 years (maximum) |
| Colombia | MINCIENCIAS | Ecosistemas Científicos | The program supports alliances formed by different actors in universities, firms, governments, and the community to promote regional development through research, development, and innovation programs that usually seek to address a specific problem in a set amount of time. | Alliance between universities, research institutions, and firms. | Matching grant | US$3,000,000 (maximum) | 3 years |

*Source:* Original table for this volume.
*Note:* "Funded unit" is the funding recipient. All dollar amounts are in purchasing power parity (PPP) dollars. For the PPP conversion for Argentina, a nominal exchange rate of 1,000 Argentine pesos per dollar was used, and the projected 2024 implied PPP conversion rate was used (the 2023 implied PPP conversion rate was used for the other countries).

## Notes

1. Murmann (2003, 55) on why Germany surpassed Britain.
2. Data for full-time equivalent researchers for 2012–21 [original calculations for this volume, using the Global Innovation Index based on UNESCO Institute for Statistics (UIS); Eurostat database; OECD, Main Science and Technology Indicators (MSTI) database; and Ibero-American and Inter-American Network of Science and Technology Indicators (RICYT)].
3. World Bank Enterprise Survey, using the last year of data available per country.
4. Survey of Adult Skills, using the last year available per country between 2011 and 2017.
5. A country's H-index is the number of publications by authors from the country that have been cited by other authors at least that number of times. For instance, a country's H-index of 20 means that authors from the country have published 20 papers that have each been cited at least 20 times.
6. Original calculations for this volume using the OECD REGPAT patent database, based on EPO PATSTAT.
7. Ferro and Romero (2021) study the efficiency of R&D activities across nations using stochastic frontier methods. They find that LAC is the region with the lowest efficiency, a result that is robust across specifications.
8. Original calculations for this volume based on OECD'S PISA 2022 Database.
9. UNESCO Institute for Statistics, circa 2019.
10. Bianchi and Giorcelli (2019) show that greater access to STEM and vocational and technical programs in Italy in the 1960s led to an increase in patenting. For Finland, Toivanen and Väänänen (2016) find large effects of greater access to engineering master's programs on patenting. On the role of engineers in development and growth, refer to Maloney and Valencia Caicedo (2022).
11. Original calculations for this volume based on UNESCO Institute for Statistics. Comparisons are based on weighted average (over countries) by region.
12. Federico Leloir (Argentina) and Mario Molina (Mexico) received the Chemistry Nobel Prize in 1970 and 1995, respectively; Bernardo Houssay (Argentina), Baruj Benacerraf (República Bolivariana de Venezuela), and Cesar Milstein (Argentina) received the Physiology or Medicine Nobel Prize in 1947, 1980, and 1984, respectively.
13. Original calculations for this volume based on UNESCO Institute for Statistics.
14. On the correlation between basic school quality and parental income or wealth in multiple regions of the world, see, for instance, the *World Development Report 2018* (World Bank 2018).
15. The *World Development Report 2018* (World Bank 2018) documents that, controlling for GDP, there is no association between education spending and learning outcomes across the world.
16. Calculations are for full-time equivalent researchers. RICYT (http://www.ricyt.org/en/category/en/indicators/).
17. RICYT (http://www.ricyt.org/en/category/en/indicators/).
18. Bryan and Williams (2021) discuss these trade-offs.
19. Personal interviews conducted for this chapter.
20. Personal interviews conducted for this chapter.
21. Original calculations for this volume based on World Economic Forum (most recent year available per country).

22. Orduña-Malea (2020), based on Scopus data. Chile leads the region, with 115.5 papers in university–industry collaboration per 1,000,000 people. Uruguay and Brazil follow, with 82 and 62.5 papers, respectively. Most of these collaborations involve technological, pharmaceutical, or oil companies.
23. This paragraph is based on Confraria and Vargas (2019).
24. This section draws on Barletta and Pereira (2024), a background paper for this report. For their paper, the authors interviewed staff and directors of the science and technology and innovation agencies of these five countries. Only national (or federal) agencies were represented in the paper, except for Fundação de Amparo à Pesquisa do Estado de São Paulo (FAPESP) in the state of São Paulo (Brazil), which was included due to its operational volume and widespread impact. The paper reports information as of March 2024. All dollar amounts in this section are in PPP dollars.
25. RICYT for researchers (2021); SCImago for research output (2022); and World Intellectual Property Organization for patents (2020).
26. Information on grants in Europe and the United States is as of March 2024. For NSF, https://nsf-gov-resources.nsf.gov/about/budget/fy2022/tables/st_02.xlsx. For NIH, https://report.nih.gov/nihdatabook/report/155.
27. For NSF, https://nsf-gov-resources.nsf.gov/about/budget/fy2023/pdf/04_fy2023.pdf. For NIH, https://grants.nih.gov/grants/funding/r01.htm. For the European Research Council, https://ec.europa.eu/info/funding-tenders/opportunities/docs/2021-2027/horizon/wp-call/2024/wp_horizon-erc-2024_en.pdf.
28. While science and technology agencies are typically concerned with research in all fields of knowledge, innovation agencies are concerned with the productivity and competitiveness of the economy. They seek to promote investment, innovation, and entrepreneurship, while strengthening human capital and technological capabilities.
29. The governance of a consortium is complex, and it takes time to build trust and effectiveness among all partners. Refer to Barletta and Pereira (2024) and the references therein.
30. Colombia has not adopted such legislation yet, nor has Chile. However, since 2011, Chile's Corporación de Fomento de la Producción (CORFO) has had a program to create and strengthen TTOs in Chilean universities.
31. In the United States, the Bayh-Dole Act gave universities ownership of their inventions made under federal research funding, with universities expected to file for patent protection and economically exploit the patent. Royalties are split among the inventors, the university or department, and the Technology Transfer Office. Refer to https://techtransfer.syr.edu/about/bayh-dole/.
32. https://www.richardspatentlaw.com/faq/how-much-does-a-patent-cost/.
33. In Brazilian universities, for instance, patenting is relatively high, but licensing revenues are low. In some universities, only 10 percent of the patents have been licensed.
34. The system in Colombia includes the Autonomous University of Manizales, Catholic University of Manizales, Luis Amigo Catholic University, National University of Colombia, the University of Caldas, and the University of Manizales.
35. Biasi, Deming, and Moser (2021) review the literature on education and innovation. Bloom, Van Reenen, and Williams (2019) and Van Reenen (2021) discuss human capital policies for innovation.
36. Ferreyra et al. (2021) provide a full discussion of the short-cycle program landscape in LAC and offer policy recommendations.
37. Refer to Fordham Institute (2023) for a discussion of policy options for top-talent development in the United States.

38. Fontaine and Urzúa (2018) provide evidence of the success of selective high schools at placing students into the country's top universities. Admission into these institutions is no longer selective but rather lottery-based.
39. For more information on ProUni, refer to https://acessounico.mec.gov.br/prouni. Londoño-Vélez, Rodríguez, and Sánchez (2020) and Londoño-Vélez et al. (2023) find positive effects of Ser Pilo Paga on enrollment, graduation, likelihood of obtaining STEM degrees, and earnings.
40. For more on VelezReyes+, refer to https://velezreyesmas.com/en/press_release/la-plataforma-filantropica-velezreyes-impulsa-el-futuro-de-las-iniciativas-stem-en-el-caribe/.
41. This portal is mifuturo.cl. For every higher education program taught in the country, the portal shows information such as graduation rate and graduates' employment rate and average salary.
42. Refer to CEDEFOP (2023); Peters et al. (2010); and the sources cited therein.
43. Refer to Shi, Liu, and Wang (2023) and references therein.
44. For more information, refer to https://www.argentina.gob.ar/ciencia/seppcti/raices and https://secihti.mx/becas_posgrados/repatriaciones-y-retenciones/.
45. The project is titled "Strengthening the Science, Technology, and Innovation (STI) System in Peru."
46. This paragraph draws from Kuznetsov (2013).

## References


Adelman, M., and R. Lemos. 2021. *Managing for Learning: Measuring and Strengthening Education Management in Latin America and the Caribbean.* Washington, DC: World Bank.

Akyeampong, K., T. Andrabi, A. Banerjee, R. Banerji, S. Dynarski, R. Glennerster, S. Grantham-McGregor, K. Muralidharan, B. Piper, S. Ruto, J. Saavedra, S. Schmelkes, and H. Yoshikawa. 2023. *Cost-Effective Approaches to Improve Global Learning—What Does Recent Evidence Tell Us Are "Smart Buys" for Improving Learning in Low- and Middle-income Countries?* London, Washington, DC, and New York: UK Federal and Commonwealth Development Office (FCDO), the World Bank, United Nations' Childrens' Fund (UNICEF), and United States Agency for International Development (USAID).

Alvarez, P., J. M. Benavente, and I. Tejeda. 2018. *Formación de Capital Humano Avanzado en Chile.* Santiago, Chile. Unpublished.

Angrist, N., D. K. Evans, D. Filmer, R. Glennerster, F. H. Rogers, and S. Sabarwal. 2023. "How to Improve Education Outcomes Most Efficiently? A Comparison of 150 Interventions Using the New Learning-Adjusted Years of Schooling Metric." Policy Research Working Paper 9450, World Bank, Washington, DC.

Barletta, F., and M. Pereira. 2024. "Governance and Policies to Promote the University–Industry Collaboration in Latin America: The Cases of Brazil, Mexico, Argentina, Colombia, and Chile." Background paper prepared for *Reclaiming the Last Century of Growth: Building Learning Economies in Latin America and the Caribbean*, World Bank, Washington, DC.

Benavente, J. M., G. Crespi, L. F. Garone, and A. Maffioli. 2012. "The Impact of National Research Funds: A Regression Discontinuity Approach to the Chilean FONDECYT." Working Paper 356, Universidad de Chile, Santiago, Chile.

Bianchi, N., and M. Giorcelli. 2019. "Not All Management Training Is Created Equal: Evidence from the Training within Industry Program." *SSRN Electronic Journal* 3457878. https://dx.doi.org/10.2139/ssrn.3457878.

Biasi, B., D. J. Deming, and P. Moser. 2021. "Education and Innovation." NBER Working Paper 28544, National Bureau of Economic Research, Cambridge, MA.

Bloom, N., R. Lemos, R. Sadun, and J. Van Reenen. 2015. "Does Management Matter in Schools?" *Economic Journal* 125 (584): 647–74.

Bloom, N., J. Van Reenen, and H. Williams. 2019. "A Toolkit of Policies to Promote Innovation." *Journal of Economic Perspectives* 33 (3): 163–84.

Braguinsky, S., and D. A. Hounshell. 2016. "History and Nanoeconomics in Strategy and Industry Evolution Research: Lessons from the Meiji-Era Japanese Cotton Spinning Industry." *Strategic Management Journal* 37 (1): 45–65.

Bryan, K. A., and H. L. Williams. 2021. "Innovation: Market Failures and Public Policies." In *Handbook of Industrial Organization*, Vol. 5, No. 1, edited by K. Ho, A. Hortaçsu, and A. Lizzeri, 281–388. Amsterdam: North-Holland.

CEDEFOP (European Centre for the Development of Vocational Training). 2023. "Skills Anticipation in Denmark (2022 Update)|CEDEFOP." CEDEFOP, Thessaloniki. https://www.cedefop.europa.eu/en/data-insights/skills-anticipation-denmark.

CINDA (Centro Interuniversitario de Desarrollo). 2015. *La transferencia de I+D, la innovación y el emprendimiento en las universidades. Educación superior en Iberoamérica–Informe 2015*. Santiago, Chile: Centro Interuniversitario de Desarrollo (CINDA).

Ciocca, D. R., and G. Delgado. 2017. "The Reality of Scientific Research in Latin America: An Insider's Perspective." *Cell Stress and Chaperones* 22 (6): 847–52.

Cirera, X., J. Frías, J. Hill, and Y. Li. 2020. *A Practitioner's Guide to Innovation Policy: Instruments to Build Firm Capabilities and Accelerate Technological Catch-Up in Developing Countries*. Washington, DC: World Bank.

Cliodinámica. 2021. *Evaluación de Resultados e Impacto FONDECYT*. Santiago, Chile: Ministerio de Ciencia, Tecnología, Conocimiento e Innovación. https://observa.minciencia.gob.cl/estudios/evaluacion-de-resultados-e-impacto-fondecyt.

Confraria, H., and F. Vargas. 2019. "Scientific Systems in Latin America: Performance, Networks, and Collaborations with Industry." *Journal of Technology Transfer* 44 (3): 874–915.

Crawford, M. F., C. C. Yammal, H. Yang, and R. L. Brezenoff. 2006. "Review of World Bank Lending for Science and Technology, 1980–2004." Science, Technology, and Innovation Discussion Paper Series 1, 35254, World Bank, Washington, DC.

Crawley, E., J. Hegarty, K. Edström, and J. C. Garcia Sanchez. 2020. *Universities as Engines of Economic Development: Making Knowledge Exchange Work*. Cham, Switzerland: Springer.

de Souza, G. 2023. "R&D Subsidy and Import Substitution: Growing in the Shadow of Protection." Federal Reserve Bank of Chicago Working Paper 2023-37, Federal Reserve Bank, Chicago.

Dinarte-Diaz, L., M. M. Ferreyra, S. Urzúa, and M. Bassi. 2023. "What Makes a Program Good? Evidence from Short-Cycle Higher Education Programs in Five Developing Countries." *World Development* 169: 106294.

Dornelles, J., J. Pertuzé, and D. Epstein. 2018. "Efecto de la relación universidad–empresa en proyectos de I+D sobre las exportaciones de las empresas chilenas." Centro de Innovación, UC-Anacleto Angelini, Santiago, Chile.

Ewers, J. 2018. "Inova Unicamp celebra 15 anos." Inova–Agência de Inovação da Unicamp. https://www.inova.unicamp.br/2018/08/15-anos-de-inovacao/.

Fedit (Federación Española de Centros Tecnológicos). 2021. *#Desafío2027: Hacia un Nuevo Modelo de I+D+I.* Fedit, Madrid. https://fedit.com/wp-content/uploads/2024/12//Informe_Fedit_Desafio2027.pdf.

Ferreyra, M. M., C. Avitabile, J. Botero Álvarez, F. Haimovich Paz, and S. Urzúa. 2017. *At a Crossroads: Higher Education in Latin America and the Caribbean.* Washington, DC: World Bank.

Ferreyra, M. M., L. Dinarte Díaz, S. Urzúa, and M. Bassi. 2021. *The Fast Track to New Skills: Short-Cycle Higher Education Programs in Latin America and the Caribbean.* Washington, DC: World Bank.

Ferro, G., and C. A. Romero. 2021. "The Productive Efficiency of Science and Technology Worldwide: A Frontier Analysis." *Journal on Efficiency and Responsibility in Education and Science* 14 (4): 217–30.

Fontaine, A., and S. Urzúa. 2018. *Educación con patines.* Santiago, Chile: Ediciones El Mercurio.

Fordham Institute. 2023. "Building a Wider, More Diverse Pipeline of Advanced Learners: Final Report of the National Working Group on Advanced Education." Thomas B. Fordham Institute. https://fordhaminstitute.org/national/research/building-wider-more-diverse-pipeline-advanced-learners.

Ghezan, L., and M. Pereira. 2016. *Evaluación de Impacto del Financiamiento de Proyectos de Investigación Científica y Tecnológica.* Centro Interdisciplinario de Estudios en Ciencia, Tecnología e Innovación (CIECTI). https://www.ciecti.org.ar/wp-content/uploads/2016/01/IT1-Evaluación-impacto-PICT.pdf.

Guimón, J., and C. Paunov. 2019. "Science-Industry Knowledge Exchange: A Mapping of Policy Instruments and their Interactions." OECD Science, Technology and Industry Policy Papers, No. 66, OECD Publishing, Paris.

Gurcanlar, T., A. Criscuolo, D. Gomez Gaviria, and X. Cirera. 2021. *Spurring Innovation-Led Growth in Argentina: Performance, Policy Response, and the Future.* International Development in Focus. Washington, DC: World Bank.

Hall, B., A. Link, and J. Scott. 2003. "Universities as Research Partners." *Review of Economics and Statistics* 85 (2): 485–91.

Innovos. 2015. *Servicio de consultoría para la elaboración del estudio de productividad científica de los centros del programa iniciativa científica milenio.* Subsecretaria de Economia y Empresas de Menor Tamaño, Milenio. https://www.iniciativamilenio.cl/wp-content/uploads/2017/11/ESTUDIOS-DE-PRODUCTIVIDAD.pdf.

Inova Unicamp Innovation Agency. 2022. *Annual Report of the Inova Unicamp Innovation Agency.* Campinas, Brazil: State University of Campinas. https://www.inova.unicamp.br/wp-content/uploads/2022/09/Annual-Report-Inova-Unicamp-2021.pdf.

Knobel, M., and R. Pedrosa. 2016. "The Challenge of Building a Research University." *University World News.* https://www.universityworldnews.com/post.php?story=20160501081123822.

Kuznetsov, Y. 2006. *Diaspora Networks and the International Migration of Skills: How Countries Can Draw on Their Talent Abroad.* WBI Development Studies Series. Washington, DC: World Bank.

Kuznetsov, Y. 2013. *How Can Talent Abroad Induce Development at Home? Towards a Pragmatic Diaspora Agenda.* Washington, DC: Migration Policy Institute.

Larsen, K., D. C. Bandara, M. Esham, and R. Unantenne. 2016. *Promoting University–Industry Collaboration in Sri Lanka: Status, Case Studies, and Policy Options.* Directions in Development–Human Development. Washington, DC: World Bank.

Lee, K.-R. 2014. "University–Industry R&D Collaboration in Korea's National Innovation System." *Science, Technology, and Society* 19 (1): 1–25.

Link, A. N., and J. T. Scott. 2009. "The Role of Public Research Institutions in a National Innovation System: An Economic Perspective." Working Paper, World Bank, Washington, DC.

Londoño-Vélez, J., C. Rodríguez, and F. Sánchez. 2020. "Upstream and Downstream Impacts of College Merit-Based Financial Aid for Low-Income Students: Ser Pilo Paga in Colombia." *American Economic Journal: Economic Policy* 12 (2): 193–227.

Londoño-Vélez, J., C. Rodriguez, F. Sánchez, and L. E. Álvarez-Arango. 2023. "Financial Aid and Social Mobility: Evidence from Colombia's Ser Pilo Paga." NBER Working Paper 31737, National Bureau of Economic Research, Cambridge, MA.

MacLeod, W. B., and M. Urquiola. 2021. "Why Does the United States Have the Best Research Universities? Incentives, Resources, and Virtuous Circles." *Journal of Economic Perspectives* 35 (1): 185–206.

Maloney, W. F., and F. Valencia Caicedo. 2022. "Engineering Growth." *Journal of the European Economic Association* 20 (4): 1554–94.

Mas Verdú, F. 2021. "Transferencia de conocimiento e intermediarios de innovación." *Papeles de Economía Española* 169: 104–18.

Murmann, J. P. 2003. *Knowledge and Competitive Advantage: The Coevolution of Firms, Technology, and National Institutions.* Cambridge, UK: Cambridge University Press.

Nieminen, M., and E. Kaukonen. 2001. *Universities and R&D Networking in a Knowledge-Based Economy: A Glance at Finnish Developments.* Sitra Report Series 11. Helsinki: Sitra.

OECD/IDB (Organisation for Economic Co-operation and Development/Inter-American Development Bank). 2022. *Innovative and Entrepreneurial Universities in Latin America.* OECD Skills Studies. Paris: OECD Publishing.

Orduña-Malea, E. 2020. "Do Latin American Universities Engage Industry in Scientific Publication? A Bibliometrics Approach through Scopus." *Palabra Clave* 10 (1): 100.

Peters, M., K. Meijer, E. van Nuland, T. Viertelhauzen, and E. Sincer. 2010. *Sector Councils on Employment and Skills at EU Level.* Rotterdam: ECORYS Nederland BV in Cooperation with KBA for the European Commission.

Rasiah, R., Y. Lin, and A. Muniratha. 2015. "The Role of the Diaspora in Supporting Innovation Systems: The Experience of India, Malaysia and Taiwan." In *Emerging Economies: Food and Energy Security, and Technology and Innovation*, edited by P. Shome and P. Sharma, 353–73. New Delhi: Springer.

Salmi, J. 2009. *The Challenge of Establishing World-Class Universities.* Directions in Development: Human Development. Washington, DC: World Bank.

Science Initiative Group. 2019. *MSI Projects.* https://sig.ias.edu/msi/initiatives.html.

Serrano, R., J. Varisco, M. Morzán, J. Damiani, E. Martínez Calvo, and F. Terentino. 2023. *Actividad de patentamiento en el sistema universitario argentino: Investigación, desarrollo e innovación.* University Patenting Report 2023. Universidad Nacional del Litoral, Santa Fe, Argentina.

Shi, D., W. Liu, and Y. Wang. 2023. "Has China's Young Thousand Talents Program Been Successful in Recruiting and Nurturing Top-Calibre Scientists?" *Science* 379 (2023): 62–5.

Tello, C., F. Magna, S. González, M. Fulgueiras, J. Parra, F. Torres, and A. Zahler. 2022. *Qué fortalecer y hacia dónde orientar los esfuerzos en Investigación Aplicada y Desarrollo Tecnológico por medio de FONDEF.* https://observa.minciencia.gob.cl/estudios/que-fortalecer-y-hacia-donde-orientar-los-esfuerzos-en-investigacion-aplicada-y-desarrollo-tecnologico-por-medio-de-fondef.

THE (Times Higher Education). 2020. *University Industry Collaboration: The Vital Role of Tech Companies' Support for Higher Education Research.* Times Higher Education. https://www.timeshighereducation.com/sites/default/files/the_consultancy_university_industry_collaboration_final_report_051120.pdf.

Toivanen, O., and L. Väänänen. 2016. "Education and Invention." *Review of Economics and Statistics* 98 (2): 382–96.

UC Davis Chile Life Sciences Innovation Center. No date. *5-Year Report.* University of California, Davis. https://chile.ucdavis.edu/sites/g/files/dgvnsk4826/files/inline-files/UC%20Davis%20Chile%205year%20report_English.pdf.

Van Reenen, J. 2021. "Innovation and Human Capital Policy." NBER Working Paper 28713, National Bureau of Economic Research, Cambridge, MA.

World Bank. 2002. "Implementation Completion Report on a Loan to Chile: Millennium Science Initiative." World Bank, Washington, DC. https://documents1.worldbank.org/curated/en/187371474636135095/pdf/000020051-20140607171016.pdf.

World Bank. 2005a. "Implementation Completion Report on a Loan to Brazil: Science and Technology Reform Support Project—PADCT III." World Bank, Washington, DC. https://documents1.worldbank.org/curated/en/677451468770146179/pdf/31601.pdf.

World Bank. 2005b. "Implementation Completion Report on a Loan to the Bolivarian Republic of Venezuela: Millennium Science Initiative." World Bank, Washington, DC. https://documents1.worldbank.org/curated/en/666381468130818368/pdf/317310rev.pdf.

World Bank. 2016. "Project Performance Assessment Report: Uganda Millennium Science Initiative." World Bank, Washington, DC. https://ieg.worldbankgroup.org/sites/default/files/Data/reports/ppar_uganda2016.pdf.

World Bank. 2018. *World Development Report 2018: Learning to Realize Education's Promise.* Washington, DC: World Bank.

World Bank. 2023. *World Development Report 2023: Migrants, Refugees, and Societies.* Washington, DC: World Bank.

World Bank. 2024. *World Development Report 2024: The Middle-Income Trap.* Washington, DC: World Bank.

World Economic Forum. 2017. *Global Competitiveness Report 2017–2018.* Cologny/Geneva: World Economic Forum.

# New Firms, New Sectors: Creating Experimental Economies and High-Quality Entrepreneurship

4

*"At any moment in time, we're really just laying a whole bunch of bets."*

—Stefanie Tompkins, Director, US Defense Advanced Research Projects Agency (DARPA)[1]

## Introduction

It is not only the low rate of technological uptake and use by existing firms discussed in chapter 2 that poses an "innovation paradox." Given the potential high returns to technological adoption, an ample cadre of aspiring entrepreneurs should be expected to emerge in developing countries to exploit the possibilities of catch-up. But as chapter 1 showed, this has not been the case historically, and it is not the case now. This chapter documents the entrepreneurial side of the innovation paradox: what factors explain the low number of capable entrepreneurs in Latin America and the Caribbean (LAC) (and developing countries more generally), given the available technological opportunities. It then offers a simple framework for thinking about why this might be so, comprising factors in both the operational environment and those relating to the quality of entrepreneurs.

## Entrepreneurship as Experimentation

While technological adoption by incumbent firms is a critical contributor to growth and job creation, the entry of new firms is arguably the more important channel of national learning and the process of creative destruction that drives growth. The entry of more productive firms and exit of less productive firms account for 25 percent of productivity growth in the United States (Foster, Haltiwanger, and Krizan 2001), but 72 percent in China (Brandt, Van Biesebroeck, and Zhang 2012). In Colombia from 1993 to 2012, about 50 percent of productivity growth occurred through this channel, and in Chile from 1996 to 2006, almost 65 percent (Cusolito and Maloney 2018). In Chile, the entry of more productive firms contributes up to half of growth in periods of high growth (Asturias et al. 2023). The literature suggests shows that job growth in the United States is disproportionately driven by new firms.[2]

Entrepreneurship is fundamentally a process of experimentation. The success of a start-up that introduces a new product, process, or technology, even if established abroad, is fundamentally uncertain. Hence, a well-functioning entrepreneurial ecosystem is one that is populated by individuals who are open to and can perceive new opportunities and are able to manage the risk associated with technological arbitrage over an extended period of time, as well as a regulatory framework and set of institutions that support their efforts. Truly big bets—the internet, global positioning systems, weather satellites, COVID-19 vaccines, drones—are often placed by heavily resourced coordinators like the United States Defense Advanced Research Projects Agency (DARPA), but the great bulk of productivity increasing innovation is by new private sector ventures.

However, in developing countries in general, the contribution of entering firms to growth relative to incumbents is lower than in high-income countries due to the lower productivity of entering firms, suggesting deficiencies on both fronts. A sample of firms from the World Bank Firm-level Adoption of Technology survey suggests that in advanced economies, entrants have similar levels of labor productivity as incumbents (consistent with Foster, Haltiwanger, and Syverson 2008) in the United States for a revenue-based measure of total factor productivity (TFPR), but because incumbents frequently lower prices to enter markets, the actual physical efficiency (quantity-based total factor productivity, or TFPQ) is higher (Haltiwanger, Jarmin, and Miranda 2013).[3] In developing countries, entrants appear to have lower labor productivity than incumbents (figure 4.1). That is, the high level of business churning—the entry and exit of firms—is not translating into an increase in national learning that would sustain productivity increases and fuel growth.

**FIGURE 4.1 Differences in Labor Productivity between Entrants and Incumbents Are Large in Developing Countries**

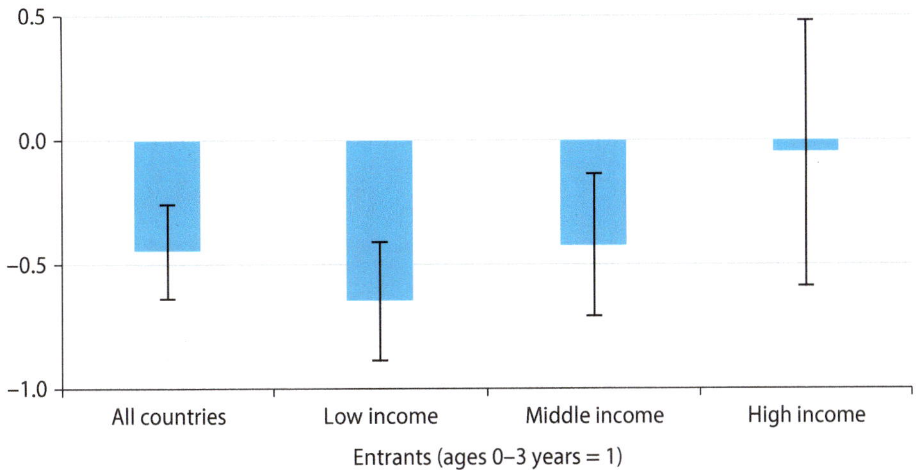


*Sources:* Original figure for this volume based on Cirera and Ding, forthcoming, and World Bank Firm-level Adoption of Technology survey data.
*Note:* The figure shows the labor productivity premium of entrants by income level and controlling for country-sector fixed effects. Entrants are firms between 0 and 3 years old.

## Is LAC, in Fact, Entrepreneurial? Density versus Quality of Entrepreneurship

This finding is a bit puzzling given that Latin America ranks high on entrepreneurship ratings—getting high marks, for instance, in the Global Entrepreneurship Monitor (GEM)—and a larger share of the workforce is employed in entrepreneurial activities than would be predicted by the level of development (Cusolito and Maloney 2018, chapter 4). However, in advanced economies, the growth rate distribution of young firms is highly skewed, suggesting that growth is not driven by the overall quantity of new firm activity, but rather by a smaller subset of more sophisticated start-ups, often driven by innovation (Botelho, Fehder, and Hochberg 2021; Decker et al. 2014; Haltiwanger, Jarmin, and Miranda 2013). The GEM data set includes the 40 percent share of the workforce in developing countries, on average, that engages in low-productivity self-employment or works in microfirms that engage in unproductive churning rather than technological arbitrage. The share of the workforce dedicated to these types of firms decreases steadily with development, suggesting that the absence of more attractive salaried jobs, rather than true entrepreneurial opportunity, is the driver (Maloney 2004).

By contrast, the share of the workforce that is self-employed and has a tertiary degree, and the share of tertiary educated workers who are entrepreneurs, rises steeply with development—the opposite of what would be expected given the technological gaps and hence abundant opportunities for technology arbitrage in developing countries. This pattern suggests various types of economic and social barriers to high-quality entrepreneurship. Figure 4.2 shows that in terms of new modern "registered" firms per 1,000 people ages 15–64, LAC, at 3.2, substantially underperforms most other regions, falling well behind Europe and Central Asia (4.5) and—especially—East Asia and Pacific (6.5). It also lags middle-income countries (3.3), the world average (3.5), and upper-middle-income countries (6.3).

Taking a narrower focus on technology-based firms, the number of start-ups has increased dramatically, but their density remains low. The Inter-American Development Bank counted 1,005 technology start-ups in LAC in 2021 that had raised more than US$1 million each, along with a number of larger *technolatinas*[4] whose total value grew from US$7 billion to US$221 billion over the past decade (Peña 2021). The region has also experienced a dramatic rise in unicorns—firms with capitalization of more than US$1 billion—from 4 in 2018 to 52 in 2022. While this is good news, New York City alone is home to 9,000 tech start-ups worth more than US$189 billion (Teare 2022; Tech:NYC 2024). The low value of LAC unicorns as a share of gross domestic product (GDP) (1.4 percent) is above only one other region: Sub-Saharan Africa (Rudolph, Miguel, and Gonzalez-Uribe 2023).

**FIGURE 4.2 The Density of New Businesses Is Low in LAC**

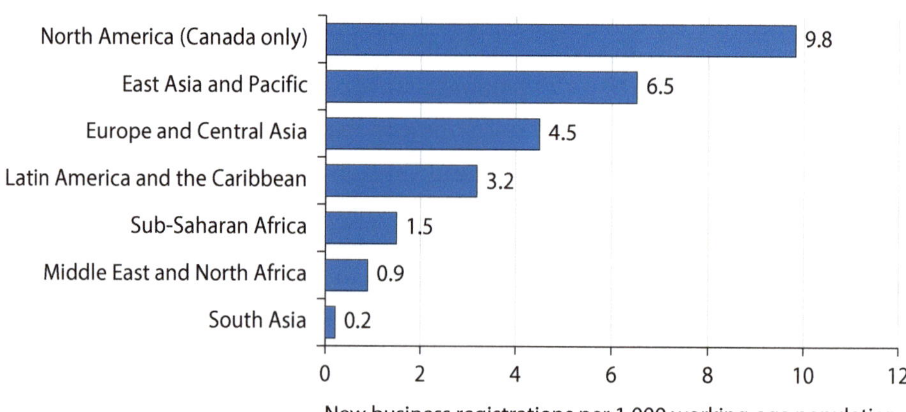


*Sources:* Original figure for this volume based on World Bank Group Open Data (https://data.worldbank.org/) and World Bank Entrepreneurship Database (https://www.worldbank.org/en/programs/entrepreneurship).
*Note:* The indicator reflects new business registrations per 1,000 people between ages 15–64. All data are from 2020, except for data for Haiti (2010); the Republic of Korea (2016); and Argentina, Bolivia, and the Dominican Republic (2018). LAC = Latin America and the Caribbean.

In sum, as Lederman et al. (2014) note, LAC has a lot of entrepreneurship but little innovation. This is somewhat strange because the region has long-established multinational technology industries and respectable technological universities (for instance, in Guadalajara, Mexico; refer to box 4.1). It makes us ask, what is going wrong?

### BOX 4.1 Why Don't Engineers Become High-Tech Entrepreneurs in Guadalajara?

Given the long experience of Mexican engineers working in high-tech companies, why aren't there more high-tech entrepreneurs in Guadalajara? A survey of 412 engineers working in Guadalajara and 408 faculty members within a major engineering university reveals a set of three factors: less willingness to become an entrepreneur; multiple perceived obstacles to venturing; and the unsupportive environment and employment situation.

*Less willingness to become an entrepreneur.* Only 30 percent of engineers and 37 percent of faculty perceived opportunities for entrepreneurship, while an even smaller share—6 percent of engineers and 13 percent of faculty—intended to start a business within 3 years. Fear of failure is high, cited by 78 percent of engineers and 53 percent of faculty. The perception of risk is similarly high, with 87 percent of engineers and 70 percent of faculty citing risk as an obstacle to starting a business venture.

*Deficient entrepreneurial skills or capital.* Only 35 percent of engineers and 45 percent of faculty think they can open a firm with the technical knowledge they have. While 36 percent of engineers and 38 percent of faculty believe they have the required skills and knowledge to start a company, only 14 percent of engineers and 28 percent of faculty believe they have the necessary entrepreneurial acumen and the practical ability to understand various business scenarios, can exercise sound judgment, and can cope with challenges that lead to a good outcome to start a tech venture. As noted in chapter 1, a lack of the ability to process information about opportunities can lead to behavior that is observationally equivalent to risk aversion.

*High opportunity costs.* Another reason hindering business creation is the existing job responsibilities that constrain potential entrepreneur's time, focus, and resources. More than 80 percent of the participants concurred that they are focused on keeping their jobs and did not intend to start a venture. Four out of five engineers felt overworked and stressed; as a result, participants emphasized not being able to start a business.

*(Continued on next page)*

**BOX 4.1 Why Don't Engineers Become High-Tech Entrepreneurs in Guadalajara? *(continued)***

**Deficiencies in the Enabling Environment**

Interviewees identified several deficiencies in the enabling environment.

*Lack of capital.* More than 89 percent of participants cited the lack of capital as an obstacle. This was the top obstacle cited, although the shortfall may be exaggerated by the reported low levels of confidence in financial literacy.

*Weak networks and support.* More than 80 percent of the participants identified a lack of formal support and a lack of assistance for business viability as an obstacle to starting a venture. In addition, 80 percent of the engineers stated that the lack of family support impedes venturing.

*Government and macro impediments.* Participants complained about bureaucracy, paperwork, and the difficulty of opening a business.

*Inhospitable macroeconomic environment.* Some 75 percent of faculty and 57 percent of practitioners cited the current economic situation as a barrier for starting a venture.

*Source:* Garcia Sanchez 2024.

## Drivers of Technological Entrepreneurship and the Entrepreneurial Ecosystem

The lack of high-quality entrepreneurship in LAC suggests the need for an entrepreneurial ecosystem that can generate and support a larger mass of entrepreneurs, the kind of risk-taking firms that are likely to arbitrage existing knowledge, create new knowledge, and leverage it for growth.[5] As figure 4.3 describes, the drivers of growth (technology adoption) are some function of the environment—and hence the overall returns from entrepreneurship, as well as underlying entrepreneurial capabilities to take advantage of it. The enabling environment affects the return to entrepreneurship and the availability of necessary complementary factors, as well as the costs of experimentation (including ease of information flows, institutional and legal barriers or support, and financing and the ability to diversify risk) and the cost of failure (including ease of liquidation or

**FIGURE 4.3 Drivers of Technological Arbitrage**

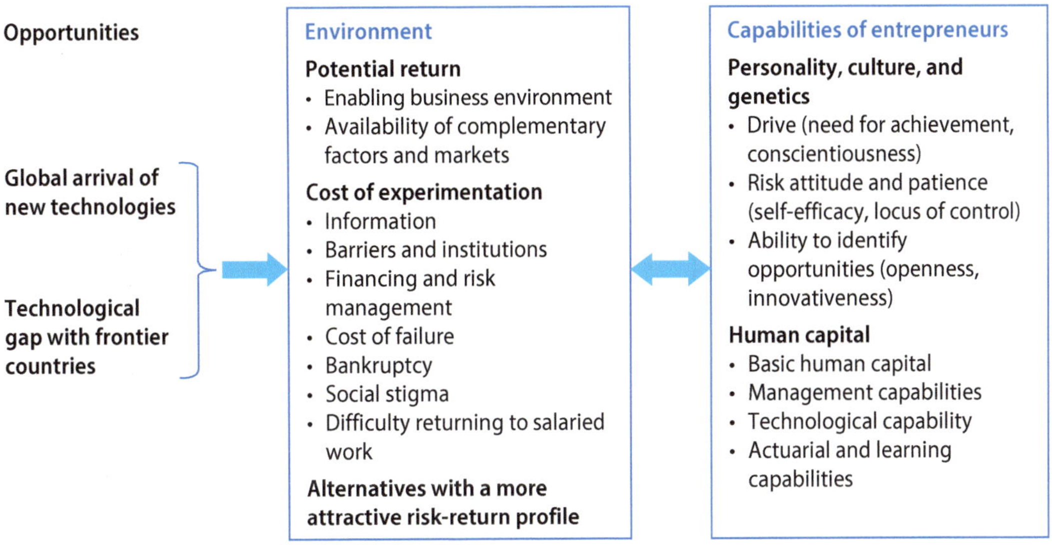

*Source:* Cusolito and Maloney 2018.

bankruptcy, social stigma, and the difficulty of rejoining the salaried work force). Finally, the presence of alternatives with a more attractive risk-return profile—ranging from real estate investment to rent seeking—can divert entrepreneurial energies. Without a suitable enabling environment, capable entrepreneurs will be unable to enter the market or succeed if they do.

However, dynamism will be limited in even the best regulatory environment without capable entrepreneurs. Studies of entrepreneurial personality have enjoyed a resurgence, partly as a result of radical increases in data, and partly due to a 21st-century fascination with start-up culture, as Kerr, Kerr, and Xu (2017) argue. This resurgence has occurred jointly with the focus on behavioral economics (Astebro et al. 2014), psychology, and advances in the study of management quality (Bloom, Bond, and Van Reenen 2007).

## Are Entrepreneurs Born or Made? Cultivating Knowledge-Intensive Entrepreneurship as Part of National Learning

The experimentation process intrinsic to entrepreneurship requires a set of skills that, as chapter 1 argues, have been historically absent from the LAC region: the ability to use information; the willingness to take on and manage risk; and the ability to learn from the experimentation process and to become better learners over time. A more psychologically oriented literature focuses on several entrepreneurial characteristics such as drive or grit (including aggressiveness and proactivity, autonomy, and innovativeness), risk attitude and patience, and openness to new opportunities—all of which are related to exploiting technological opportunities. Underlying these are psychological traits affecting, for instance, attitudes toward risks. "Self-efficacy" describes a person's belief that he or she can perform tasks and fulfill a role. It is directly related to expectations, goals, and motivation (Cassar, Friedman, and Schneider 2009). "Locus of control" is the degree to which people believe that they have control over the outcome of events in their lives, as opposed to external forces beyond their control. Box 4.1 suggests that these characteristics emerge as part of the reason for disappointing rates of technological entrepreneurship in Guadalajara. Though studies of entrepreneurial behavior of separated twins suggest some possible genetic component ("nature") behind these characteristics, the literature overall puts a greater weight on "nurture"—how agents learn to be modern entrepreneurs.[6] Culture looms large in the literature on entrepreneurship,[7] ranging from attitudes toward child raising (Cramer et al. 2002; Kihlstrom and Laffont 1979; Van Praag and Cramer 2001) to Latin America's anti-entrepreneurial inheritance from Rome via Spain (Baumol 2010). The "lazy hacendado" trope is frequently invoked in diagnoses of LAC's historical performance (Maloney and Zambrano 2022).

But in practice, the line between culture, institutions, and education broadly considered blurs. It is hard to distinguish a psychological aversion to risk from an absence of "entrepreneurial capital"—the ability to use existing information to correctly evaluate the risk profile of a new opportunity, and then to confidently exploit it. The examples of Antioquia, Colombia, and Brazil in chapter 1 suggest that whatever the inherited colonial cultural characteristics, for a period they were overcome, largely by building human capital and supporting institutions.

The notion that these deeper entrepreneurial skills can be taught is backed by increasing evidence. The largest determinant of entrepreneurship is whether a parent, especially an adoptive parent, was an entrepreneur, suggesting a transmission of attitude or skills (Akcigit and Goldschlag 2023a). This also suggests that countries without an established tradition of transformational entrepreneurship need to deliberately cultivate one, and recent studies suggest they can. Programs targeted at youth, such as Skills for Effective Entrepreneurship Development (SEED) evaluated in Uganda, have shown that teaching both hard skills (such as accounting, finance, economics, marketing, and so on) and soft skills (such as negotiation, persuasion, grit, emotional regulation, and so on) to varying degrees have led to higher self-efficacy, more start-ups, and higher earnings in developing country settings (Chioda et al. 2023).[8]

US management training programs in World War II led to a rise in the share of participants starting new firms (Giorcelli 2023). In Mexico, 1 year of managerial consulting services led to an increase in "entrepreneurial spirit" (an index that measures entrepreneurial confidence and goal setting) and a 50 percent increase in firm size (Bruhn, Karlan, and Schoar 2018). In the Dominican Republic, beneficiaries of random lotteries for government contracts to manage construction projects were more likely subsequently to be owners of formal firms and less likely to be private sector employees, and their firms were more likely to hire and survive (Pecenco, Schmidt-Padilla, and Taveras 2020). The vast majority of managers overseeing LAC's unicorns had previous entrepreneurial experience. Programs like Start-Up Chile precisely tried to "change the chip" of the country to be more open to entrepreneurship, with some success (refer to the discussion later in the chapter).

But chapter 3 also stresses that the lag in formal education, both in coverage and quality, limits the pool from which potential entrepreneurs of all kinds can be drawn. Though the share of tertiary graduates in the LAC population (19 percent) is at the global average, it is lower than the shares in both East Asia and Pacific and Europe and Central Asia, and in particular of the member countries of the Organisation for Economic Co-operation and Development (OECD) (39 percent) (OECD 2017, 203). Only about 20 percent of students from Brazil, Colombia, and Mexico major in science, technology, engineering, and mathematics (STEM) fields compared to more than 60 percent of undergraduate and graduate students from India and the Islamic Republic of Iran. This might not seem critical given that most unicorn founders majored in Economics and Business Administration (42 percent), followed by Engineering (22 percent) and Computer Science (20 percent). Moreover, most founding teams (60 percent) have at least one member with a master's degree in business administration, suggesting the need for standard business skills. However, most unicorns are found in fintech industries (35 percent) followed by e-commerce and direct-to consumer (23.1 percent); supply chain, logistics, and delivery (9.6 percent); and internet software and services (9.6 percent): mostly sectors that require relatively little technical investment, in which an administrative background, rather than a technical one, may be more appropriate. Sectors ranging, for instance, from biomedicine to artificial intelligence (AI) to electric vehicles to green technologies that are among the fast-growing sectors in both developing countries and advanced economies will require much more intensive use of STEM skills—and LAC is largely absent from these fields.

This said, it is unlikely that simply training more engineers and scientists will suddenly lead to the region entering these fields. The frustrating mystery of Guadalajara is that it prides itself on several excellent engineering programs, and the presence of a multitude of high-tech multinationals where on-the-job experience is available, yet there has not yet been an explosion of national high-tech engineers. Interviews summarized in box 4.1 suggest core psychological or cultural factors, deficient entrepreneurial or managerial skills, and high opportunity costs of giving up their current attractive alternatives to pursue entrepreneurship. Some of these problems can be remedied by teaching business skills. But several major impediments persist in the enabling environment, ranging from deficient capital to lack of support mechanisms to government impediments. These factors should be viewed as merely a list of possible candidates; the relative importance of each item needs to be investigated, and the relevant locality—whether city or state—needs to be engaged precisely in that activity.

## Reducing and Managing the Cost of Experimentation

While attitudes and entrepreneurial culture are critical for technological entrepreneurship, entrepreneurial decisions also depend on the costs of experimentation. When costs are high, the risks are also high, which works as a deterrent to generate new ventures. Several factors can reduce or help manage the costs of experimentation arising from technological entrepreneurship.

### *Cost of Information*

Experimentation requires, to begin, information about potential technological arbitrage or, in the case of new-to-the-world ideas, close familiarity with the existing related knowledge. This aspect offers a plausible explanation of why, with similar initial technological abilities and institutions, Spain, as proximate to and part of the technologically advanced European Union, has caught up so much faster than LAC

### *Connectivity*

Clearly, connectivity and the ability to connect through newspapers, electronic journals, online conferences, and other means dramatically reduces the costs of gaining at least a superficial knowledge of where the technological frontier is relative to 30 years ago. Barriers to fully "wiring" parts of LAC remain (Beylis et al. 2023; World Bank 2016).

***Proximity to Universities***

A deeper understanding and ability to manage these technologies is necessary, and the more specialized mechanisms for spotting and refining new ideas are in the universities that historically have been the facilitators of national learning (box 4.2). The United States' leveraging of copper as a basis of growth was made possible by the establishment of mining programs at the University of California, Berkeley and Columbia University, as well as the Colorado School of Mines. The entrepreneurial success of Antioquia, Colombia, was anchored in the School of Mines patterned after Berkeley's. Major high-tech entrepreneurial hot spots, such as Silicon Valley and Route 128 near Boston, are anchored by world-class research universities—Berkeley and Stanford in the former case, and Harvard and MIT in the latter. Numerous studies, including those for Brazil and China, similarly find that high-tech entrepreneurship is highest in locales with strong universities (Fischer, Queiroz, and Vonortas 2018; Lai and Vonortas 2019). Brazilian unicorns tend to be affiliated with either the University of São Paulo or Fundação Getulio Vargas. This pattern partially reflects the concentration of talented individuals, but there is no question that the institutions serve as collectors and generators of potentially actionable knowledge. Linking this knowledge to the private sector is often facilitated by technological transfer agencies, and affiliated incubators, and accelerators, attempt to institutionalize the linkages.

This said, the design and objectives of the universities are critical to realizing this "third mission." As discussed in chapter 3, Latin America ties for last place with Sub-Saharan Africa for collaboration with the private sector, perhaps for reasons of perceived low quality of the research, but as likely because of a lack of incentives for academics to tailor their research agendas to the needs of the local productive sector. Further, one diagnostic for why there is so little high-tech entrepreneurship in Guadalajara, despite a well-developed tech sector and several high-quality universities, has to do with deficient focus on entrepreneurial skills or support in the curriculum. Box 4.2 suggests that of greater importance is an entrepreneurial culture that connects students to industry as part of the curriculum, given existing entrepreneurial gaps. Yet, the University of São Paulo and the Fundação Getulio Vargas both in Brazil have 19 and 16 co-founders of unicorns, respectively (Rudolph, Miguel, and Gonzalez-Uribe 2023), suggesting that something is working well and there may be potential lessons to be drawn from that experience (box 3.3 in chapter 3 highlights some successful experiences).

### BOX 4.2 The Effect of Universities on Recent Graduates' Drive to Foster Innovation and Create Start-Ups

Research beginning in the 1980s documents the importance of faculty and research staff in creating technological advances via spin-off firms. While faculty spin-offs are an important impact of universities, the effect on graduates goes beyond spin-offs. Successful university support to graduates hinges on collaboration between faculty, students, and the private sector, along with enabling access to research and the entrepreneurial ecosystem.

Three cases studied by Astebro, Bazzazian, and Braguinsky (2012) document the importance of creating an entrepreneurial culture that connects students to local industry as part of the university curriculum, rather than merely offering a set of specific entrepreneurship courses. These cases also underscore the importance of a collaborative environment within the student body to support students' decisions to create start-ups. Finally, these programs show that strong technical skills also play an important role for graduates to be able to create start-ups, and that the universities can help address initial financing constraints for these businesses.

The *Massachusetts Institute of Technology* (MIT) is one of the world's premier entrepreneurial launchpads. It is endowed with highly favorable conditions to foster the creation of start-ups, such as high expenditures on research and development and applied engineering, a longstanding entrepreneurial culture, and ties with private industry and local venture capital. The assessment highlights the importance of faculty in stimulating and supporting start-ups by students and graduates, particularly among engineering students. The report also shows that the number of alumni start-ups exceeds the number of faculty spin-offs, even up to two decades after graduation. This fact is particularly remarkable given that the number of tech spin-offs originating from MIT faculty exceeds all other US institutions.

The study identifies "positive feedback" as a major factor in creating such an entrepreneurial environment. Also worth noting is that MIT taught only one entrepreneurship class until 1990; thus, specific entrepreneurship classes played a limited role in creating the entrepreneurial atmosphere at MIT. Successful graduate start-ups (beginning in the 1950s) form an integral part of this atmosphere and have become early role models for future students, many of whom chose MIT because of its entrepreneurial environment. By the 1990s, 42 percent of graduate entrepreneurs claimed they went to MIT specifically because of this environment. In addition to this student selection effect, the study mentions the importance of university student-run

*(Continued on next page)*

**BOX 4.2 The Effect of Universities on Recent Graduates' Drive to Foster Innovation and Create Start-Ups *(continued)***

activities in fostering a more entrepreneurial environment and developing the necessary skills among graduates. Other important factors are the high-quality research faculty, local venture capital, ample industry funding for engineering and science research, and development of an entrepreneurship center with the university at its core.

*Halmstad University* in Sweden has also produced a notable number of entrepreneurs even without access to the same suite of local factors as MIT (such as local venture capital or an entrepreneurship center). The Innovation Engineering or "Inventor Program" focuses on combining broad engineering knowledge with business skills. A survey in 1992 examining cohorts from 1979 to 1991 found that 36 percent of alumni started new businesses. Contributing to this high start-up rate is the requirement that students pursue thesis projects geared toward developing a technical idea into a product in cooperation with an established local company, fostering student independence and maturity and closeness to industry. The Innovation Engineering curriculum ensures a strong foundation in math, engineering, and business courses to prepare students for the third year, which focuses exclusively on the thesis. Additionally, the university provides base funding for direct development and some start-up costs, along with lab space, equipment, and advice from a patent agent.

*Chalmers University of Technology* in Sweden founded an Entrepreneurship School (E-school) in 1997. The E-school pairs Chalmers undergrads with Chalmers inventions developed in the laboratory by Chalmers faculty and staff to create spin-offs—combining formal coursework with tasking students to create real companies over the course of the program. An important program feature is that these students do not bring or develop their own venture ideas, instead working to commercialize inventions developed by Chalmers faculty and staff. Each project is provided a small cash infusion for patenting, legal, and other costs, raised by Chalmers from local public seed funds, along with other services provided at a reduced rate or in-kind. About half of the E-school graduates continue in a leading position in the newly incorporated business, and approximately 80 percent of these businesses remain in the region. Graduates also often return to Chalmers as guest speakers, to provide further opportunities for students and provide contract research.

*Source:* Astebro, Bazzazian, and Braguinsky 2012.

### *Getting Out of the Region to Learn*

Learning from abroad has historically been an essential vector of transfer, from espionage by colonial Americans in Great Britain to Japan's sending of students abroad—especially to the United Kingdom and Scotland—in the Meiji period. It remains true today that the advanced economies are where the bulk of the ideas, networks, and finance are centered. Two-thirds of LAC unicorn founders have had international exposure through their university studies (almost 45 percent studied in the United States) or work experience. Harvard University and Stanford University are hubs for networking, with numerous co-founders attending one of the two schools (Rudolph, Miguel, and Gonzalez-Uribe 2023). Put differently, Mexico, and the LAC region, are located next to the largest generators of new technology in the history of mankind, and the deepest sources of start-up funding on the planet. This offers an extraordinary opportunity for national learning. More profoundly, would-be and new entrepreneurs may be challenged to be more open to new ways of organizing a business, ecosystem, or society, much the way Pedro Nel and Tulio Ospina were in the previous century, when they brought mining expertise from the United States to Colombia. Yet LAC sends relatively few students to study in the United States (figure 3.9), for instance, compared to Hong Kong SAR, China; the Republic of Korea; or Singapore—even though they all have very good universities.

### *Agencies or Funds that Actively Pursue Relevant Technologies*

In addition to imparting a more growth-oriented mission in the universities, many countries establish institutions that actively pursue new technologies. Finland's TEKES (Center for Advancement of Technology) makes periodic tours of world technology hubs and universities to map the frontier. The Nordic Innovation House is a co-working and virtual office for Nordic tech companies, investors, and local advisors in Silicon Valley that seeks to engineer a "soft landing" for entrepreneurs entering the US market, enabling them to tap into the local community of technology partners, investors, and service providers.[9] Often with the backing of the Chinese government, Chinese firms invested 13 percent of all foreign venture capital financing in the United States, largely as a learning strategy. For example, in 2016, the Chinese private equity firm Hone Capital engineered a partnership with AngelList, then the biggest portal for matching US start-ups with seed capital, and invested in 400 high-tech start-ups across the spectrum, with the specific goal of "accelerating the introduction of foreign high-tech technologies" into China (Kinder 2024).

By these standards, LAC export and innovation promotion agencies are relatively passive—and in some cases, missing altogether. This may reflect disappointment with previous efforts. If these agencies cannot be reformed or built to function as instruments along the lines of Nordic Innovation House, doubling or tripling the number of students in global technology hubs is probably the most cost-effective way of building networks and transferring technology.

## The Business Enabling Environment

Intermediating between entrepreneurship-related human capital and the actual exploitation of technological opportunities is the business enabling environment. As noted in *The Innovation Paradox* (Cirera and Maloney 2017; Goñi and Maloney 2017), distortions and missing markets dramatically reduce returns to technological adoption, and in turn reduce the number of successful entrepreneurs a given economy can produce. Higher costs of experimentation, including rigidities and barriers to starting businesses, lower the value of the project and deter market entry (Kerr, Nanda, and Rhodes-Kropf 2014). A substantial literature finds that more numerous and more onerous procedures required to start a business and larger minimum capital requirements are detrimental to entrepreneurship (refer to Djankov 2009; Dreher and Gassebner 2013, among others). A 2024 report by the European Commission confirms earlier findings (such as those by Klapper, Laeven, and Rajan 2006) that costly regulations hamper the creation of new firms in Europe, force new entrants to be larger, and cause incumbent firms to grow more slowly. It is also the case, however, that the slow and cumbersome process for resolving insolvency present in many countries in LAC, particularly when combined with social sanctions against failure, discourages taking risks in the first place.

### Excessive Regulation

Excessive regulation can act as a barrier to entrepreneurship when it is cumbersome. For example, it is argued that the technological lag of the European Union with the United States in technology is not mainly due to deficient research and development (R&D) spending, which, while more fragmented, is only slightly below the magnitude in the United States, but because government regulation is poorly designed and burdensome (Wolf 2024). LAC's regulatory, taxation, and labor codes are worse than the EU's and are seemingly designed to prevent entrepreneurship. After Sub-Saharan Africa, LAC is the costliest region worldwide in terms of start-up procedures (figure 4.4, panel a). It also ranks poorly on insolvency laws (figure 4.4, panel b),[10] discouraging entry and the development of deeper financial markets. It ranks poorly in registering property, too (Doing Business Archive 2020a).

**FIGURE 4.4 Entry and Exit Costs Are Higher in Follower Countries Than in Frontier Countries**

a. Cost of business start-up procedures

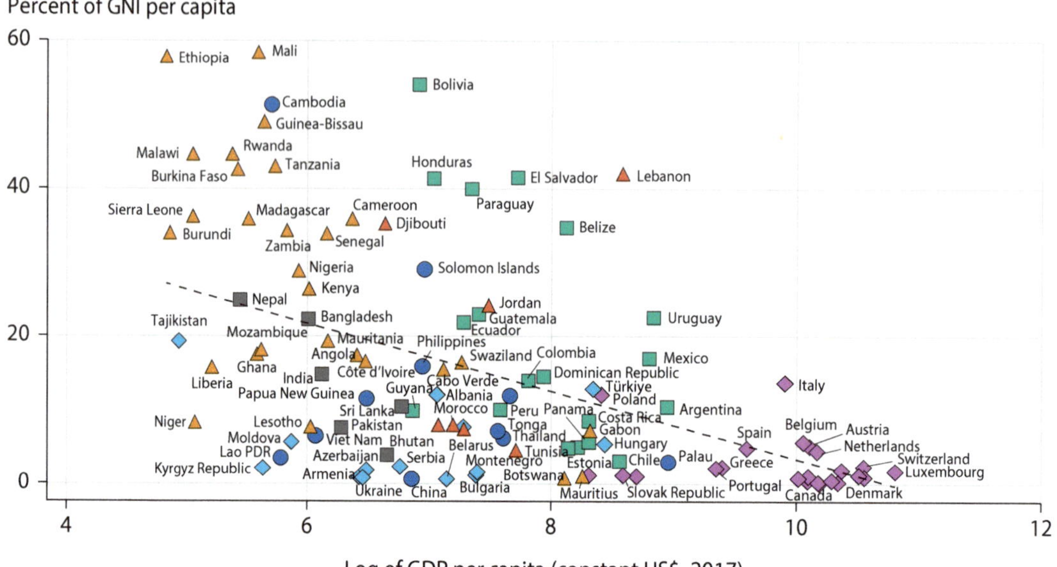


b. Time to resolve insolvency

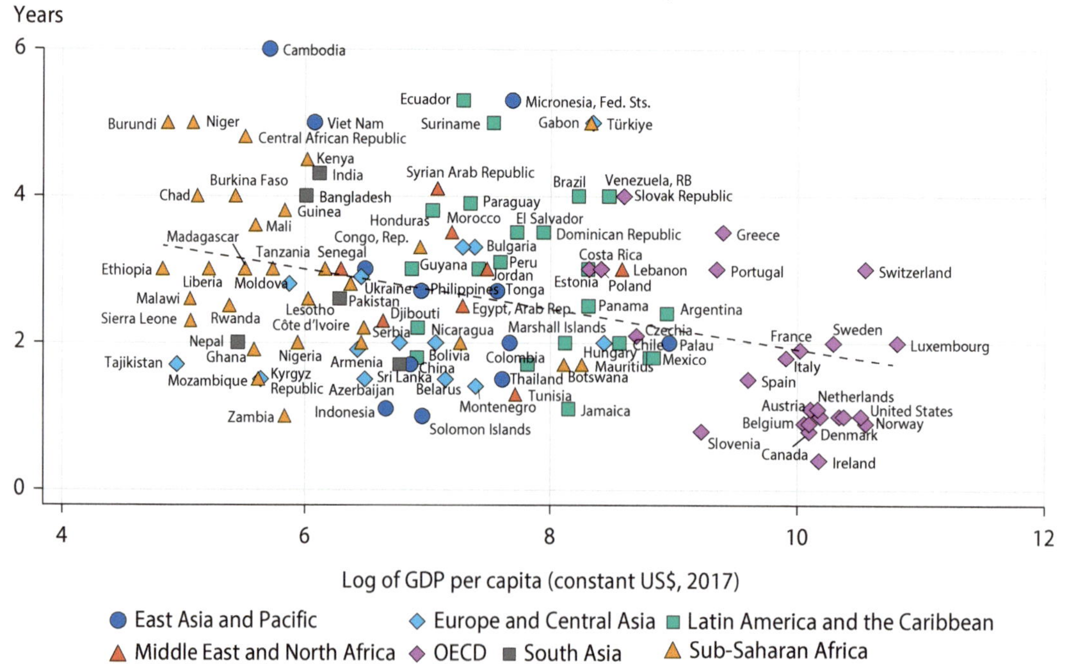


*Source:* Cusolito and Maloney 2018.

*Note:* GDP = gross domestic product; GNI = gross national income.

## High and Inefficient Taxation

LAC countries have tax systems that punish global competitiveness and discourage entry. Corporate tax rates exceed those in Asia or Europe. Total business tax rates average 47 percent of profits, exceeding the average rate of OECD nations, at 40 percent, and every other region except Africa. More importantly, the time required to comply with them is the highest in the world and about double that in OECD countries (Doing Business Archive 2020b). A typical firm in LAC must spend almost twice as long as a firm in East Asia and Pacific on paying taxes (table 4.1). A recent World Bank study shows that even income taxes, which are concentrated in the top decile of the distribution, have a negative impact on entrepreneurship (Venturi, Riera-Crichton, and Vuletin, forthcoming; Vuletin, forthcoming). In general, the region would benefit from shifting toward wealth taxes and in particular property taxes, and away from taxes that stifle productive activity (refer to the October 2024 volume of the Latin American and Caribbean Review series; Maloney et al. 2024).

## Labor Markets for Innovation

Recent work on why Europe lags the United States in tech entrepreneurship stresses that the costs of restructuring in the face of unforeseen shocks—which, itself, is a function of the continents' rigid employment protection legislation—is 10 times higher in Europe, and this has a major impact constraining tech industries. More generally, institutionalized resistance to technological adoption has been highlighted as a major determinant of low growth (Parente and Prescott 2000). LAC's labor protection system is, in general, poorly designed either to enable entrepreneurship or to protect

**TABLE 4.1 Efficiency in Paying Taxes in LAC Versus Other Regions**

| Location | Paying taxes score | Payments (number per year) | Time (hours per year) | Total tax and contribution rate (% of profit) |
|---|---|---|---|---|
| **Region** | | | | |
| East Asia and Pacific | 73.6 | 20.6 | 173.0 | 33.6 |
| Europe and Central Asia | 77.9 | 14.4 | 213.1 | 31.7 |
| Latin America and the Caribbean | 60.5 | 28.2 | 317.1 | 47.0 |
| Middle East and North Africa | 75.1 | 16.5 | 202.6 | 32.5 |
| OECD high income | 84.3 | 10.3 | 158.8 | 39.9 |
| South Asia | 60.2 | 26.7 | 273.5 | 43.9 |
| Sub-Saharan Africa | 57.8 | 36.6 | 280.6 | 47.3 |

*Source:* Doing Business Archive 2020b.
*Note:* LAC = Latin America and the Caribbean; OECD = Organisation for Economic Co-operation and Development.

workers (Coatanlem and Coste 2024; for Chile, refer to Caballero et al. 2013). In Mexican labor law, the prescribed costs of letting workers go for reasons of technology adoption are higher than for general business distress (Maloney 2009). What is needed are systems that protect the worker but not the particular job and facilitate the adjustments firms need to make as they respond to new technologies (Eslava and Melendez, forthcoming; Wolf 2024). In addition, excessively rigid markets may discourage risk taking if entrepreneurs perceive that it would be hard to get another salaried job should the venture fail or that reentering salaried work would imply beginning again at the bottom of the ladder.

## Distortions and Rent-Seeking

Distortions to economic activity can also create demand for rent-seeking activities away from entrepreneurship. Most talented individuals prefer to follow the largest returns in protected activities than risky entrepreneurial activities. A long tradition focuses on how rent-seeking activities in developing countries divert potentially transformative engineers to nonproductive activities, offering a strong rationale for eliminating distortions or interventions that generate such options (Murphy, Schleifer, and Vishny 1991). In addition, 40 percent of LAC firms note that corruption hinders their daily operations significantly, while another fifth catalogs the courts systems as a major constraint—levels comparable to those in the Middle East and North Africa and considerably above those in other developing regions (World Bank 2020).

An alternative interpretation inverts the causality and is consistent with the timing of protectionism in the region long before the Great Depression: an absence of entrepreneurial capital discouraged entrepreneurship under competitive conditions and led to the generation of rent-seeking activities (Maloney and Zambrano 2022).

More recently, the literature has shifted the focus toward the competition for technical talent by large incumbent firms. In trying to explain the 44 percent decline in inventors starting firms over the last 15 years in the United States, Akcigit and Goldschlag (2023b) suggest that this decrease is due partly to a preference for large incumbent firms, where salaries are 12 percent higher but inventiveness is lower. In places like Guadalajara where high demand for technical talent by established multinational firms yields high-paying and stable career trajectories, the expected return from experimentation needs to be very high, particularly in a context where there is weak tradition of high-end entrepreneurship.

### Trade Costs

The cost associated with export regulations in LAC is the highest worldwide with the exception of Sub-Saharan Africa (Doing Business Archive 2020c). Pursuit of deep trade agreements and other behind-the-border reforms could facilitate international integration and generate scale (Rocha and Ruta 2022). Export promotion agencies, which can help establish networks and assist young firms in navigating foreign systems, are shown to be effective in general (Lederman, Olarreaga, and Payton 2010) but are often inert in LAC.

## Enabling Early-Stage and Risk Finance

Early-stage and risk finance are also essential for generating entrepreneurship across the region, whether as a source of liquidity, a means of diversifying risk, or a source of managerial capabilities. For example, in the United States, among firms that went public between 2005 and 2019 and are still operating, the 51 percent funded with venture capital account for 72 percent of market capitalization and 88 percent of R&D expenditures (Lerner et al. 2024).[11] In developing countries outside of China, although relatively few firms are backed by venture capital, those that are accounted for 31 percent of citation-weighted patenting (Lerner et al. 2024).[12] It is not coincidental that China expanded to be the second largest venture capital market in the world while it developed a dynamic technology sector. Further, the annual return of venture capital funds in China, at 70–80 percent, is more than double the return in the United States (30–35 percent) (Malkin 2021). This gap suggests that the absence of risk financing is a major explanation for the innovation paradox. There are, in fact, high returns to be had in some lagging countries if the risk financing—and everything that is necessary for its emergence—is in place.

As discussed in chapter 2, LAC's financial systems remain underdeveloped in key respects. Even after controlling for several possible economic and structural determinants, including size, LAC's banks lend less and charge more than expected.[13] Allocation to small innovative firms is especially low in middle-income countries, as documented in *Unleashing Productivity through Firm Financing* (Didier and Cusolito 2024). Firms with fewer than 100 employees face the largest financing gaps. Debt-to-assets ratios are 40 percent in middle-income countries, compared to 65 percent in high-income countries. Though most high-growth firms are not high-tech and prefer bond financing that does not dilute their ownership (Brown, Mawson, and Mason 2017), among innovative high-tech companies where intellectual property is difficult to collateralize, bond or bank markets are poor sources of finance, but equity financing is still scarce and winds up being targeted toward larger firms. In middle-income countries, firms with more than 350 employees accounted for about 70 percent of venture capital investments, compared to 35 percent in high-income countries (Didier and Cusolito 2024). The common policy response that the government provides venture capital financing is generally not successful. Venture capital does more than finance; it sorts firms, governs them, and then certifies them. In these ways, it serves as a signal of viability.

Entrepreneurial financing also has an essential learning dimension that dictates that venture capital markets need to evolve organically. Funding for innovative start-ups is far riskier and more specialized than can be handled by standard financial institutions (refer to box 4.3). Recipients of venture capital, for example, state that the managerial guidance and mentorship are almost as equally important as the financing received (De Carvalho, Calomiris, and de Matos 2008). This finding implies that the issue of deficient risk financing cannot be treated purely as a question of the state providing financing or loosening restrictions on pension fund investments. It is also a question of building capabilities in both managers and domestic financial agents. Hence, over the medium term, the region needs to work with external established venture capital firms (Berger, Dechezleprêtre, and Fadic 2024). China initially tried to brute force venture capital creation but wound up with the usual while elephants. The successful establishment of a venture capital industry was due to the return of diaspora with precisely the experience and networks needed (Ahlstrom, Bruton, and Yeh 2007). The more successful expansion phase of Chinese venture capital occurred as the government paired its assets with these diaspora-led and outside firms. Chinese-owned Hone Capital's efforts to team up with a US angel investment firm in the United States can be seen as developing a shortcut to developing the evaluation and managerial capital needed to follow global technology trends immediately in house. More broadly, "access to finance" and "ecosystem support for capability building" are intrinsically intertwined.

As with any start-up industry, reforms to the enabling environment are critical, ranging from protection of minority shareholder rights to legal enforcement, and to efficient insolvency resolution mechanisms. Further, the entire chain of risk capital needs to be developed at the same time. Latin America's venture capital industry has a lower rate of return than Asia's, partly because of the absence of the ability to exit—to have the firm go public and get off the books of the venture capital firm.

## BOX 4.3 Venture Capital as Facilitator of Technology Adoption and Contributor to the Innovation Ecosystem

As Rudolph, Miguel, and Gonzalez-Uribe (2023, 7) note: "Venture capitalists are said to provide smart money because they provide more than just financing. A rich literature in finance shows that, relative to other financiers, venture capitalists use two broad mechanisms to add value while mitigating the challenges of financing innovative companies. Notably, before providing capital, they scrutinize companies through a rigorous process called due diligence. This involves various evaluation and selection activities following the initial screening for adherence to the fund's mandate, as described by Gompers et al. (2020). After investment, these investors then monitor and add value to their portfolio companies in a variety of ways. These include: (1) designing financial contracts and compensation schemes that help align the incentives of entrepreneurs and investors (Lerner and Nanda 2020); (2) guiding entrepreneurs through their active involvement with the businesses (Bernstein, Giroud, and Townsend 2016; Ewens and Malenko 2020; Hellmann and Puri 2002; Lerner 1995); and (3) facilitating the efficient reallocation of resources between portfolio companies (Gonzalez-Uribe 2020; Lindsey 2008).

"Recent research suggests that venture capitalists are not only investors but also ecosystem builders that can provide value to companies beyond their portfolio. A study by Gonzalez-Uribe et al. (2023) shows that venture capitalists' due diligence can have a substantial impact on business development—even if the venture capitalist decides not to invest. This is likely because the due diligence can help entrepreneurs overcome the constraints that limit their business development, such as financial difficulties (Kerr and Nanda 2015); information gaps (Yu 2020); and limited firm capabilities (Gonzalez-Uribe and Reyes 2021). Other investors and institutions designed to support entrepreneurs, such as business accelerators, play similar roles in building ecosystems in high-growth company clusters. Business accelerators are support programs for entrepreneurs that train, coach, and sometimes fund them (Gonzalez-Uribe and Hmaddi 2022). In the United Kingdom and the United States, accelerators have been shown to help attract venture capital and talent to their surrounding region(s). This makes it easier for entrepreneurs to raise financing and grow—including even those that do not participate in accelerators (Gonzalez-Uribe and Hmaddi 2022).

"Until 2020, the high-growth company ecosystem in Latin America and the Caribbean (LAC) was still in the developmental stage. High-growth companies in LAC were scarcer

*(Continued on next page)*

**BOX 4.3 Venture Capital as Facilitator of Technology Adoption and Contributor to the Innovation Ecosystem *(continued)***

than they were in the United States, and this difference in company growth distribution was at the root of LAC's development problem (Eslava, Haltiwanger, and Pinzón 2022). Closing the gap by unleashing the development of companies in LAC with high growth potential was not only a problem of financing, but also of capabilities (Gonzalez-Uribe and Leatherbee 2018a; Gonzalez-Uribe and Reyes 2021). Access to smart money from venture capitalists, as well as the opportunities that venture capitalists and other early-stage investors provide entrepreneurs to get them investment-ready, are important resources for unleashing the high-growth company ecosystem."

*Source:* Rudolph, Miguel, and Gonzalez-Uribe 2023, 7.

On the borrowers' side, there is some evidence that reported financial constraints may be as much related to limitations in the ability of entrepreneurs to perceive opportunities and solve problems as to the true absence of finance. Even established firms are often limited by their own inability to generate the basic financial data that financial institutions need. Among start-ups, it is unclear how insurmountable reported financial constraints really are. The vast majority of US start-ups bootstrap relying on their own savings or that of family and friends (Hurst and Lusardy 2004). Edelman and Yli-Renko (2010) argue that entrepreneurs' perceptions of opportunity mediate between objective characteristics of the business enabling environment and the entrepreneurs' efforts to start a new venture: neither objective evaluations nor perceptions of missing finance affect entrepreneurs' efforts. Bischoff et al. (2013) argue that capital constraints are only binding when nascent entrepreneurs have a mental model common to novice entrepreneurs, but not to experienced entrepreneurs. That is, part of the process of releasing financial constraints in the enabling environment may, in fact, be the process of learning entrepreneurship. This said, there is ample microevidence that early-stage financing liquidity is a binding constraint on entrepreneurship. Recent evidence from the Spanish Christmas Lottery shows that such a large-scale random distribution of significant liquidity increases the entry of start-ups, job creation, and self-employment in winning regions and does so more in areas with limited access to credit (Bermejo et al. 2024).

LAC lags in most of the early stages of financing, ranging from pre-seed support to liquid markets that would facilitate exit to non-risk sources, although major improvements have occurred in the last decade (figure 4.5, panel a). As one crude measure, private equity and venture capital (PEVC) investments in the LAC region rose from less than US$500 million in 2017 to exceeded US$16 billion in 2021 before falling back to US$2.8 billion in 2023. As a share of GDP, this places them at about one-third the level of Asia, at US$50.4 billion.[14] The sharp rise in risk financing, upon which LACs unicorns have been dependent, while welcome, does not reflect a deepening of domestic markets but rather a short-term spike in funding a few very large and generally late-stage investments. Foreign investors participated in about 90 percent of the value of the deals conducted during 2013–21. In all, almost 70 percent of the surge in foreign venture capital investment since 2019 has been driven by deals involving the Big 4 investors: SoftBank (the Japanese multinational with investment funds headquartered in Hong Kong SAR, China; the United Kingdom; and the United States), and DST Global, Ribbit Capital, and Tiger Global (based in the United States) (Rudolph, Miguel, and Gonzalez-Uribe 2023). The region continues to lag as a recipient of venture capital investments from global high-income investors (figure 4.5, panel b). Of the US$192 billion invested by venture capital firms headquartered in Canada, Europe, and the United States between 2021 and 2023, LAC received only 10 percent (US$19.3 billion), compared to the US$115.6 billion captured by Asia.[15] Data from the top 30 global investors show that only 30 percent invest in LAC, with only 1.3 percent of this LAC investment channeled toward early-stage or innovative ventures. This low level is comparable only to Africa (0.4 percent), and well below emerging markets in Asia (13 percent).

**FIGURE 4.5 Venture Capital Investments in LAC Lag**

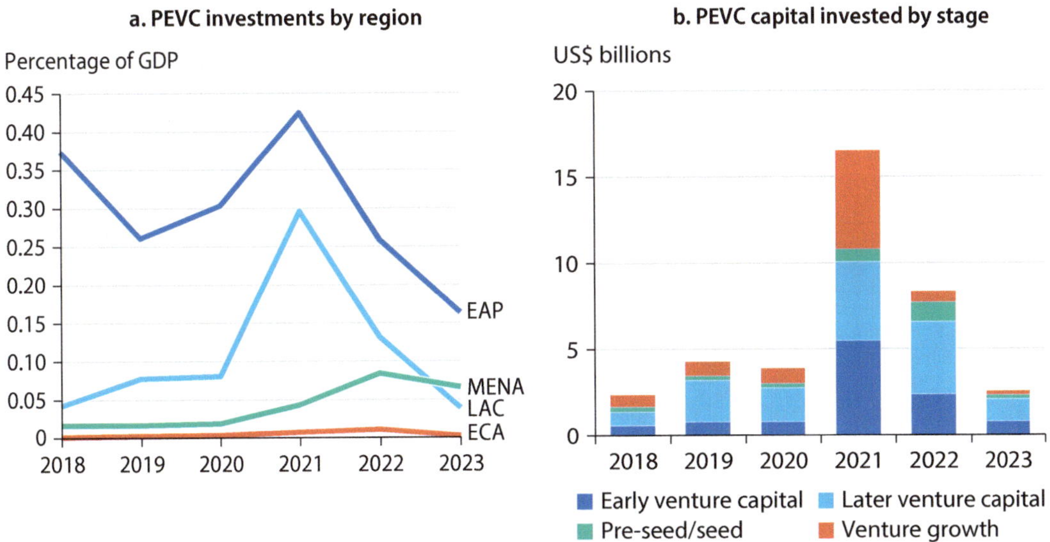


*Source:* Original figure for this volume based on PitchBook data (https://pitchbook.com/data).
*Note:* The figure shows private equity venture capital by region. EAP = East Asia and Pacific; ECA = Europe and Central Asia; GDP = gross domestic product; LAC = Latin America and the Caribbean; MENA = Middle East and North Africa; PEVC = private equity venture capital.

Addressing the reasons why more foreign venture capital firms do not invest in LAC is critical because generating their managerial experience takes decades, and venture capital firms headquartered in Canada, the European Union, and the United States finance 82 percent (US$1.1 trillion) of all global venture capital investment around the world in start-ups.[16] Some of these firms are among the world's most experienced and capable in terms of building and promoting new companies and tech start-ups and enabling innovation at large. Ninety percent of global seed and angel funds in 2023 originated from North America (primarily the United States), with the remainder from Europe. None of the 10 most active regional venture capital firms in LAC by deal count in the past 5 years are among the global top 50 (Robbins 2024).

Various investor surveys conducted between 2014 and 2020 cite several reasons for not investing in LAC: (1) difficulty in finding experienced local fund managers who know how to create value in companies funded by risk capital (EMPEA 2014); (2) currency crises and volatile political changes (EMPEA 2019); (3) lack of more robust capital markets to provide exit opportunities; and (4) limited adoption of AI solutions and software to compete with more developed markets (EMPEA 2020). These concerns again highlight the need to develop local capabilities in the financial sector, as well as the obvious point that the region needs to defend its macro stability tenaciously. The lack of exit possibilities has improved somewhat in the past few years, but geographical and institutional concentration remains high. By number of deals, most exits in the last 5 years occurred in Brazil (68 percent), followed by Mexico at 10 percent.[17] In Brazil, two institutions, Bovespa Mais and Novo Mercado, have proven critical to developing Brazil's venture capital market by facilitating exit.[18]

These discouraging factors also have likely influenced why most LAC start-ups backed by venture capital are generally not at the technological frontier. LAC PEVC investments also skew heavily toward information technology (IT) and financial services in terms of both capital invested and number of deals. IT investments are in line with global trends, but financial services investments exceed the global trend of 9.9 percent of capital invested (Imtiaz and Sabater 2024). Less than 7 percent of LAC venture capital funding is directed to sectors such as AI, cybersecurity, the Internet-of-Things, automotive and other robotics, biotech, advanced materials, and nanotech, Rudolph, Miguel, and Gonzalez Uribe (2023) find. "Part of this results from the region's lack of legitimacy in the eyes of foreign investors, which has steered founders toward safer bets, such as importing 'X for LAC' ideas from the advanced economies. Other factors include the costly bureaucracy and red tape underlying personal and commercial transactions in some countries in the region" (Rudolph, Miguel, and Gonzalez-Uribe 2023, 24). All these factors reduce the returns to innovation.

In sum, early-stage and venture capital are critical to starting and expanding the kinds of firms that are likely to propel the next wave of LAC growth. Facilitating their increase requires a cross-section of reforms, ranging from streamlining bankruptcy procedures laws to making government more effective in building the relevant technical and business capital to defending macroeconomic stability. In the medium term, it will be essential to pair with diaspora-led and foreign venture capital firms. This not only ensures the presence of venture management skills but also guarantees the best available market signals about the viability of any particular venture.

## Strong Entrepreneurship Support Organizations

Support in strengthening capabilities and assisting latent entrepreneurs in the region has improved over the past few decades. Notably, LAC has seen an expansion of entrepreneurship support organizations (ESOs) that provide financing with accompanying support (such as training, mentorship, and networking). More than 80 incubator and accelerator programs have been created in LAC since 2003, leading to a per capita density similar to that found in Asia (figure 4.6), although most are concentrated in Brazil, Chile, and Mexico (refer to annex 4A). Some of the most prominent early-stage foreign investors in LAC include incubators and accelerators such as Y Combinator, Google for Startups, 500 Global, and Fj Labs, which have ranked in the top 10 in LAC in the last 5 years based on number of deals.[19]

These ESOs have been critical to financing high-growth start-ups. Endeavor's Catalyst Fund has backed 22 of LAC's unicorns, including as one of its first investments, Mercado Libre, now worth at least US$10 billion. Regional incubators have supported hundreds, or in the case of Start-Up Chile, thousands of startups (annex 4A.1). More than one-third of LAC's unicorn companies are alumni of accelerator or incubator programs. Successful businesses have also reinvested in the region and supported overall growth of access to funding opportunities for entrepreneurs. Start-Up Chile's support is associated with higher business creation rates in target industries and the area near Santiago (refer to box 4.4).

**FIGURE 4.6 The Per Capita Density of Incubators and Accelerators in LAC Is Improving Compared to Other Regions**

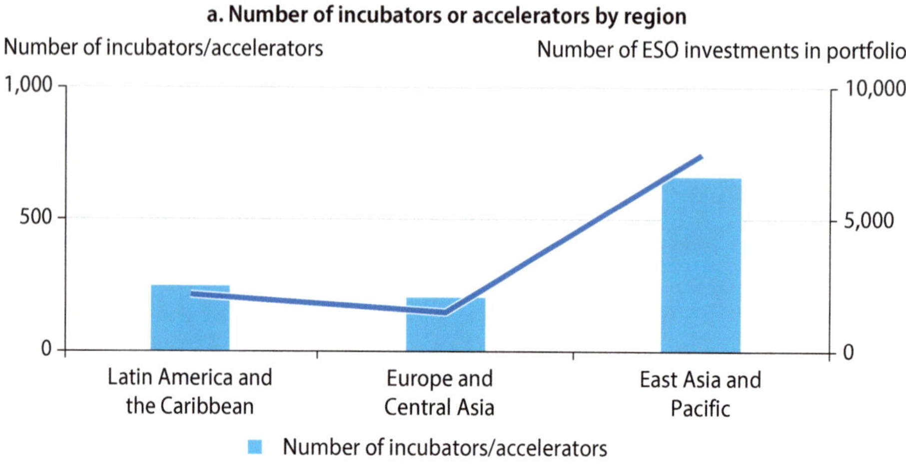


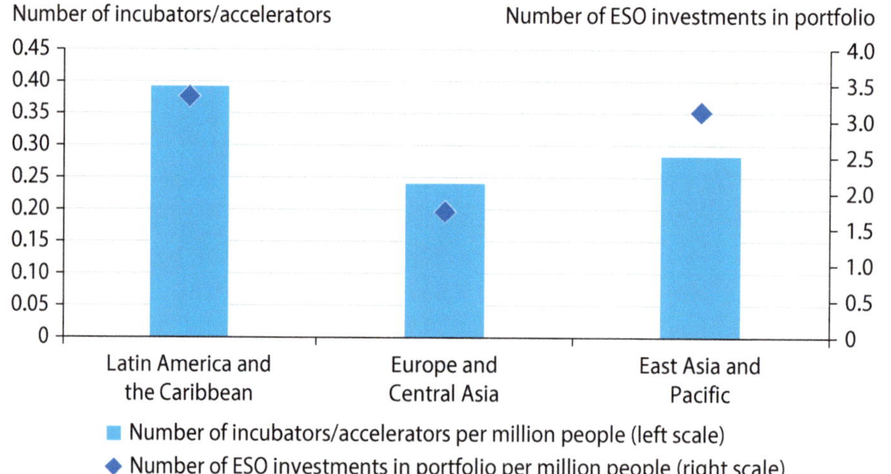


*Source:* Original figure for this volume based on PitchBook data (https://pitchbook.com/data).
*Note:* ESO = Entrepreneurship Support Organization.

**BOX 4.4 InnovaChile and Start-Up Chile**

The *InnovaChile* program was created as part of an initiative to help innovative companies in Chile connect and collaborate with academia to promote the development of research and development (R&D) by defining policies, strategies, and resources to foster innovation and competitiveness. It is supported by CORFO (Corporación de Fomento de la Producción), a public institution responsible for

*(Continued on next page)*

## BOX 4.4 InnovaChile and Start-Up Chile *(continued)*

supporting entrepreneurship, innovation, and competitiveness, and strengthening human capital and technological capabilities. InnovaChile manages five financing lines: (1) promotion of business innovation; (2) adoption and generation of technological capacities for innovation; (3) public goods for competitiveness; (4) diffusion and extension for competitive small and medium enterprises; and (5) strengthening the program for the innovation ecosystem (Chandra and Medrano Silva 2012).

The results for the 2019–22 period show that a solid network of 214 partners and more than 1,000 strategic business connections were established via CORFO support, including events, mentorship programs, and business rounds, among others. On average, less complex projects tend to establish more connections, as opposed to more complex R&D-intensive ones. Beneficiaries outside CORFO's program were also reached by the impacts of this initiative (CORFO 2022).

A recent impact evaluation for InnovaChile has not yet demonstrated positive results on patent and brand generation and innovation in the period under study. In fact, the program shows a negative impact on patent generation (iCuantix SPA 2022). One potential explanation is that beneficiary firms focus on development of existing products as opposed to developing new ones. The study also showed that patent generation appeared higher for programs that financed more sophisticated and advanced-stage innovations as opposed to early-stage innovation voucher programs. These results could have been affected by both the COVID-19 pandemic and the short period for results (iCuantix SPA 2022).

*Start-Up Chile* was established in 2010 to increase the incidence of high-potential entrepreneurship in Chile, strengthen the entrepreneurial ecosystem, and position Chile as an innovation and entrepreneurship hub. It has welcomed 2,000 foreign beneficiaries and their start-up teams to Chile since 2010, making it the top backer of Latin America and the Caribbean start-ups, according to Sling Hub.

Although the share of Chilean entrepreneurs participating in the program has grown to 40 percent over time, the program aimed to provide a soft landing for foreign entrepreneurs in Chile, facilitated by a partner in the Chilean business community. Participants receive free office space in downtown Santiago and a US$40,000 grant. In addition to providing capital to companies that would otherwise find it difficult to raise financing, Start-Up Chile also adds value through the capacity-building

*(Continued on next page)*

### BOX 4.4 InnovaChile and Start-Up Chile *(continued)*

activities it offers participants, including business training, mentoring, and networking opportunities (Gonzalez-Uribe and Leatherbee 2018b), as well as helping participants refine their pitches. Assistance is based mainly on peer-to-peer teaching, all in a collaborative environment. By bringing entrepreneurs to Chile from around the world, Start-Up Chile seeks not only to connect Chile better to the rest of the world but to contribute to a cultural change that creates more openness toward entrepreneurship and prepares Chilean entrepreneurs to be competitive globally. According to Nicolas Shea, founder of the program, "to accelerate was never the objective. What we wanted was a cultural change in Chile. To reach that goal, all you need is a group of highly qualified entrepreneurs. Making sure they came to Chile was our job, making sure they succeeded was, and will always be, theirs" (Gonzalez-Uribe and Leatherbee 2015).

The results to date have been mixed. Some studies argue that for domestic entrepreneurs, the program has had no clear effect on a variety of economic variables (survival, profitability, exports, employment, future projects of the head of the project). It has, however, led to greater access to funds, suggesting that the process of selection into the program has served as a signal of quality. Semi-structured interviews with key players suggest that the program had attracted talent. An increase in firm creation of about 6 percent has been attributed to the program (Rudolph, Miguel, and Gonzalez-Uribe 2023).

However, concerns about the attractiveness of the investment environment, the relatively low selectivity, and the inability to retain good foreign firms have reduced the impact. The program has contributed to the image of the country as a destination for entrepreneurship and innovation. It also has promoted a culture of entrepreneurship in the country by strengthening the community of entrepreneurs, improving the perception of entrepreneurship, legitimizing it as a career, increasing appreciation of entrepreneurial skills and values, and diffusing new techniques. It has strengthened interactions among agents of the entrepreneurial ecosystem. The interviews also revealed some confusion over Start-Up Chile's four goals: attracting and retaining foreign entrepreneurs, strengthening domestic entrepreneurs, strengthening local institutions, and branding the country. The interviews stressed that it is especially necessary to retain foreign start-ups as an anchor to achieve the other goals. It has proven difficult to evaluate the program's impact on establishing a better ecosystem or a country brand. The relatively modest size of the grants has likely led to a modest effect.

*(Continued on next page)*

**BOX 4.4 InnovaChile and Start-Up Chile *(continued)***

The Chilean experience has influenced the creation of 50 entrepreneurship programs around the world. Brazil, Jamaica, the Republic of Korea, Malaysia, Peru, and Puerto Rico have directly replicated the model.

*Sources:* Melo 2012; Rudolph, Miguel, and Gonzalez-Uribe 2023; Start-Up Chile 2024; Verde 2016.

ESOs can fill the critical gap in the pre-seed and seed stages. ESOs that have the capabilities can help provide start-ups with access to a network of investors, along with developing their pitches and business plans. In principle, ESOs, including incubators and accelerators, can address both financing and capacity gaps in the entrepreneurial ecosystem. Additionally, the skills training offered by ESOs tends to be targeted to specific needs for start-ups, along with providing mentorship and advice throughout the start-up journey.

Therefore, it is important to consider the evolution and quality of ESOs in Latin America. According to a survey by think tank Startup Genome, only 10 percent of start-ups in emerging markets have access to strong mentorship networks, underscoring the importance of supporting ESOs in LAC (Ospina 2023). This said, the network of ESOs in LAC operates more in silos than as a regional ecosystem. Greater collaboration across ESOs, investors, mentors, and other support mechanisms would help develop the cadre of high-tech entrepreneurs the region needs. Table 4A.1 in annex 4A presents information about 10 well-established ESOs in the region.

## Conclusion

This chapter explores an extension to the innovation paradox: why, given the vast potential for national learning and growth through the adoption of existing technologies in follower countries, there are not cadres of entrepreneurs aggressively trying to arbitrage these opportunities. The entrepreneurs captaining new firms are the irreplaceable vectors who enable technological change and have the greatest potential to disrupt the status quo, especially moribund incumbent firms. Though the region has high rates of churning and multitudes of low-skilled entrepreneurs, it lacks the density of those with the education and capabilities to start and maintain truly transformative companies.

The chapter has argued that developing highly successful entrepreneurs in the region requires facilitating and reducing the costs of the experimentation that is intrinsic to the national learning process. This requires entrepreneurial skills that range from basic technical and administrative skills to skills that are harder to develop: distinguishing good new projects and managing the risk and financing—the entrepreneurial capital discussed in chapter 1.

But it also requires an enabling environment that lowers the cost of information, raises the returns to innovation, and helps finance and diffuse the risks of complex investments with long time horizons. This requires the reforms needed to deepen and broaden financial markets, and more generally facilitate and encourage the accumulation of all types of capital; it also requires reorienting the supporting institutions in the National Innovation System that would offset the standard market failures associated with knowledge flows and provide fertile ground for new experiments, as described in chapter 3. At present, there are ecosystems in the region that would seem to have all the necessary elements—high-tech foreign companies and entrepreneurs, good higher education institutions, and financial sectors of growing sophistication—but the factors that remain missing, as well as the coordination mechanisms that need to be improved, are not well understood. Working on both fronts—improving entrepreneurs' capabilities and strengthening the overall National Innovation System—is essential to animate the latent technology-intensive entrepreneurship that has the potential to transform LAC's economies. The next chapter provides some guidance.

## ANNEX 4A: Entrepreneurship Support Organizations in LAC

Table 4A.1 provides information on 10 major organizations operating in Latin America and the Caribbean that support start-ups.

**TABLE 4A.1 Ten Established Entrepreneurship Support Organizations Operating in LAC**

| Name | Location | Start-ups supported (number) | Program length | Average investment size |
|---|---|---|---|---|
| 500 Startups | Mexico | 170+ | 4 months | US$60,000 |
| ACE Startups | Brazil | 300+ | n/a | R$1 million |
| Founder Institute | Argentina, Bolivia, Brazil, Chile, Colombia, Ecuador, Mexico, Peru, Venezuela, RB | 200+ | 4 months | n/a |
| Google for Startups | Mexico | 75+ | 3 months | None |

(Continued on next page)

**TABLE 4A.1 Ten Established Entrepreneurship Support Organizations Operating in LAC *(continued)***

| Name | Location | Start-ups supported (number) | Program length | Average investment size |
|---|---|---|---|---|
| Mass Challenge | Mexico | 160+ | 4 months | US$100,000 |
| Rockstart Colombia | Colombia | 50+ | 5 months | US$70,000 |
| Start-Up Chile | Chile | 1,900+ | 4–12 months | Up to US$90,000 |
| Startup Farm | Brazil | 300+ | 6 months | Up to R$150,000 (for 5 percent equity) |
| Startup Mexico | Mexico | 100+ | 6–10 months | n/a |
| Wayra | Argentina, Brazil, Chile, Colombia, Mexico, Peru | 200+ | n/a | Up to US$150,000 |

*Source:* Original table for this volume based on Sharp Sheets data (https://sharpsheets.io/).
*Note:* n/a = not available.

Beyond the international ESOs that are headquartered locally to provide support in LAC, many locally operating ESOs are linked to universities or government agencies. Some examples include the following.

*Argentina.* EMPRETECNO is an Agencia I+D+i program that provides financing for new product and/or market development to existing technology-based small and medium enterprises, along with accompanying technical assistance. Agencia I+D+i is an independently run government agency under the Ministry of Science and Technology with a mandate to support innovation and entrepreneurship within Argentina.

*Chile.* After the launch of its first incubator in the 1990s (Chandra and Medrano Silva 2012), Chile developed two programs in the 2000s to subsidize incubator creation, along with the incubator run by the Association of Chilean Businesses. Public resources to support these efforts were decentralized through the specialized government agency CORFO (Corporación de Fomento de la Producción) to develop additional programs based on regional gaps and priorities, support existing incubators and accelerators, and provide additional support to Chilean entrepreneurs and ESOs (CORFO 2019). Several Chilean ESOs have also received international awards, positioning the country well relative to regional peers (Ramirez, da Silva, and Amestica 2019). Santiago Innova, the first incubator in Chile, was started in 1992 by the municipal government of Santiago, with a mandate to create jobs for the local economy. More than 27 ESOs are now part of the national association, each of which has also developed wider mentor networks to support entrepreneurs within the ecosystem. The ESO network in Chile also includes linkages to government, universities, industry, and entrepreneurs. For more information about the program and its results, refer to box 4.4.

*Mexico*. In the early 1990s, the Mexican government decentralized management of ESO resources and support to hybrid public agencies (Guerrero and Urbano 2017). The ESO space has been dominated by incubators at public and private universities (Molina et al. 2011), notably the National University of Mexico, the National Polytechnic University, and the Monterrey Institute of Technology and Higher Education (Tec). Tec is often considered a best practice example of an ESO system within a university to foster entrepreneurship within academia (Cantu-Ortiz et al. 2017); promote graduate studies in STEM fields (Guerrero, Urbano, and Gajón 2017; Guerrero et al. 2018); and foster entrepreneurial and innovative practices (Guerrero, Urbano, and Herrera 2019; Herrera, Guerrero, and Urbano 2018) (box 3.3 in chapter 3).

## Notes

1. Quoted in *The Economist*, https://www.economist.com/special-report/2024/10/14/american-productivity-still-leads-the-world.
2. Refer to Davis and Haltiwanger (1992, 1998); Decker et al. (2014); Fairlie, Miranda, and Zolas (2019); Haltiwanger, Jarmin, and Miranda (2013).
3. The revenue-based measure of total factor productivity (TFPR) measures the value of sales given input costs. Because value necessarily includes the price of the product, it may be capturing the quality of the product, which should be included as a measure of increased productivity, but also market power. A monopolist will show higher TFPR simply by virtue of being able to charge more in the absence of competitors. TFPQ strips out the price of the good in the calculation, leading to a measure of "efficiency." This implies it misses the positive impact of quality growth but also strips out noncompetitive effects.
4. *Technolatinas* are defined as technology-based private companies born in LAC and owned by founders from the region. The definition includes the wide range between early-stage start-ups and well-established companies worth tens of billions of dollars with thousands of employees. Most are entrepreneur-driven digital ventures.
5. For a review of entrepreneurial systems, refer to Alves, Fischer, and Vonortas (2021).
6. Nicolaou et al. (2008) and Nicolaou and Shane (2010) provide some support for biological underpinnings, arguing that up to 40 percent of variance in entrepreneurship choices is explained by genes. However, Lindquist, Sol, and van Praag (2015), comparing biological and adopted children, find that while children of entrepreneurs are 60 percent more likely to become entrepreneurs than others in Sweden, the influence of adoptive parents is twice as large as the influence of biological parents. That is, characteristics related to nurture or environment wind up being more important. Zumbuehl, Dohmen, and Pfann (2013) find that parents who invest more in child-rearing show a greater intergenerational similarity in attitudes toward risk. Nanda and Sørensen (2010) find that Danes are more likely to become entrepreneurs if their coworkers have previously been entrepreneurs.
7. Spolaore and Wacziarg (2009, 471) show that the distance from the technological frontier captured by genetic characteristics, proxying for "customs, habits, biases,

conventions, etc. that are transmitted across generations—biologically and/or culturally—with high persistence," is correlated with economic performance. Putterman and Weil (2008) demonstrate that backgrounds of the ancestors migrating to a country are correlated with economic performance. At a more microlevel, Guiso, Sapienza, and Zingales (2006) offer the example of how culture defined by religion and ethnicity affects beliefs about trust and show that entrepreneurship is sensitive to such beliefs. Trustworthy individuals have a comparative advantage in the kinds of incomplete contracts based on handshakes. Trusting others (and being trusted) increased the likelihood of becoming an entrepreneur. More generally, they find that cultural variables, such as agreeing that thriftiness is a value that should be taught to children, can explain half of the cross-country difference in national savings rates.

8. SEED is "an innovative in-residence 3-week mini-MBA [master's of business administration] program for high school students modeled after western business school curricula." Chioda et al. (2023) evaluated the program as it was adapted to the Ugandan context.
9. "The Nordic Innovation House's goals are to create value for the Nordic companies wanting to scale, reduce barriers and to kick-start Nordic businesses" (Finland Abroad 2016).
10. This indicator measures the time, cost, and outcome of insolvency proceedings involving domestic legal entities. These variables were used to calculate the recovery rate, which was recorded as cents on the dollar recovered by secured creditors through reorganization, liquidation, or debt enforcement (foreclosure or receivership) proceedings. Data are drawn from the World Bank World Development Indicators, the International Monetary Fund, and the Economist Intelligence Unit.
11. In an earlier estimate, companies backed by venture capital account for approximately 50 percent of the total market capitalization and 60 percent of the innovation in the United States (Gornall and Strebulaev 2015).
12. Citation-weighted patenting measures patent importance by considering not just the number of patents a company holds, but also how often those patents are cited by others.
13. Original finding in De la Torre, Ize, and Schmukler (2011), supported by more recent data in World Bank (2023).
14. PitchBook data, 2015–23 (https://pitchbook.com/data).
15. PitchBook data, 2023 (https://pitchbook.com/data).
16. PitchBook data, 2023 (https://pitchbook.com/data).
17. Top acquiring companies in the last 5 years include MercadoLibre, B3, XP Investimentos, Globant, and DNA Capital. Less than one-quarter of the top 30 (exits by) acquisitions in the last 5 years involved non-LAC actors.
18. Novo Mercado is a premium listing tier that requires firms to adopt governance standards that are stronger than legally demanded. The increased transparency has helped stimulate Brazil's venture capital and private equity market Bovespa Mais, which broadly holds to Novo Mercado standards and targets small and mid-cap firms, seeking to host companies with a gradual strategy of gaining access to capital markets. It helps companies improve their transparency, grow their shareholder base, and increase liquidity.
19. Eight cities in LAC saw their first deal by a pioneer (first in the city) accelerator during the period from 2015 to 2018, including: Aguascalientes (Mexico),

Apodaca (Mexico), Kingston (Jamaica), Mendoza (Argentina), Santa Fe (Argentina), São Leopoldo (Brazil), Sunchales (Argentina), and Temuco (Chile). An additional 23 cities saw non-pioneer accelerator deals forged during the same time period.

## References

Ahlstrom, D., G. D. Bruton, and K. S. Yeh. 2007. "Venture Capital in China: Past, Present, and Future." *Asia Pacific Journal of Management* 24: 247–68.

Akcigit, U., and N. Goldschlag. 2023a. "Measuring the Characteristics and Employment Dynamics of U.S. Inventors." Becker Friedman Institute for Economics Working Paper No. 2023-49, University of Chicago, Chicago.

Akcigit, U., and N. Goldschlag. 2023b. "Where Have All the 'Creative Talents' Gone? Employment Dynamics of US Inventors." NBER Working Paper 31085, National Bureau of Economic Research, Cambridge, MA.

Alves, A. C., B. B. Fischer, and N. S. Vonortas. 2021. "Ecosystems of Entrepreneurship: Configurations and Critical Dimensions." *Annals of Regional Science* 67: 73–106.

Astebro, T., N. Bazzazian, and S. Braguinsky. 2012. "Startups by Recent University Graduates and their Faculty: Implications for University Entrepreneurship Policy." *Research Policy* 41 (4): 663–77.

Astebro, T., H. Herz, R. Nanda, and R. A. Weber. 2014. "Seeking the Roots of Entrepreneurship: Insights from Behavioral Economics." *Journal of Economic Perspectives* 28 (3): 49–70.

Asturias, J., S. Hur, T. J. Kehoe, and K. J. Ruhl. 2023. "Firm Entry and Exit and Aggregate Growth." *American Economic Journal: Macroeconomics* 15 (1): 48–105.

Baumol, W. J. 2010. *The Microtheory of Innovative Entrepreneurship*. Princeton, NJ: Princeton University Press.

Berger, M., A. Dechezleprêtre, and M. Fadic. 2024. "What Is the Role of Government Venture Capital for Innovation-Driven Entrepreneurship?" OECD Science, Technology and Industry Working Papers 2024/10, OECD Publishing, Paris.

Bermejo, V. J., M. A. Ferreira, D. Wolfenzon, and R. Zambrana. 2024. "How Do Cash Windfalls Affect Entrepreneurship? Evidence from the Spanish Christmas Lottery." *Journal of Financial and Quantitative Analysis, First View* 1–30. https://doi.org/10.1017/S0022109024000371.

Bernstein, S., X. Giroud, and R. R. Townsend. 2016. "The Impact of Venture Capital Monitoring." *Journal of Finance* 71 (4): 1591–622.

Beylis, G., W. F. Maloney, G. Vuletin, and A. Zambrano. 2023. *Wired: Digital Connectivity for Inclusion and Growth*. Washington, DC: World Bank.

Bischoff, K. M., M. M. Gielnik, M. Frese, and T. Dlugosch. 2013. "Limited Access to Capital, Start-Ups, and the Moderating Effect of an Entrepreneurship Training: Integrating Economic and Psychological Theories in the Context of New Venture Creation (Summary)." *Frontiers of Entrepreneurship Research* 33 (5): 3.

Bloom, N., S. Bond, and J. Van Reenen. 2007. "Uncertainty and Investment Dynamics." *Review of Economic Studies* 74 (2): 391–415.

Botelho, T. L., D. Fehder, and Y. Hochberg. 2021. "Innovation-Driven Entrepreneurship." NBER Working Paper 28990, National Bureau of Economic Research, Cambridge, MA.

Brandt, L., J. Van Biesebroeck, and Y. Zhang. 2012. "Creative Accounting or Creative Destruction? Firm-level Productivity Growth in Chinese Manufacturing." *Journal of Development Economics* 97 (2): 339–51.

Brown, R., S. Mawson, and C. Mason. 2017. "Myth-Busting and Entrepreneurship Policy: The Case of High Growth Firms." *Entrepreneurship & Regional Development* 29 (5–6): 414–43.

Bruhn, M., D. Karlan, and A. Schoar. 2018. "The Impact of Consulting Services on Small and Medium Enterprises: Evidence from a Randomized Trial in Mexico." *Journal of Political Economy* 126 (2): 635–87.

Caballero, R. J., K. Cowan, E. Engel, and A. Micco. 2013. "Effective Labor Regulation and Microeconomic Flexibility." *Journal of Development Economics* 101 (1): 92–104.

Cantu-Ortiz, F. J., N. Galeano, P. Mora-Castro, and J. Fangmeyer, Jr. 2017. "Spreading Academic Entrepreneurship: Made in Mexico." *Business Horizons* 60: 541–50.

Cassar, A., D. Friedman, and P. H. Schneider. 2009. "Cheating in Markets: A Laboratory Experiment." *Journal of Economic Behavior & Organization* 72 (1): 240–59.

Chandra, A., and M. A. Medrano Silva. 2012. "Business Incubation in Chile: Development, Financing and Financial Services." *Journal of Technology Management and Innovation* 7 (2): 1–13.

Chioda, L., D. Contreras-Loya, P. Gertler, and D. Carney. 2023. "Making Entrepreneurs: The Return Training Youth in Soft versus Hard Business Skills." World Bank, Washington, DC.

Cirera, X., and Y. Ding. Forthcoming. "Entrants and Technology Adoption in Developing Countries." World Bank, Washington, DC.

Cirera, X., and W. F. Maloney. 2017. *The Innovation Paradox: Developing-Country Capabilities and the Unrealized Promise of Technological Catch-Up.* Washington, DC: World Bank.

Coatanlem, Y., and O. Coste. 2024. "Cost of Failure and Competitiveness in Disruptive Innovation." IEP@BU Policy Brief, Institute for European Policymaking, Università Bocconi.

CORFO (Corporación de Fomento de la Producción). 2019. *Balance de Gestión Integral.* Santiago, Chile: CORFO.

CORFO (Corporación de Fomento de la Producción). 2022. *Resultados de Corfo Conecta. Análisis Exploratorio de Resultado de Redes.* Santiago, Chile: CORFO.

Cramer, J. S., J. Hartog, N. Jonker, and C. M. van Praag. 2002. "Low Risk Aversion Encourages the Choice for Entrepreneurship: An Empirical Test of a Truism." *Journal of Economic Behavior & Organization* 48 (1): 29–36.

Cusolito, A. P., and W. F. Maloney. 2018. *Productivity Revisited: Shifting Paradigms in Analysis and Policy.* Washington, DC: World Bank.

Davis, S. J., and J. Haltiwanger. 1992. "Gross Job Creation, Gross Job Destruction, and Employment Reallocation." *Quarterly Journal of Economics* 107 (3): 819–63.

Davis, S. J., and J. Haltiwanger. 1998. "Measuring Gross Worker and Job Flows." In *Labor Statistics Measurement Issues*, edited by J. Haltiwanger, M. E. Manser, and R. H. Topel, 77–122. Chicago: University of Chicago Press.

De Carvalho, A. G., C. W. Calomiris, and J. A. de Matos. 2008. "Venture Capital as Human Resource Management." *Journal of Economics and Business* 60 (3): 223–55.

De la Torre, A., A. Ize, and S. L. Schmukler. 2011. *Financial Development in Latin America and the Caribbean: The Road Ahead.* Washington, DC: World Bank.

Decker, R., J. Haltiwanger, R. Jarmin, and J. Miranda. 2014. "The Role of Entrepreneurship in US Job Creation and Economic Dynamism." *Journal of Economic Perspectives* 28 (3): 3–24.

Didier, T., and A. P. Cusolito. 2024. *Unleashing Productivity through Firm Financing.* Washington, DC: World Bank.

Djankov, S. 2009. "The Regulation of Entry: A Survey." *World Bank Research Observer* 24 (2): 183–203.

Doing Business Archive. 2020a. *Registering Property.* Washington, DC: World Bank.

Doing Business Archive. 2020b. *Paying Taxes.* Washington, DC: World Bank.

Doing Business Archive. 2020c. *Trading across Borders.* Washington, DC: World Bank.

Dreher, A., and M. Gassebner. 2013. "Greasing the Wheels? The Impact of Regulations and Corruption on Firm Entry." *Public Choice* 155 (3/4): 413–32.

Edelman, L., and H. Yli-Renko. 2010. "The Impact of Environment and Entrepreneurial Perceptions on Venture-Creation Efforts: Bridging the Discovery and Creation Views of Entrepreneurship." *Entrepreneurship Theory and Practice* 34 (5): 833–56.

EMPEA (Emerging Markets Private Equity Association). 2014. *Global Limited Partners Survey. Investors' Views of Private Equity in Emerging Markets.* Washington, DC: EMPEA.

EMPEA (Emerging Markets Private Equity Association). 2019. *Global Limited Partners Survey. Investors' Views of Private Equity in Emerging Markets.* Washington, DC: EMPEA.

EMPEA (Emerging Markets Private Equity Association). 2020. *Global Limited Partners Survey. Investors' Views of Private Equity in Emerging Markets.* Washington, DC: EMPEA.

Eslava, M., J. Haltiwanger, and A. Pinzón. 2022. "Job Creation in Colombia versus the USA: 'Up-or-Out Dynamics' Meet 'The Life Cycle of Plants'." *Economica* 89 (355): 511–39.

Eslava, M., and M. Melendez. Forthcoming. *Shaping the Playing Field for Economic Growth: Critical Regulatory Frameworks for Business in Latin America.* Washington, DC: World Bank.

European Commission. 2024. *The Future of European Competitiveness.* European Commission.

Ewens, M., and N. Malenko. 2020. "Board Dynamics over the Startup Life Cycle." NBER Working Paper 27769, National Bureau of Economic Research, Cambridge, MA.

Fairlie, R. W., J. Miranda, and N. Zolas. 2019. "Measuring Job Creation, Growth, and Survival among the Universe of Start-Ups in the United States Using a Combined Start-up Panel Data Set." *ILR Review* 72 (5): 1262–77.

Finland Abroad. 2016. "Nordic Cooperation in Silicon Valley." Helsinki: Ministry for Foreign Affairs of Finland and Finland's Missions Abroad.

Fischer, B. B., S. Queiroz, and N. S. Vonortas. 2018. "On the Location of Knowledge-intensive Entrepreneurship in Developing Countries: Lessons from São Paulo, Brazil." *Entrepreneurship & Regional Development* 30 (5–6): 612–38.

Foster, L., J. Haltiwanger, and C. J. Krizan. 2001. "Aggregate Productivity Growth: Lessons from Microeconomic Evidence." In *New Developments in Productivity Analysis*, edited by C. R. Hulten, E. R. Dean, and M. J. Harper, 303–72. Chicago: University of Chicago Press for the National Bureau of Economic Research.

Foster, L., J. Haltiwanger, and C. Syverson. 2008. "Reallocation, Firm Turnover, and Efficiency: Selection on Productivity or Profitability?" *American Economic Review* 98 (1): 394–425.

Garcia Sanchez, J. C. 2024. "Why Guadalajara Has Not Taken Off as a Generator of Innovative Entrepreneurship? An Extended Case Study." In *Emergent Ecosystems: Overcoming Systemic Obstacles for Technology Entrepreneurship*. Washington, DC: World Bank. Unpublished.

Giorcelli, M. 2023. "The Effects of Business School Education on Manager Career Outcomes." *SSRN Electronic Journal* 4468594. https://dx.doi.org/10.2139/ssrn.4468594.

Gompers, P. A., W. Gornall, S. N. Kaplan, and I. A. Strebulaev. 2020. "How Do Venture Capitalists Make Decisions?" *Journal of Financial Economics* 135 (1): 169–90.

Goñi, E., and W. F. Maloney. 2017. "Why Don't Poor Countries Do R&D? Varying Rates of Factor Returns across the Development Process." *European Economic Review* 94: 126–47.

Gonzalez-Uribe, J. 2020. "Exchanges of Innovation Resources Inside Venture Capital Portfolios." *Journal of Financial Economics* 135 (1): 144–68.

Gonzalez-Uribe, J., and O. Hmaddi. 2022. "The Multi-Dimensional Impacts of Business Accelerators: What Does the Research Tell Us?" LSE Research Online Documents on Economics 115461, London School of Economics and Political Science, LSE Library.

Gonzalez-Uribe, J., R. Klingler-Vidra, S. Wang, and X. Yin. 2023. "The Broader Impact of Venture Capital on Innovation: Reducing Entrepreneurial Capability Constraints through Due Diligence." *SSRN Electronic Journal* 4516863. https://dx.doi.org/10.2139/ssrn.4516863.

González-Uribe, J., and M. Leatherbee. 2015. "Business Accelerators and New-Venture Performance: Evidence from Start-Up Chile." https://api.semanticscholar.org/CorpusID:34225894.

Gonzalez-Uribe, J., and M. Leatherbee. 2018a. "Selection Issues." In *Accelerators: Successful Venture Creation and Growth*, edited by M. Wright and I. Drori, 81–99. Cheltenham, UK: Elgar.

Gonzalez-Uribe, J., and M. Leatherbee. 2018b. "The Effects of Business Accelerators on Venture Performance: Evidence from Start-Up Chile." *Review of Financial Studies* 31 (4): 1566–603.

Gonzalez-Uribe, J., and S. Reyes. 2021. "Identifying and Boosting 'Gazelles': Evidence from Business Accelerators." *Journal of Financial Economics* 139 (1): 206–87.

Gornall, W., and I. A. Strebulaev. 2015. "The Economic Impact of Venture Capital: Evidence from Public Companies." *SSRN Electronic Journal* 2681841. http://dx.doi.org/10.2139/ssrn.2681841.

Guerrero, M., and D. Urbano. 2017. "The Impact of Triple Helix Agents on Entrepreneurial Innovations' Performance: An Inside Look at Enterprises Located in an Emerging Economy." *Technological Forecasting and Social Change* 119: 294–309.

Guerrero, M., D. Urbano, J. A. Cunningham, and E. Gajón. 2018. "Determinants of Graduates' Start-Ups Creation across a Multi-Campus Entrepreneurial University: The Case of Monterrey Institute of Technology and Higher Education." *Journal of Small Business Management* 56 (1): 150–78.

Guerrero, M., D. Urbano, and E. Gajón. 2017. "Higher Education Entrepreneurial Ecosystems: Exploring the Role of Business Incubators in an Emerging Economy." *International Review of Entrepreneurship* 15 (2): 175–202.

Guerrero, M., D. Urbano, and F. Herrera. 2019. "Innovation Practices in Emerging Economies: Do University Partnerships Matter?" *Journal of Technology Transfer* 44: 615–46.

Guiso, L., P. Sapienza, and L. Zingales. 2006. "Does Culture Affect Economic Outcomes?" *Journal of Economic Perspectives* 20 (2): 23–48.

Haltiwanger, J., R. Jarmin, and J. Miranda. 2013. "Who Creates Jobs? Small versus Large versus Young." *Review of Economics and Statistics* 95 (2): 347–61.

Hellmann, T., and M. Puri. 2002. "Venture Capital and the Professionalization of Start-Up Firms: Empirical Evidence." *Journal of Finance* 57 (1): 169–97.

Herrera, F., M. Guerrero, and D. Urbano. 2018. "Entrepreneurship and Innovation Ecosystem's Drivers: The Role of Higher Education Organizations." In *Entrepreneurial, Innovative and Sustainable Ecosystems: Best Practices and Implications for Quality of Life*, edited by J. Leitão, H. Alves, N. Krueger, and J. Park, 109–28. Cham, Switzerland: Springer.

Hurst, E., and A. Lusardy. 2004. "Liquidity Constraints, Household Wealth and Entrepreneurship." *Journal of Political Economy* 112 (1): 319–47.

iCuantix SPA. 2022. *Evaluación de Impacto Retorno de la Innovación: Impacto de la Inversión de CORFO en Instrumentos de Fomento de la Innovación*. Santiago, Chile: Dirección de Presupuestos.

Imtiaz, M., and A. Sabater. 2024. "Global Venture Capital Investments Continue Downtrend in December 2023." S&P Global Market Intelligence.

Kerr, S. P., W. R. Kerr, and T. Xu. 2017. "Personality Traits of Entrepreneurs: A Review of Recent Literature." NBER Working Paper 24097, National Bureau of Economic Research, Cambridge, MA.

Kerr, W. R., and R. Nanda. 2015. "Financing Innovation." *Annual Review of Financial Economics* 7 (1): 445–62.

Kerr, W. R., R. Nanda, and M. Rhodes-Kropf. 2014. "Entrepreneurship as Experimentation." *Journal of Economic Perspectives* 28 (3): 25–48.

Kihlstrom, R. E., and J. J. Laffont. 1979. "A General Equilibrium Entrepreneurial Theory of Firm Formation Based on Risk Aversion." *Journal of Political Economy* 87 (4): 719–48.

Kinder, T. 2024. "How a Chinese Billionaire's Silicon Valley Splurge Caught the Eye of the FBI." *Financial Times*, September 26.

Klapper, L., L. Laeven, and R. Rajan. 2006. "Entry Regulation as a Barrier to Entrepreneurship." *Journal of Financial Economics* 82 (3): 591–629.

Lai, Y., and N. S. Vonortas. 2019. "Regional Entrepreneurial Ecosystems in China." *Industrial and Corporate Change* 28 (4): 875–97.

Lederman, D., J. Messina, S. Pienknagura, and J. Rigolini. 2014. *Latin American Entrepreneurs: Many Firms but Little Innovation*. Washington, DC: World Bank.

Lederman, D., M. Olarreaga, and L. Payton. 2010. "Export Promotion Agencies: Do They Work?" *Journal of Development Economics* 91 (2): 257–65.

Lerner, J. 1995. "Venture Capitalists and the Oversight of Private Firms." *Journal of Finance* 50 (1): 301–18.

Lerner, J., J. Liu, J. Moscona, and D. Y. Yang. 2024. "Appropriate Entrepreneurship? The Rise of China and the Developing World." NBER Working Paper 32193, National Bureau of Economic Research, Cambridge, MA.

Lerner, J., and R. Nanda. 2020. "Venture Capital's Role in Financing Innovation: What We Know and How Much We Still Need to Learn." *Journal of Economic Perspectives* 34 (3): 237–61.

Lindquist, M. J., J. Sol, and M. van Praag. 2015. "Why Do Entrepreneurial Parents Have Entrepreneurial Children?" *Journal of Labor Economics* 33 (2): 269–96.

Lindsey, L. 2008. "Blurring Firm Boundaries: The Role of Venture Capital in Strategic Alliances." *Journal of Finance* 63 (3): 1137–68.

Malkin, A. 2021. "China's Experience in Building a Venture Capital Sector: Four Lessons for Policy Makers." CIGI Paper No. 248, Centre for International Governance Innovation (CIGI), Waterloo, ON, Canada.

Maloney, W. F. 2004. "Informality Revisited." *World Development* 32 (7): 1159–78.

Maloney, W. F. 2009. "Mexican Labor Markets: Protection, Productivity, and Power." In *No Growth Without Equity? Inequality, Interests, and Competition in Mexico*, edited by S. Levy and M. Walton, 245–81. Washington, DC: World Bank.

Maloney, W. F., and A. Zambrano. 2022. "Learning to Learn: Experimentation, Entrepreneurial Capital, and Development." Documentos CEDE 19940, Universidad de los Andes, Facultad de Economía, CEDE.

Maloney, W., J. A. Zambrano, G. Vuletin, G. Beylis, and P. Garriga. 2024. *Taxing Wealth for Equity and Growth*. Latin America and the Caribbean Economic Review, October. Washington, DC: World Bank.

Melo, H. 2012. "Prosperity through Connectedness (Innovations Case Narrative: Start-Up Chile)." *Innovations: Technology, Governance, Globalization* 7 (2): 19–23.

Molina, A., J. M. Aguirre, M. Breceda, and C. Cambero. 2011. "Technology Parks and Knowledge-based Development in Mexico: Tecnológico de Monterrey CIT2 Experience." *International Journal of Entrepreneurship and Innovation Management* 13 (2): 199–224.

Murphy, K. M., A. Shleifer, and R. W. Vishny. 1991. "The Allocation of Talent: Implications for Growth." *Quarterly Journal of Economics* 106 (2): 503–30.

Nanda, R., and J. B. Sørensen. 2010. "Workplace Peers and Entrepreneurship." *Management Science* 56 (7): 1116–26.

Nicolaou, N., and S. Shane. 2010. "Entrepreneurship and Occupational Choice: Genetic and Environmental Influences." *Journal of Economic Behavior & Organization* 76 (1): 3–14.

Nicolaou, N., S. Shane, L. Cherkas, J. Hunkin, and T. D. Spector. 2008. "Is the Tendency to Engage in Entrepreneurship Genetic?" *Management Science* 54 (1): 167–79.

OECD (Organisation for Economic Co-operation and Development). 2017. *Latin American Economic Outlook 2017: Youth, Skills and Entrepreneurship*. Paris: OECD Publishing.

Ospina, D. 2023. "Why Accelerators Matter in Emerging Regions: The Case of LatAm." Open VC. https://openvc.app/blog/why-accelerators-matter-in-emerging-regions-the-case-of-latam.

Parente, S. L., and E. C. Prescott. 2000. *Barriers to Riches*. Cambridge, MA: MIT Press.

Pecenco, M., C. Schmidt-Padilla, and H. Taveras. 2020. "Opportunities and Entrepreneurship: Evidence on Advanced Labor Market Experience." Job Market Paper, Department of Agricultural and Resource Economics (ARE), UC Berkeley.

Peña, I. 2021. *Tecnolatinas 2021: The LAC Startup Ecosystem Comes of Age.* Washington, DC: Inter-American Development Bank.

Putterman, L., and D. Weil. 2008. "Post-1500 Population Flows and the Long-Run Determinants of Economic Growth and Inequality." NBER Working Paper 14448, National Bureau of Economic Research, Cambridge, MA.

Ramirez, C. P., S. S. da Silva, and L. Amestica. 2019. "Incubadoras en red: Capital relacional de incubadoras de negocios y la relación con su éxito." *Revista de Administração Sociedade e Inovação* 5 (2): 162–79.

Robbins, J. 2024. "Meet the Most Active VC Investors in Latin American Startups." *Pitchbook News & Analysis.* https://pitchbook.com/news/articles/most-active-vcs-latin-america-2024.

Rocha, N., and M. Ruta, eds. 2022. *Deep Trade Agreements: Anchoring Global Value Chains in Latin America and the Caribbean.* Washington, DC: World Bank.

Rudolph, H. P., F. Miguel, and J. Gonzalez-Uribe. 2023. *Venture Capital in Latin America and the Caribbean.* Washington, DC: World Bank.

Spolaore, E., and R. Wacziarg. 2009. "The Diffusion of Development." *Quarterly Journal of Economics* 124 (2): 469–529.

Start-Up Chile. 2024. *Our Impact.* Santiago, Chile: CORFO.

Teare, G. 2022. "Global Venture Funding and Unicorn Creation in 2021 Shattered All Records." *Crunchbase News.* https://news.crunchbase.com/business/global-vc-funding-unicorns-2021-monthly-recap/.

Tech:NYC. 2024. "NYC Tech Ecosystem Overview." Tech:NYC. https://www.technyc.org/nyc-tech-snapshot.

Van Praag, C. M., and J. S. Cramer. 2001. "The Roots of Entrepreneurship and Labour Demand: Individual Ability and Low Risk Aversion." *Economica* 68 (269): 45–62.

Venturi, L., D. Riera-Crichton, and G. Vuletin. Forthcoming. "The Income and Labor Effects of Individual Income Tax Changes in Latin America: Evidence from a New Measure of Tax Shocks in Latin America." Working Paper Series, World Bank, Washington, DC.

Verde. 2016. *Evaluación del Programa Start-Up Chile de CORFO.* Santiago, Chile.

Vuletin. G. Forthcoming. *Rethinking Taxation in LAC: Objectives, Instruments, and Behavioral Responses.* Washington, DC: World Bank.

Wolf, M. 2024. "How to Make European Industrial Policy Work." *Financial Times*, September 24, 2024. https://www.ft.com/content/4e884cb1-7300-460d-885d-f667640c7812.

World Bank. 2016. *World Development Report 2016: Digital Dividends.* Washington, DC: World Bank.

World Bank. 2020. *Enterprise Surveys: Corruption.* Washington, DC: World Bank.

World Bank. 2023. *Global Economic Prospects: January 2023.* Washington, DC: World Bank.

Yu, S. 2020. "How Do Accelerators Impact the Performance of High-Technology Ventures?" *Management Science* 66 (2): 530–52.

Zumbuehl, M., T. J. Dohmen, and G. A. Pfann. 2013. "Parental Investment and the Intergenerational Transmission of Economic Preferences and Attitudes." IZA Discussion Paper 7476, Institute of Labor Economics, Bonn.

# Policy Guidelines for Creating Learning Economies | 5

*"The best time to plant a tree is 100 years ago, the second-best time is now."*

—Adapted from a Chinese proverb.

## Introduction

Creating economies that can learn to identify opportunities to use new technologies, products, and processes and thereby increase productivity and diversify is the only long-term solution to alleviating poverty and generating fulfilling jobs in Latin America and the Caribbean (LAC). The only possible way to increase productivity, in turn, is to adapt and eventually invent new technologies. Other shortcuts—such as mimicking import substitution, as in the past, and some new attempts at industrial policy today—will eventually lead to stagnant growth and disappointment.

Numerous resources are now available to guide specific policies to promote innovation. Among them, the World Bank Productivity Project offers a series of reports detailing policies to stimulate productivity growth and innovation. *The Innovation Paradox: Developing-Country Capabilities and the Unrealized Promise of Technological Catch-Up* (Cirera and Maloney 2017), as well as its companion volume, *A Practitioner's Guide to Innovation Policy: Instruments to Build Firm Capabilities and Accelerate Technological Catch-Up in Developing Countries* (Cirera et al. 2020), offer specific recommendations on building individual's capabilities (human capital) and innovation policies. More recently, *Bridging the Technological Divide: Technology Adoption by Firms in Developing Countries* (Cirera, Comin, and Cruz 2022) provides insights into technology transfer per se. An earlier work, *Quality Systems and Standards for a Competitive Edge* (Diop et al. 2007), focuses on how transfer of best practices can increase value added through quality increases. *Harvesting Prosperity: Technology and Productivity Growth in Agriculture* (Fuglie et al. 2019) highlights the relevance of these issues to that sector. *At Your Service? The Promise of Services-Led Development* (Nayyar, Hallward-Driemeier, and Davies 2021) explores the conditions to exploit high-end services. The *World Development Report 2024* on the middle-income trap also provides broad guidelines on how to use innovation for growth in developing countries (World Bank 2024). The reader is referred to these resources for more details about these policies.

This section instead presents some broad policy guidelines that can accelerate the process of learning and knowledge diffusion in Latin American and Caribbean countries. While some gaps related to specific policy design remain in most countries, creating learning economies needs a change of approach and direction to industrial and innovation policies.

## Building Learning Economies

### 1. Growth in the Region Requires a Strategy of "Learning How to Learn" to Identify and Exploit Technological Opportunities

Development is fundamentally an experimental learning process about what new technology or idea leads to a profitable firm or a new area of national comparative advantage. It is a series of informed bets, with attendant risks, that requires the capacity to identify new technologies, evaluate their profitability relative to existing alternatives, finance and implement them over a long gestation period, and manage risk and failure. These capabilities and supporting institutions need to evolve as the economy grows more complex and the technological frontier shifts out (Murmann 2003; Nelson 2005). As noted by Nobel Prize winner Kenneth Arrow, quoted on the first page of this report, it is not enough that information flows freely; countries need to learn how to learn from experimenting with the opportunities it presents. This applies both to the efficiency and quality upgrading of incumbent firms, and to the cultivation of sophisticated new entrants that arbitrage new technological opportunities.

As highlighted by *The Innovation Paradox* (Cirera and Maloney 2017) and by the *World Development Report 2024* on the middle-income trap

(World Bank 2024), the nature of this process of experimentation varies by level of development. For many developing countries, there is great value added in simply adopting existing technologies, processes, and practices to improve quality and efficiency (for instance, management techniques) to diffuse existing best practices. It is also critical to stress that innovation for developing countries focuses less on research and development (R&D) projects at the frontier, and much more in taking advantage of the opportunities within the frontier offered by working with existing technologies.

### 2. Industrial Policy Must Focus on Building Capabilities and Institutions that Facilitate Identifying, Adopting, and Using Knowledge

Industrial policies conceived as policies to promote structural transformation of the economy have received more attention by mainstream economists, albeit with varying degrees of rigor. However, as chapter 1 shows, history is clear that *how* you produce a good is at least as important as *what* you produce. It is true that some new sectors—such as information technology (IT), and likely knowledge-intensive services—offer more potential for bets with a large upside and hence greater potential for growth than others such as mining or textiles. However, very similar production structures—indeed, identical industries—have yielded very different development outcomes depending on a country's capacity to exploit and apply available knowledge. LAC continues to underleverage the sectors it currently produces. Even within finely disaggregated sectors, LAC places fewer technological bets. This means that the pursuit of lofty missions inspired by a "Moon Shot" to alter a nation's productive structure will fail if they do not focus on developing the underlying "dark matter"—human capabilities and supporting institutions—that permit placing the necessary bets on innovation in the first place.

This poses a double challenge for advocates of industrial policies. First, governments need to have the capabilities to identify which potential sectors might have large positive externalities and should be encouraged. Second, they need to ensure the necessary managerial and technological capabilities and institutions are in place to support entering that sector. In line with these caveats, some proponents, such as Aghion (2014), have modest ambitions, arguing that industrial policies should be limited to (1) sectors currently inactive but that are close "input-wise" to existing sectors; and (2) sectors where the country clearly has missing complementary factors—such as shallow financial markets, low labor mobility, or low educational attainment. These sectors can benefit from learning spillovers from the existing sector that has similar capability endowments, while government addresses or compensates for the missing complementarities in the National Innovation System (NIS).

Bolder attempts at structural transformation magnify the challenges. In some advanced economies, a myriad of private sector actors has capabilities for experimentation, the market ensures exit of failed bets and firms, and the state deploys nudges (incentives) to correct market failures. However, few states in developing countries have the installed capabilities to place high-quality big bets—to confidently pick winners—or the discipline to close down losers. Hence, building the capabilities and institutions, including those of the state, to support experimentation by the private sector is the *sine qua non* of growth policy.

One practical implication, central to this report, is *the need to prioritize capabilities over targets*. Any quantity targets—be they growth of particular sectors, increased R&D or patenting, or cultivating suppliers for multinationals in new resource sectors—needs to first ensure the capabilities to support them.

## 3. LAC Needs to Actively Engage with the Global Knowledge Economy

However possible it was for countries to learn by doing and reinvent frontier technologies in the past, it is not today (refer to chapter 1). Hence, countries need to aggressively engage with the global knowledge frontier as they seek to rejuvenate traditional extractive industries, build linkages around foreign direct investment (FDI), or enter new green industries. The increasing barriers emerging in, and uncertainty around, the rules of the global trade regime only intensify the need for greater competitiveness; hence, the need for technology adoption and co-invention with foreign partners.

On the supply side, this requires access to technologies whose access ranges from being free and easily available through licensing to closely protected proprietary assets. As chapter 2 shows, developing countries are slower at adopting even the former, and the Firm-level Adoption of Technology survey suggests that LAC accesses them more slowly than Eastern Europe or Asia. Further, it is also clear that most firms in LAC do not soon follow early adopters that have demonstrated locally the possibilities of these technologies.

### *The Need for Active Learning*

Part of the problem stems from a lack of information, or irrational overconfidence, as described in chapter 2. Openness to trade and FDI is a powerful remedy to both. But what is also needed is a mindset to use trade and FDI more than as a source of jobs or taxes, and rather as a source of learning. This learning does not happen automatically. Part of the lack of adoption arises from an inability to use available information to take advantage of new opportunities. History's lesson from the mining industry and import substitution industrialization in LAC is that production and even exporting in itself does not lead to technological transfer or upgrading. Policies to facilitate adoption of off-the-shelf or easily licensed technologies—including management extension, International Standards Organization (ISO) quality systems, and so on—were a feature of the East Asian miracles, while the reverse has been true in some LAC countries, which have encouraged technological self-sufficiency by making imported technology more costly. Cooperative international platforms, such as the partnership between Chile and University of California, Davis that led to the explosion of fruit and wine exports, make knowledge more available, and also develop capabilities. Collaboration agreements are linked to more rapid adoption of green technologies (Bastos and Castro 2025).

#### *The Challenge of Proprietary Knowledge*

In other cases, technologies may be more closely protected proprietary assets. Knowledge flows become the result of a bargaining equilibrium that is a function of the leverage of the potential host country and the likely benefits to the origin firm (Sampson 2024). China leveraged its market size to negotiate transfer of know-how and capabilities in manufacturing, and Norway leveraged access to its oil and gas reserves (Villen and Wicken 2013).

In such bargains, the source firm clearly weighs any lost value of rents from transferring technology, but also the potential benefits arising from developing local providers or other linkages. Here, again, a key condition is that there are both the installed capabilities and the absence of insurmountable barriers in the enabling environment in the receiving country.

These options are not available to every country or sector. The Republic of Korea experienced difficulties in accessing key manufacturing technologies at critical moments. This may explain its stated goal of "technological self-reliance," which clearly is not an omnibus policy toward displacing technology imports, as Korea spends greatly on licensing. Filling in those gaps by local invention, as with advancing the frontier more generally, clearly requires investment in frontier levels of technical and managerial capabilities. This is where Brazil's industrial policies of the 2010s stumbled. Mobilizing the resources and ensuring the underlying capabilities are heavy policy "lifts." In the Asian Miracle economies, the successful achievement of both was often driven by security concerns that made these particular "Moon Shots" of existential importance.

## The Innovation Systems Supporting National Learning Need to Be Broader in LAC than in Advanced Economies

### 4. The Innovation System Needs to Be Conceived of More Broadly than in Advanced Economies

Conceptually, innovation-related externalities can justify government interventions on a large scale, ranging from innovation subsidies to public agencies like the Defense Advanced Research Projects Agency (DARPA) in the United States or Fundación Chile. However, the innovation paradox—why despite the expected high returns to innovation, so few firms and governments prioritize innovation investments—suggests distortions and absent complementary factors in the enabling environment ranging from top technical talent, to entrepreneurs capable of taking ideas to market, to workers capable of managing sophisticated technologies, to financial sectors deep enough to diffuse risk, to distortions in trade, to anticompetitive behavior that reduce the expected returns from investment. This implies that continuing progress on market-friendly reforms remains a central innovation policy. The ecosystem supporting innovative start-ups is a central subsystem for promoting the entry of start-ups that will have transformative positive impacts.

### 5. Managing Risk Is a Critical Role of the National Innovation System

The inherent riskiness in technological adoption and investment, and indeed growth, moves risk mitigation and management to center stage.

#### *Financial Systems Are Critical to Managing Risk*

Deepening the region's financial sectors is critical to funding investments of any type and diffusing the risk faced by new or incumbent firms and farms. This requires improvements in the enabling environment, such as better dispute or insolvency resolution procedures. There is also a process of learning as banks gain capabilities to evaluate riskier projects.

#### *Developing the Chain of Equity Finance Is Essential to Promote High-Innovation Firms*

In fact, this learning process is both more systemic and challenging. Equity finance is more suited to high-risk innovative firms whose principle assets are intellectual property that is hard to collateralize. Given that in advanced economies and to a surprisingly large extent in emerging economies, R&D-intensive or innovative firms are financed by venture capital, this agenda needs to move to center stage. But developing the chain of risk capital from angel investors to venture capital to public stock markets requires the time-consuming acquisition of risk management skills. Venture capital firms have the capability of vetting high-risk projects and guiding their management, and then the credibility to certify the firm's potential. Only 10–20 percent of companies backed by venture capital generate significant returns (Mulcahy, Weeks, and Bradley 2012), so choosing and nurturing incipient winners well is a developed skill. But venture capital firms need to be cultivated as part of the entire chain of risk capital—including developing the markets, such as Bovespa Mais and Novo Mercado, that facilitate exit.

This process needs to occur organically and requires a host of associated reforms. It is difficult for the state to fill the gap, both because of the absence of necessary risk evaluation and management capabilities, and because democratic states often find it difficult to justify the failure of a large fraction of their investments to their citizens. Even in the United States, which invests in R&D at perhaps half of the level that is justified by estimated social returns, Department of Energy loan loss rates are only 3.1 percent, suggesting deficient risk taking. In countries where it is difficult to separate a sensible but ultimately unsuccessful bet from corruption, this effect is multiplied (Zoffer 2024). As in China, government funding can help kick-start the local industry, but by working closely with private venture capital managed by foreign investors or expatriates (Berger, Dechezleprêtre, and Fadic 2024).

## 6. Competition and Capabilities Are Complementary

LAC needs to increase competition in many sectors. As or more important as the supply of technological knowledge is the demand for it by firms. Without the need to compete, there is no imperative to innovate, and without such an imperative, innovation incentives are pushing on a string. However, increasing competition without having firms capable of responding to it will lead to contraction of both innovation and production. Hence, fostering competition and building capabilities are complementary policies. These two agendas in the NIS need to march in parallel.

In sum, the conception of the NIS needs to extend beyond standard innovation-related market failures to all related factor markets and barriers to experimentation. In addition, the educational and research institutions normally associated with the NIS also require reform in most of LAC.

## Educational and Research Institutions Are Critical to Both Developing Capabilities and Supporting Innovation

### 7. There Is No Shortcut around Building Capabilities (Human Capital) at All Levels

Taking advantage of technological opportunities does not happen by chance: it requires individuals with technical, professional, scientific, managerial, and entrepreneurial capabilities. LAC needs to address its shortfalls across the spectrum of human capital—and must do so vigorously—while aligning the supply of skills with the needs of the economy and society. Currently, the dearth of foundational skills not only renders good jobs and entrepreneurship inaccessible to millions of young people but also shrinks the talent pool that should give rise to top high-quality scientists and entrepreneurs. Fixing their ineffective and inefficient education systems should be a first-order priority for LAC countries. No country in recent history has accomplished sustained growth while displaying the low average achievement and learning levels of LAC youth. Successful educational reforms—both at the basic and higher education levels—will require changing what is taught and how it is taught, while pivoting toward experiential learning. Innovative engineering schools are providing a blueprint for these changes, including incorporating outside work in curriculums.

#### *LAC Needs to Increase the Density of Transformational Entrepreneurs*

Entrepreneurs themselves can be "made," but their cultivation is a poorly understood combination of cultural and psychological attitudes, rigorous educational systems, study abroad and mentorship programs, university entrepreneurship training—and experience. Building the ecosystem that would support the emergence of entrepreneurs and ensuring their flourishing requires an integrated and iterative approach as a subpart of the NIS. Focusing only on finance or only building incubators or attracting anchor FDI is not likely to yield positive results unless complementary ingredients are present as well.

#### *LAC Needs to Find the Right Balance between Spending on Basic and Higher Education*

The right balance between investment in basic versus higher education is debated, but the discourse to date has probably been too biased toward the former. While it is critical to prepare workers for the modern economy with good-quality elementary education and training, high-quality jobs are created by individuals with advanced professional skills—often in science, technology, engineering, and mathematics (STEM)—as well as entrepreneurial skills, who start and grow firms. Both basic and higher education are therefore essential for poverty and inequality reduction. In the 1900s, the United States had a well-articulated engineering infrastructure with specializations in the major subfields that drove the country's industrialization, although only 4 percent of the population was enrolled in secondary school. Whatever the correct balance, it is certainly true that LAC gets poor educational results for the amount it spends, so reforms at both the primary and secondary level, as well as university level, are necessary to get more bang per peso spent.

***Expand technical education and align higher education with private sector needs.*** The introduction of short-cycle "junior college"–type programs as an alternative to a university education could help redress the perennial shortage of technical workers. High-quality technical programs are often costly to provide and, in some countries, must be redesigned with incentives to ensure quality and alignment with industry needs. The supply of higher education graduates needs to shift toward more technical fields of strategic importance to LAC economies. LAC has no shortage of Nobel Prizes, yet few of them are in STEM.

***Engage the diaspora.*** Both Latin America and—especially—the Caribbean have a large diaspora of talent abroad. This needs to be thought of less as brain drain than as brain circulation. The experience gained in foreign technological centers like Silicon Valley—not just learning skills but also building networks for risk finance—is critical. While repatriating talent might not be feasible, the region could strengthen efforts to engage the diaspora and tap into that source of talent to build research and business networks, provide mentorship, and access the knowledge frontier and finance.

***Reorient and strengthen universities and public research institutions.*** Government support of public universities can be seen as long-term underwriting of both the risks involved with research as well as the underlying appropriability externalities. However, a sustained reform effort is required to enhance the third mission of universities (particularly the public ones) to contribute to society through knowledge development and transfer. Volumes such as *Universities as Engines of Economic Development* (Crawley et al. 2020) explore the roles universities around the world have played not only identifying and adapting frontier technologies developed abroad, but serving as seedbeds for new firms and sectors. Whereas universities like the Massachusetts Institute of Technology (MIT) and the University of California, Berkeley in the United States were founded with this mission in their DNA, in other countries, moving away from a historical ivory tower vision of universities as separate from productive sector has required both a change of the institutional "chip" and a realignment of incentives to promote collaboration with the private sector.

An equally important agenda is to clarify the role of publicly supported research institutions and technology transfer organizations as providers of public goods in the identification and dissemination of new technologies. This would require clear, purposeful mission statements as well as strong incentives to guarantee quality and alignment with private sector needs.

Progress with public universities and research institutes can ensure that scarce R&D public funding, often filtered mostly through these institutions, supports firms and sectors as they attempt to become globally competitive. Because these institutions are less market-driven by nature, public spending must be designed to foster university–industry collaboration. Tax incentives or subsidies to firms or research grants to universities may be less successful than well-designed and efficient matching grant programs for collaboration (Cirera et al. 2020).

## Developing Governance Capabilities Is Critical Growth Policy

### 8. Building a More Capable and Efficient State Is Necessary for Creating Learning Economies

Developing national learning capabilities requires not necessarily a larger or more interventionist state, but a more capable one. The state plays a role in the NIS intervening to remedy failures, overseeing and encouraging linkages among nonmarket institutions, guiding the process of gaining national learning capacity, and, in countries with more capabilities, placing bets itself, as is the case with DARPA in the United States or Fundación Chile. Generating well-functioning policies in these areas is necessarily also an experimental and long- term process that requires a capable state with the autonomy to resist lobbying and to end losing policies or investments.

The nondemocratic nature or episodes of several of the success stories—China, Japan, Korea, and Singapore—is sometimes seen as more suitable to managing these tasks. However, LAC's nondemocratic experiences, ranging from the Porfiriato in Mexico to the regimes of the 1980s, generated few Tigers, while Finland, Ireland, and Spain engineered rapid growth under democratic auspices. A more useful distinction is that between high-capacity and low-capacity states, both democratic and authoritarian (Mazzuca and Munck 2020) that suggests that improving government performance is a key pillar of the learning agenda. Indeed, in the 1950s in Spain, modernizing public administration—bringing private sector management tools to the public sector, particularly in recruitment and procurement, and cultivating public-private partnerships—was a critical focus of the emerging technocracy, and central to Spain's take-off (Calvo-Gonzalez 2021). Mainstreaming the frontier literature on government analytics and policy best practice is precisely the focus of *The Government Analytics Handbook: Leveraging Data to Strengthen Public Administration* (Rogger and Schuster 2023) and *Data for Better Governance: Building Government Analytics Ecosystems in Latin America and the Caribbean* (Santini et al. 2024). LAC has extensive information systems that can be used for a broad range of government analytics and for monitoring improvement programs (Santini et al. 2024).

Specifically, for the learning agenda, there are good practices for diagnosing poor functioning in the NIS, designing appropriate remedial programs, and then implementing them—all of them with the caveats around maintaining the independence of the state from undue distortionary lobbying (Rogger and Schuster 2023).

#### Better Understand the Local Problems to Be Solved

Extrapolating from other countries' experience is broadly informative, but in the end, countries need to conduct more nuanced diagnostics of what local market failures or missing factors or markets are impeding technological adoption and innovation. Often governments stuck in a low-level "capability trap" will engage in "isomorphic mimicry" (Andrews, Pritchett, and Woolcock 2017)—the tendency to replicate others' solution programs without understanding the local problems to be solved, which can lead to simply adding inert new boxes on the NIS organogram with limited functionality or, in the worst case, be counterproductive.

***Address the source and locate policy in the context of the overall innovation system.*** As always, the goal is to redress distortions or failures at the source. As an example, while there are market failures dictating subsidies to R&D, low R&D investment may reflect low firm capabilities, distortions in the NIS, and barriers to accumulation more generally, which government support to R&D will not address and may exacerbate, for instance, by de facto subsidizing inefficient incumbents.

*Design policies to connect elements of the innovation system.* Dissemination of new technologies, know-how, or ways of learning requires interaction among the various agents and institutions of the innovation system, many of which are not market driven. Mission statements and funding design of universities and public research institutions should emphasize interactions with the private sector and other internal and external actors. Matching grant schemes are likely preferable to blanket R&D subsidies or tax write-offs because they similarly encourage interactions.

*Focus on the local level.* Understanding why firms or clusters are not innovating more will often require undertaking detailed and nuanced analysis of local conditions. Examples include Guadalajara, Mexico, where major players in the ecosystem have joined forces to understand why high-tech entrepreneurship remains elusive, and Manizales, Colombia, which is working with the MIT Regional Entrepreneurship Accelerations Program (REAP) to understand the barriers to more dynamic firms and exports. This approach suggests that diagnostics from the "bottom up" at the local level are a necessary complement to national-level diagnoses of elements of the overall innovation system. It is also often easier to coördinate the various actors in a local ecosystem than ministries at a national level.

*Make evaluation an ongoing and systematic process.* The necessary follow-up to experimenting with new policies ensures ongoing evaluation to ensure effective spending of public resources and optimal design of initiatives. At the design phase, ideally, every program would include a monitoring and evaluation system as well as a cost-benefit analysis, and some robust impact evaluations, to learn whether the program accomplishes its intended goals—and at what cost. By their mere existence, these evaluations can create a culture of accountability and learning—and can help build the capabilities necessary for the successful design and implementation of the next generation of programs.

### *Improve the Efficacy of Implementation*

Strengthening the capacity to implement needed steps efficiently, reliably, and undistorted by lobbying is critical. This requires design of policies that ensure transparency but that are supported by the requisite capacities. The state also has to be able to course-correct if evaluations suggest disappointing results. Short-term policies designed to subsidize structural change, for instance, should have sunset clauses built in, which are an automatic way to ensure that subsidies or protections are always visible and not the long-term default.

***Be coldly objective about government capabilities to execute initiatives.*** Many initiatives that might seem to be simply about budgeting money or establishing a new institution, in fact, demand scarce capabilities for them to have impact. Venture capital cannot be simulated by governments simply allocating funds because venture management skills are a critical ingredient. At the most extreme end of the spectrum, the DARPA-type models of decentralized and autonomous decision-making to take risks on innovative projects cannot succeed without clear governance structures and truly capable and experienced program managers. Science parks or incubators are sometimes seen as a mechanism for facilitating interaction among universities, foreign sources of knowledge, and entrepreneurs, but their managers need to be capable of advising entrepreneurs on solutions to problems, and coordinators who link firms to sources outside the facility (Fukugawa 2006). Government may be able to diagnose missing elements of clusters or roadmap existing industries, but they may have more trouble identifying new areas of comparative advantage and fending off distortionary lobbying.

***Reduce the dimensionality of interventions and simplify.*** Because government bandwidth is limited, effective implementation also requires limiting the scope of interventions and often targeting scarce resources. Part of the challenge is to reduce the dimensionality of the government's task list, and this is often done by being realistic at the design phase. This may imply that some programs that require coordination across multiple subprograms are not feasible, given local government capabilities. Second- or third-best policies requiring less capability and autonomy of the state may be preferable to the ideal policy.

Delegating tasks to private sector firms can reduce the burden on government. Foreign firms in global value chains, for instance, are often able to redress financial, managerial, and marketing shortfalls. Japan's dramatic gains in productivity and quality through the provision of scientific management knowledge to firms was affected by three private sector organizations working in collaboration with the government and academia (Kikuchi 2011). Spain's technology transfer Centros Tecnologicos were largely driven by the private sector. Diaspora-created or foreign venture capital firms are more able to place bets in new firms or sectors than government functionaries.

***Ensure alignment of solutions with the needs of the private sector.*** Relying more on the private sector also ensures a higher likelihood of removing barriers to its growth.[1] Spain's Centros Tecnologicos, by virtue of being largely directed and financed by the private sector, ensured relevance, while centers in Finland, Germany, and the United Kingdom need to raise at least one-third of their funding from private contracts; if they are not useful, they fail. Training systems function best when government supports investments at the margins, such as facilities or equipment, but the private sector largely directs the centers and pays the marginal costs (enrollment); again, if they are not adding value, they fail. Design of this kind ensures both alignment with the needs of the private sector and the execution capabilities within the program.

***Pursue targeting.*** Many interventions—higher education, whether national or abroad; laboratories for scientific research; firm upgrading programs; repatriation of STEM professionals, R&D spending—are costly and compete with other social imperatives. Necessarily, some targeting of the promising firms and sectors is required. This is not to advocate a strategy of government picking winners, which is challenging. The economics profession has found measuring externalities and likely spillovers difficult, and most shortcuts to identifying promising sectors are not robust (Lederman and Maloney 2012). Further, at the firm level, studies such as *High-Growth Firms: Facts, Fiction and Policy Options for Emerging Economies* stress the difficulty of identifying high-growth firms that governments might wish to back—neither high-tech nor small size nor previously fast growth are reliable signals (Grover Goswami, Medvedev, and Olafsen 2019). A promising strategy is using information from the private sector to help make more informed choices—or at least, rule out likely losers. Examples include partnerships of state venture capital support with private sector venture capital firms; replacing blanket R&D subsidies with matching grant–type programs that join university researchers with viable firms; and using information from introductory management extension programs to identify promising firms with potential to undertake more expensive and complex interventions (McKenzie 2021). Such actions can help reduce the universe of potentially dynamic firms and sectors to identify promising candidates.

#### *Strengthen the Coherence of Policies across the NIS*

LAC's innovation resources are often scattered across agencies, leading to fragmented and underfunded initiatives. Tools like public expenditure reviews can provide a map of innovation spending and suggestions for consolidation and efficiency (Correa 2014). More generally, governments need to oversee the functioning of the NIS: understanding the interactions of different policies, ensuring their coherence, and mapping gaps in necessary complementary factors. For example, countries in Europe and Central Asia are starting to adopt European Union state aid rules for R&D projects that provide frameworks to evaluate the impact of large subsidy programs in the economy and potential effects on other firms.

Yet, governments need to avoid introducing distortions that undermine other efforts to support innovation. Policy interventions are often made in the context of multiple layers of government-induced protection and distortions and a costly business environment that reduces investment of all kinds and limits the allocation of resources to more risky activities. This often translates into large shares of public R&D spending concentrated in public institutions with few linkages to the private sector, or, in the Brazilian context, allocated to protected sectors with little growth potential (de Souza 2023).

In practice, generating coherence across the system requires that agencies dedicated to private sector development, export promotion, the advancement of university research, or innovation have a mandate to work together. High-level coordinating councils of ministries need to have high-level backing for the mission to ensure coherence, lest they become inert interactions among lower-level delegates.

## 9. Political Predictability and Consistency over Time Are Needed

It takes time to build learning economies, and this is impossible to do when policy objectives and institutions change radically every political cycle. As figure 5.1 shows, ongoing political commitment to innovation—as shown by how often the topic was mentioned in national speeches (Calvo-Gonzalez, Eizmendi, and Reyes 2022)—is correlated with innovation performance. Countries need to strive toward a political consensus on the need to build national learning capabilities and the reforms that are necessary over a multidecade horizon to achieve. Generating and maintaining such a consensus is easier when building learning capability is seen as essential to national defense, as was the case historically in Japan; Korea; Singapore; Taiwan, China; and now China. Such a "mission" is less immediately compelling in LAC, and hence government attention is more easily deviated from the task. Again, however, Spain offers an example of the social coalescence around a European-inspired way forward, enabled following a coherent strategy over a long horizon with limited volatility (Calvo-Gonzalez 2021).

**FIGURE 5.1 There Is a Close Correlation between Political Commitment on Innovation and Innovation Performance in LAC**

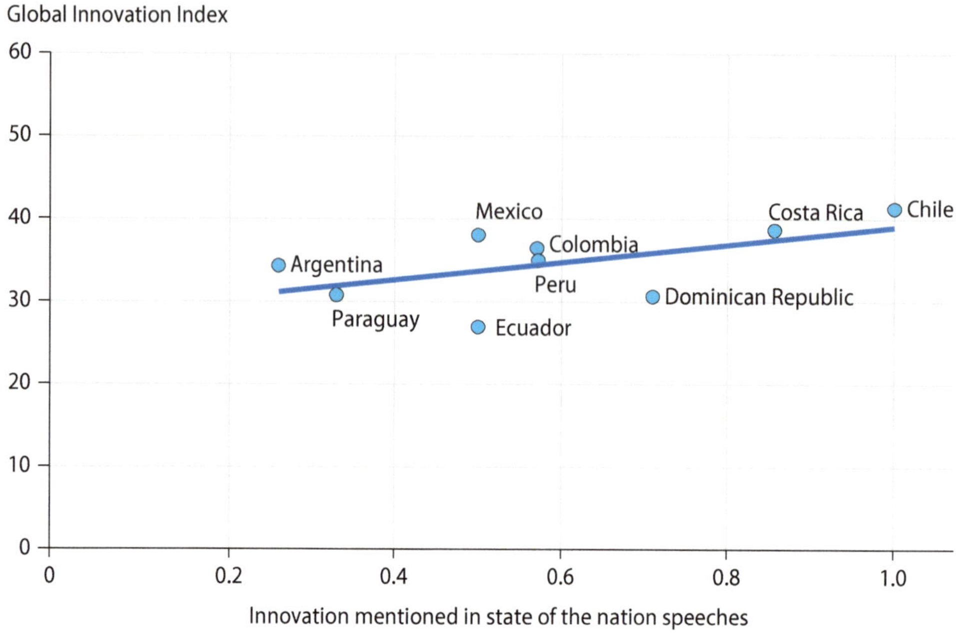

*Source:* Cirera and Maloney 2017.
*Note:* LAC = Latin America and the Caribbean.

## 10. Policy Mixes Depend on Where the Country Is on the Policy Escalator

As recognized in *The Innovation Paradox* (Cirera and Maloney 2017) and the *World Development Report 2024* on the middle-income trap (World Bank 2024), among others, the reform agenda differs depending on the level of sophistication of the overall private sector and institutional environment. *The Innovation Paradox* proposed a "capabilities escalator," where policies to support firm upgrading are sequenced in accordance with the level of capabilities of the private sector, as well as of policy makers and institutions, and ratchet up through progressively higher stages of sophistication. While within any country, and in fact within sectors within a country, there will be vast heterogeneity, with some firms at the frontier and others not, this "escalator" approach can be broadened to serve as a distillation of the discussion here and a heuristic guide to help countries define their policy agendas.

Figure 5.2 illustrates how the focus of policies should shift as countries develop in different areas. The escalator needs to be interpreted as a coalescing of objectives as state capacity and private sector capabilities accumulate and allow more complex projects to be managed. These capabilities increase along the development process but with some heterogeneity. For example, some upper-middle-income countries have more capable governments and some lower-middle income countries can have capabilities similar those of low-income countries. Countries on the top, for instance, still need to make sure that small and medium enterprises have access to finance while designing more complex venture capital programs. A first set of factors requires creating an enabling environment for innovation and learning. This implies focusing on basic investment climate reforms and competition policies that concentrate on ensuring entry and a level playing field in low- and lower-middle-income countries and moving to financial deepening and risk finance while improving competition policies toward addressing antitrust and abuse of market dominance. Then in upper-middle-income countries and high-income countries, policies can address more complex competition issues with more sophisticated antitrust enforcement in platforms and digital markets.

**FIGURE 5.2 The Policy Escalator**

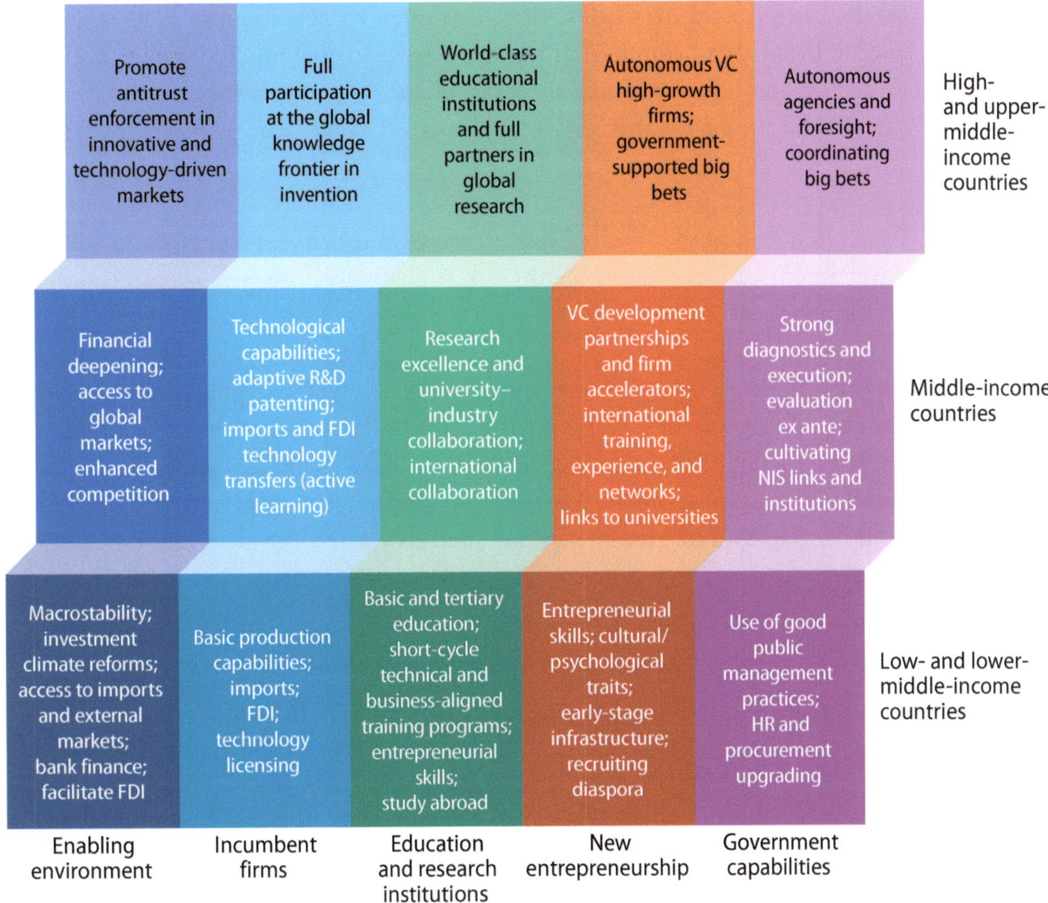


*Source:* Original figure for this volume.
*Note:* FDI = foreign direct investment; HR = human resources; NIS = National Innovation System; R&D = research and development; VC = venture capital.

More importantly, while the focus on building capabilities is important in all countries, governments should focus on basic production capabilities in low- and middle-income countries, prioritizing knowledge transfer via imports and attracting FDI to adding know-how investment transfers. As countries move up the capabilities' escalator, governments can transition to a focus on technological and invention capabilities (Cirera and Maloney 2017) and shift to more sophisticated forms of access and participation in global knowledge. This is analogous to the approach to invest, infuse, and innovate in the *World Development Report 2024* (World Bank 2024).

Regarding educational and research policies, the focus should shift from basic and tertiary education, as well as technical skills and training, to generate research excellence and industry collaboration, in order to fully participate in global research.

For entrepreneurship policies, while the focus starts with entrepreneurial skills, traits, and attitudes, and linkages to the diaspora, this should evolve toward more sophisticated policies targeting the development of risk finance and early-stage infrastructure, and at the top of the escalator the development of autonomous venture capital and supporting riskier entrepreneurial ventures.

Complementary to these policy priorities are investments in improving government capabilities to be able to implement more sophisticated policies and manage risk.

This graduation of policies should not be viewed as prescriptive because countries have sectors with varying proximity to the frontier. Rather, this approach provides heuristic guidance on how priorities should change to create learning economies. More importantly, setting objectives that are too high for the level of capabilities can lead to wasted resources and ineffective policies.

## Several Entry Points Can Help Ignite the Reform Process

### 11. Identify Entry Points for Reform

This approach requires an ambitious reform process, together with long-term commitment. A natural question is, therefore, how and where to start? While there is not a prescriptive process to start this reform, the discussion that follows offers some entry points, which differ by country and context. Ideally, demonstrating early results can provide a demonstration effect that will help diffusion of policy changes to other areas.

### *Devise Multi-Decade National Strategies to Build Learning Economies*

National planning strategies in many countries set strategic long-term focus, promulgate reforms, and coordinate across ministries to ensure coherence and long-term continuity of innovation and productivity policies. For example, Colombia's CONPES (Consejo Nacional de Política Económica y Social) is the highest national planning authority and advises the government on critical policy. Often, however, such documents remain on paper with limited impact unless championed at the highest level and ideally, with broad political support. Critically, there can be no separation between productivity policies directed at the private sector and "innovation" policies, which are sometimes slotted more toward the academic realm.

To this end, most countries in the region have adopted interministerial councils as coordination mechanisms to redress the fragmentation of policies and resources, often with contradictory objectives across ministries. However, it is important to ensure de facto coordination by, for example, having joint programs across ministries and joint decisions about new policies endorsed at the highest level. In particular, the danger is that councils once chaired by ministers lose priority within a government and are attended by progressively lower-level staff who, while fully understanding the challenges, lack the power to redress problems, resist the inevitable ministerial territoriality, or ensure continuity.

### *Use Public-Private Dialogue Mechanisms to Push the Learning Agenda*

Policies to build learning economies cannot be successfully designed without the participation of the private sector, which is most closely aware of what impedes innovation and growth. Several mechanisms and models of public-private dialogue for innovation are being applied in the region. From platforms such as Mobilização Empresarial pela Inovação in Brazil to Fundación Chile, this agenda requires a strong public-private partnership over the medium and long term. Hallak and López (2022) show how public-private councils for sectoral competitiveness have worked in different LAC countries. Sectoral roadmapping, if solely pushed by governments without buy-in from the private sector, is likely to fail given that the private sector is at the center stage of accumulating learning capabilities and can reflect market signals. Common concrete items on the agenda might be reform of insolvency and dispute resolution, restructuring of training programs to better serve the private sector, or strengthening export promotion agencies to help firms enter new markets. The private sector is often wary of engagement with governments, which may lack competence or consistency over time. Hence, ensuring necessary government capabilities is critical, as well as creating clear and transparent dialogue mechanisms.

#### *Ramp Up Active Learning from FDI*

A particularly important set of discussions is necessary with respect to FDI to identify possible areas where technology transfer and the development of local capabilities is of mutual interest. That is, FDI should be treated more as a source of learning, as China has done, and less purely as a source of employment and tax revenues. Further, such companies can help resolve failures arising from underdeveloped markets, facilitate entry into international markets, and transfer managerial technologies.

#### *Pursue Linkages and Share Incentives among Existing Institutions in the NIS*

Often the lack of articulation—for instance, between industry, universities and public agencies—is due less to low quality or interest in collaboration than to information asymmetries. Some actors, such as Austin, Texas, hire firms to map and match private sector actors and local centers of academic excellence to facilitate collaboration. However, the lack of articulation of the LAC National Innovations Systems is not entirely an information problem. Designing programs with incentives for relevant actors to collaborate is critical. Maximizing these linkages, for example, by creating joint programs and consortia with common goals and incentives, rather than competing across institutions for budgets, can lead to faster diffusion of reforms.

#### *Use Subnational Governments to Pilot and Diffuse Successful Programs*

Subnational initiatives are more fine-tuned to the local context and the missing markets or market failures to be resolved than are national or federal governments, often far away in the capital city. Initiatives such as MIT's REAP and Venture Mentoring Service can support implementation of pilot programs in cities or regions. When successful, these efforts can serve as a demonstration of results to be diffused to other contexts. Their feasibility depends on the capabilities of local governments to diagnose problems and implement policies. Hence, not all subnational innovation initiatives are viable. Further, they often work best in the partnership of local anchor firms, such as Luker Agricola in Manizales, Colombia, which has partnered with the local mayoralty to promote Manizales Mas, which seeks to strengthen the local entrepreneurial ecosystem.

## Conclusion

Growth occurs only by a process of informed bets on new technologies, processes, products, and markets that, if well selected, generate gains in value added over time. Development might be thought of as the process through which economies and societies learn how to learn—how to recognize these opportunities, develop strategies to exploit them, and then to execute. This requires learning on the part of the private sector, but also on the part of the government that needs to begin setting an enabling environment that facilitates technological adoption and then encourages learning by firms and potential entrepreneurs. LAC entered the Second Industrial Revolution unarmed—lacking capabilities across the human capital spectrum as well as supporting institutions. However, the examples of Finland, Korea, Norway, and Spain suggest that history is not destiny, that a delayed catch-up is feasible. It will, however, require a shift to a more active approach to national learning, and a setting of goals and reforms that are pursued over several decades. The rewards are large: reclaiming LAC's lost century of growth is reclaiming the hope for a more dynamic future.

## Note

1. The Meiji leap forward in textiles was driven by private firms, while the government agencies transferred inappropriate or antiquated technologies (Braguinsky and Hounshell 2016). Similarly, some Chilean agencies dedicated toward promoting innovation in mining-related small and medium enterprises were seen as insufficiently attuned to the nuances of the problems being addressed (Aroca and Stough 2016).

## References

Aghion, P. 2014. "Afterword: Rethinking Industrial Policy." In *Creating a Learning Society: A New Approach to Growth, Development, and Social Progress*, edited by J. E. Stiglitz and B. C. Greenwald, 509–22. New York: Columbia University Press.

Andrews, M., L. Pritchett, and M. Woolcock. 2017. "Looking like a State: The Seduction of Isomorphic Mimicry." In *Building State Capability: Evidence, Analysis, Action*, edited by M. Andrews, L. Pritchett, and M. Woolcock, 29–52. Oxford, UK: Oxford Academic.

Aroca, P., and R. Stough. 2016. "Lessons from a Study of Innovation in a Chilean Mining Region." CEPR Working Paper, Centre for Economic Policy Research, London.

Bastos, P., and L. Castro. 2025. "The Emergence and Diffusion of Green Technologies: Firm-Level Evidence from Textual Analysis of Patents and Earnings Calls." Policy Research Working Paper 11036, World Bank, Washington, DC.

Berger, M., A. Dechezleprêtre, and M. Fadic. 2024. "What Is the Role of Government Venture Capital for Innovation-Driven Entrepreneurship?" Science, Technology and Industry Working Paper 2024/10, Organisation for Economic Co-operation and Development, Paris.

Braguinsky, S., and D. A. Hounshell. 2016. "History and Nanoeconomics in Strategy and Industry Evolution Research: Lessons from the Meiji-Era Japanese Cotton Spinning Industry." *Strategic Management Journal* 37 (1): 45–65.

Calvo-Gonzalez, O. 2021. *Unexpected Prosperity: How Spain Escaped the Middle-Income Trap*. Oxford, UK: Oxford University Press.

Calvo-Gonzalez, O., A. Eizmendi, and G. Reyes. 2022. "The Shifting Attention of Political Leaders: Evidence from Two Centuries of Presidential Speeches." https://dx.doi.org/10.48550/arXiv.2209.00540.

Cirera, X., D. Comin, and M. Cruz. 2022. *Bridging the Technological Divide: Technology Adoption by Firms in Developing Countries.* Washington, DC: World Bank.

Cirera, X., J. Frías, J. Hill, and Y. Li. 2020. *A Practitioner's Guide to Innovation Policy: Instruments to Build Firm Capabilities and Accelerate Technological Catch-Up in Developing Countries.* Washington, DC: World Bank.

Cirera, X., and W. F. Maloney. 2017. *The Innovation Paradox: Developing-Country Capabilities and the Unrealized Promise of Technological Catch-Up.* Washington, DC: World Bank.

Correa, P. 2014. *Public Expenditure Reviews in Science, Technology, and Innovation: A Guidance Note.* Washington, DC: World Bank Group.

Crawley, E., J. Hegarty, K. Edström, and J. C. Garcia Sanchez. 2020. *Universities as Engines of Economic Development: Making Knowledge Exchange Work.* Cham, Switzerland: Springer.

de Souza, G. 2023. "R&D Subsidy and Import Substitution: Growing in the Shadow of Protection." *SSRN Electronic Journal* 4587133. https://dx.doi.org/10.2139/ssrn.4587133.

Diop, M., L. J. Guasch, J.-L. C. Racine, and M. I. Sanchez. 2007. *Quality Systems and Standards for a Competitive Edge.* Directions in Development: Trade. Washington, DC: World Bank.

Fuglie, K., M. Gautam, A. Goyal, and W. F. Maloney. 2019. *Harvesting Prosperity: Technology and Productivity Growth in Agriculture.* Washington, DC: World Bank.

Fukugawa, N. 2006. "Assessing the Impact of Science Parks on Knowledge Interaction in the Regional Innovation System." *SSRN Electronic Journal* 909464. https://dx.doi.org/10.2139/ssrn.909464.

Grover Goswami, A., D. Medvedev, and E. Olafsen. 2019. *High-Growth Firms: Facts, Fiction, and Policy Options for Emerging Economies.* Washington, DC: World Bank.

Hallak, J. C., and A. López. 2022. *¿Cómo apoyar la internacionalización productiva en América Latina?: análisis de políticas, requerimientos de capacidades estatales y riesgos.* Washington, DC: Inter-American Development Bank.

Kikuchi, T. 2011. "The Role of Private Organizations in the Introduction, Development and Diffusion of Production Management Technology in Japan." In *Kaizen National Movement: A Study of Quality and Productivity Improvement in Asia and Africa*, JICA and GRIPS Development Forum, 23–47.

Lederman, D., and W. F. Maloney. 2012. *Does What You Export Matter? In Search of Empirical Guidance for Industrial Policies.* Washington, DC: World Bank.

Mazzuca, S. L., and G. L. Munck. 2020. *A Middle-Quality Institutional Trap: Democracy and State Capacity in Latin America.* Cambridge, UK: Cambridge University Press.

McKenzie, D. 2021. "Small Business Training to Improve Management Practices in Developing Countries: Re-Assessing the Evidence for 'Training Doesn't Work'." *Oxford Review of Economic Policy* 37 (2): 276–30.

Mulcahy, D., B. Weeks, and H. Bradley. 2012. "We Have Met the Enemy ... and He Is Us: Lessons from Twenty Years of the Kauffman Foundation's Investments in Venture Capital Funds and the Triumph of Hope over Experience." *SSRN Electronic Journal* 2053258. https://dx.doi.org/10.2139/ssrn.2053258.

Murmann, J. P. 2003. *Knowledge and Competitive Advantage: The Coevolution of Firms, Technology, and National Institutions*. Cambridge, UK: Cambridge University Press.

Nayyar, G., M. Hallward-Driemeier, and E. Davies. 2021. *At Your Service? The Promise of Services-Led Development*. Washington, DC: World Bank.

Nelson, R. R. 2005. *Technology, Institutions, and Economic Growth*. Cambridge, MA: Harvard University Press.

Rogger, D., and C. Schuster, eds. 2023. *The Government Analytics Handbook: Leveraging Data to Strengthen Public Administration*. Washington, DC: World Bank.

Sampson, T. 2024. "Technology Transfer in Global Value Chains." *American Economic Journal: Microeconomics* 16 (2): 103–46.

Santini, J. F., F. S. Capurro, D. Rogger, T. Lundy, G. Kim, J. de León Miranda, S. Cocciolo, and C. Casanova. 2024. *Data for Better Governance: Building Government Analytics Ecosystems in Latin America and the Caribbean*. Washington, DC: World Bank.

Villen, S., and O. Wicken. 2013. "The Dynamics of Resource-Based Economic Development: Evidence from Australia and Norway." *Industrial and Corporate Change* 22 (5): 1341–71.

World Bank. 2024. *World Development Report 2024: The Middle-Income Trap*. Washington, DC: World Bank.

Zoffer, Joshua. 2024. "Elon Musk Needs to Teach the Government How to Lose More Money." *New York Times*, December 27, 2024 (opinion). https://www.nytimes.com/2024/12/27/opinion/elon-musk-industrial-policy.html.

www.ingramcontent.com/pod-product-compliance
Lightning Source LLC
LaVergne TN
LVHW070117110826
845147LV00002B/137

* 9 7 8 1 4 6 4 8 2 2 0 5 6 *